This Broad's Life

This Broad's Life

The Raucous, Riveting Autobiography
of the Most Outrageous Radio Talk-show Host
in America Today

BARBARA CARLSON

WITH JESS CAGLE

POCKET BOOKS
New York London Toronto Sydney Tokyo Singapore

POCKET BOOKS, a division of Simon & Schuster Inc.
1230 Avenue of the Americas, New York, NY 10020

ISBN: 0-671-52305-8

First Pocket Books hardcover printing August 1996

10 9 8 7 6 5 4 3 2 1

POCKET and colophon are registered trademarks of
Simon & Schuster Inc.

Printed in the U.S.A.

I dedicate this book to my mother, Jane Gillis Duffy. Mother, you died without knowing how much I love and appreciate you. Do you know that now? Do you know that I have forgiven you and want your forgiveness? I hope there's a bookstore in Heaven. I hope you'll stop flirting with Saint Peter and take time to read this. It will explain a lot. It says so much that I failed to say to you when you were alive.

Acknowledgments

When Pocket Books asked me to write this book, my first thought was, my God, I haven't even written the thank-you notes for my two weddings. How do they expect me to write a book?

Thank you, Jess Cagle, my dear, cute, smart collaborator, for making the task possible and for folding my underwear. Thank you, Sue Carswell (L.C.), my editor, for showing faith, tenacity, charm, and a God-given strength to accomplish deadlines while overcoming my incredible procrastination and vulnerability. Thank you, Mendes Napoli, my long-suffering agent whom I fired because he had the audacity to be a man and to tell me what to do. (P.S. We've since made up.)

Thank you, my fabulous children, Anne Carlson Davis and Tucker Carlson, for your forgiveness. Thank you, Andrew Davis, my son-in-law, for loving my daughter and for playing a major role in creating Allie Davis, my beloved granddaughter. A special thanks to my delightful stepchildren: Scott, Jerri, and Kent Anderson, who have brought me two wonderful grandchildren, Cici and Briggs, who have brought their grandmother-by-marriage great joy. And thank you, Pete Anderson, my knight in tweedy armor, my mentor, my lover, my husband, for your help and patience. All of you, my family, have given generously of yourselves for this project. You are kind and decent people.

So many others contributed their memories to this book

that I'll have to lump you together. Please know, each of you, that words here can't begin to thank you enough. But thank you, Tom Weiser, Chuck Mark, Mary Baker, Barbara McConagha, Colleen and Dick Walter, Janella Slade, Bruce and Mary Duffy, George and Diana Duffy, Gay Parker, Peter Thiele, Suzie DeLong Brixius, Donna O'Day, Sandra Purtle, Jackie Gardner, Mary Lufkin, Ginny Morris, and Sally Howard. Special thanks to Kay Miller, whose newspaper account of my trip to the fat farm provided me with invaluable memories and details. In fact, thanks to the entire staff of the *Star Tribune,* whose chronicles of Barbara Carlson helped jog my memory and filled in the gaps. Additional thanks go to Gail Eisenberg for her research, and to Pocket Books' Jo Carone, Amelia Sheldon, and Craig Hillman, for all their help and enthusiasm.

And finally, I must thank all those who have unwittingly become a part of this book, simply by virtue of being part of my life. Especially you, Governor Arne Carlson, whom I also thank for giving me the world's most wonderful children and sharing with me perhaps the most important twelve years of this broad's life.

There was a little girl
Who had a little curl
Right in the middle of her forehead;
And when she was good,
She was very, very good,
But when she was bad she was horrid.

—Henry Wadsworth Longfellow

Introduction

My name is Barbara Carlson, and I am an alcoholic and a binge eater. I wear a fur coat and have a tattoo on my behind. I am the ex-wife of the current Minnesota governor, and, as a morning shock jock/political commentator on Minneapolis' KSTP-AM, I am an advocate of a tight state budget, welfare reform, and dildos. Everyone from male strippers to conservative think-tankers to financial advisers has joined me in my hot tub, from which I sometimes broadcast my daily radio talk show.

I am also a wife, mother, and grandmother, a Junior League alumna, and a pro-choice Republican. I would have turned in this book sooner, but I was running for 1996 St. Paul Winter Carnival queen. The contestants were attractive women, eighteen-year-olds, thirty-year-olds, a couple of fifty-year-olds, and one loud-mouthed broad. Alas, the crown was bestowed on a beautiful thin massage therapist in her thirties. They *say* it wasn't a beauty pageant.

At the time of publication, I will be fifty-eight years old, and this book is the story of my strange yet typical, violent yet gratifying life up to now. I have shared in these pages my upbringing in an alcoholic household and the death from SIDS of my baby daughter, Kristin, in 1966. Looking back, I think that my story springs from those two events. I believe that those two gifts of fate have guided me to experiences that you may find at turns shocking (I was raped as a teen-ager—I survived—and I stabbed my ex-husband—he survived), funny (as a political wife, I flashed my tits at a couple of black-tie dinners), and sad (I reconciled with my mother too late in her life). Experience has given me wisdom, and I hope that you will find that wisdom in this book. I hope women of my generation will find themselves. This broad's life, in a general sense, is all of our lives. We were born to run households; then as divorced single mothers and middle-aged women in the 1970s, we ended up running for our lives.

Running. That's a good metaphor for life, isn't it? Running away, running for cover, and finally—if you're lucky—running home. Reliving my past in these pages sent me running back to a therapist I had seen twenty years ago. I talked to this therapist about a man named Lou, the love of my life—a man who could never be mine. Why did I love Lou so much, I wondered. I loved him because I could be quiet with him. I wasn't tough, I didn't say bright things, I felt sexy with him. I felt like a woman. And I wonder now if that part of me, the loving and gentle and sexy part, will ever show up again. Yet I do have love in my life. So ... why don't I weigh 120 pounds? Why aren't I a better wife? Will my self-destructive behavior ever end?

I can't promise answers here. Not for myself, much less for you. I can promise a thrilling journey through my days. But buy the book first. I've got a granddaughter who has a voracious appetite for quality children's wear. And I could use a new string of pearls.

—*Barbara Carlson*
Minneapolis, 1996

This
Broad's
Life

1

Never Again

"Arne!" I said to my husband. "That woman is blowing a bear!"

"No, Barbara," he corrected me. "It's a horse."

Goddammit. *What* did I do with my glasses?

The year was 1976, and this was the Sexual Attitude Reassessment Seminar at the University of Minnesota. Since I had begun recovery for alcoholism one year before, there was not a self-help program on earth that I wasn't willing to try; this one was a weekend of lectures, films, and discussion groups exploring various sexual issues. This particular segment of it was known as the "Fuck-o-rama."

We lounged on pillows while about a dozen films unreeled simultaneously along the walls of the auditorium. A kinky nightmare played out. To the left of the woman and her horse, three little boys performed fellatio on each other. To our right, a pig did his best to have sex with a human female, his little corkscrew tail uncoiling, coiling, uncoiling, over and over. On another screen, a woman knelt under the erection of a man bound to a crucifix by leather straps. She slit the tip of his penis with a knife and lapped up the blood.

The films were intended to desensitize counselors and clergy who might come across such peccadillos in the line of duty. So, what was I doing here? I was training to become a counselor, but thought I might use it to save my marriage, too.

1

Not that I thought bestiality and kiddie porn would do the trick. The Fuck-o-rama was only part of the program. The rest of the films we saw that weekend were beautiful takes on human sexuality, images of human beings expressing tenderness toward each other, films about gay sex and lesbian sex and sex over fifty. I had hoped that they would speak to my husband, demonstrate to him what touching another human being was all about, and I had persuaded him to come here. With some defeat in his icy blue eyes, he had agreed. "Indulge her once more," he must have been thinking, "and then I'll get on with my life."

Our marriage was dead, and by my own reckoning, it had died in 1966, on the night we lost our firstborn child, a little girl named Kristin, to crib death. On the night of her death, that terrible night, my husband wouldn't hold me. *He wouldn't hold me.* I couldn't forgive him for that, so I punished him over and over for the love he withheld. I found caring and affection with others, on the sly, out of town, in motels.

During the course of my twelve-year marriage to Arne Carlson, the man who would be elected Minnesota governor in 1990, I stabbed him twice and humiliated him countless times. He hit me once, and once told me to rot in hell. He never once touched my vagina with his hand. And through it all, I wondered if Kristin hadn't died, could we have survived?

But I had witnessed a miracle a year earlier: sobriety. Now it seemed all things were possible—even this marriage. I had dropped 50 pounds since going through recovery, down to about 130 pounds—a number that hadn't crossed my bathroom scales since I was a girl. At the age of thirty-six, sober after twenty-three years of trying to commit slow, alcoholic suicide, my bloodshot eyes had cleared. They were now a clear blue, as clear as Arne's. My complexion had become fair and rosy again.

During my spiritual housecleaning, I had uncovered something wonderful—some residual love and caring for this man, Arne Carlson. I had kept my frenetic energy and my sense of humor, even as I emptied my bottles that had held my life force for so long. I could still laugh. God, what a blessing to be able to laugh sober. I had begun to make amends to my surviving, battle-weary children, a son and daughter, the real victims of my alcoholism. I felt pretty, thin, and blond. I *wanted* my husband. At last, I hoped, I was pretty enough, thin enough, blond enough, *sober* enough to make him want me and take my hand as I reached out to him.

Lights up. The Fuck-o-rama disappeared.

We drove back to Minneapolis, to the big house on Fremont Avenue, and we got in bed. I was turned on. Arne wasn't in the mood. He must have thought he was doing me a favor when he allowed me to go down on him. When I finished the job, he rolled over and fell asleep, a Boy Scout done with the day's good deed. Every woman for herself. It was the last time that my husband and I would ever have sex.

I lay awake a mile away, on my side of the bed, frustrated and humiliated, angry as hell, and grieving for this marriage. *Defeated.* "You are never going to do this again," I thought to myself. It wasn't a vow. It was more than that; more like a sad, quiet epiphany. We would maintain the marriage through Arne's final campaign for the Minnesota legislature, but I realize now that my life started over that night as he lay sleeping. "You are never going to do this again," I repeated, softly.

I began to like the sound of it, although I knew that, before long, I would face the horrors of being a single mother and almost forty. I didn't know if I could face that without the bottle. I knew only that there would be pain ahead. Lots and lots of pain and healing and more pain. I had already survived rape, alcohol, abuse, the death of a child, cigarettes, Valium, alcoholic parents, and marriage to Arne Carlson. If God was going to test my wobbly Catholic faith with an adversity I hadn't been through, He would have to get creative. As I lay next to Arnie, I took comfort in that thought. I had been through so much. What else was there?

Well, I have learned one thing in the two decades since that night: God is one creative sonfoabitch.

2

Color Me Barbara

The first person I ever stabbed was another little girl named Barbara. I was five years old. To me, she was the anti-Barbara, all one color: beige. Beige hair, beige eyes, beige arms, and beige teeth with a slightly yellow cast. She wore perky little scarves around her neck. Her mother had a 54-inch waist, a floor you could eat off of, and wore little white anklets with big black orthopedic shoes. They were quiet people, well-behaved, living in a quiet home, where you could hear the clock ticking. Not like my house at all. I loathed these people and all they stood for. We often strolled home from elementary school together, the other Barbara and I. One day an urge took over. I removed a little sterling donkey pin from my blouse and shoved it with mighty force into the anti-Barbara's little beige ass.

She bled.

She ran home to tell her mommy.

My own mother was on the phone by the time I walked through the door of my own house. "I'm sure she could not have done something like that," my mother said. She was not very convincing.

"Why did you do it?" my mother asked me, after she hung up.

I glared.

"She drove me to it," I said.

Crooked Parts

I came gushing from the womb on June 21, 1938, delivered by my own maternal grandfather, Dr. Floyd "Daddy Doc" Gillis, in Mitchell, South Dakota. My father and mother, Harry and Jane Duffy, had made the drive from their home in Edina, a suburb of Minneapolis, for a free delivery.

My first memory: It takes place back in Minneapolis. I must have been no more than a year and a half, in my nursery, where I was busily finger painting with my poop. I was enjoying myself thoroughly and was suspiciously quiet, I guess, for I could hear my mother coming up the stairs, calling "Barbie?" (She called me Barbie, thinking wishfully.) "Barbie?" When she opened the door to the nursery, she found me naked, covered in discharge, and twirling a dirty diaper above my head. She stood there—petite, perfectly coiffed, and horrified.

I let go of that diaper. It sailed through the air and landed at her feet, soiling her little white pumps. At least I recall their being white. This must have been before Labor Day.

Whenever it was, it marked the beginning of my lifelong battle with Jane Duffy.

My mother was one of the beautiful women, one of those who took second looks for granted. Friends tell me that I would have liked her, had I ever given her a chance when I was growing up. They tell me that Jane helped us put on plays in the living room, that she would take us to the drive-in in her convertible and buy us candy at the ice show. I don't remember those things. My childhood friend Suzie DeLong, a statuesque Nordic goddess, emulated my mother. She says my mother reminded her of Jane Powell—beautiful and glamorous, a wonderful hostess with a generous laugh. My mother sculpted in clay and drew delicate little angels on her Christmas cards. She invited my girlfriends up to her bathroom, and while soaking in the tub, she drew pictures for them. How charming. How I hated her.

What do I remember about Jane Duffy? I remember lying in bed and hearing Jane as she came home from dinner late so many times. She climbed the stairs to my room.

"I love you," she whispered, leaning over to kiss me.

I could smell the alcohol and I hated it. I pretended to be asleep, thinking, "Why can't she tell me that when she's sober?" And eventually she'd stumble out and down the hall to her own room.

When I was very young she once crafted for me a doll-house with needlepoint rugs and exquisite handmade furniture. When I knew she was looking, I kicked it, and the little tiny pieces of china rattled and cracked. For Christmas, she gave me a hand-monogrammed dicky. I snipped the collar in half and threw away the part with her embroidery.

I have a photo. I call it "Alcoholic with Child," and I can stare at it for hours. I'm a toddler, and she's holding me. She is composed and poised, and I am sitting still. Imagine what she must have gone through to dress me, put me in the car, make me behave. I know it wasn't easy, because the part in her otherwise perfect hair is crooked. She had probably begun drinking early that day. I must have squirmed, turning my head from side to side, trying to avoid the stench of scotch as she combed my hair. I guess I mussed her hair, or she had to dress herself in a hurry after wrangling me. And so she has a crooked part in the picture. A crooked part. A battle scar.

My father's name was Harry Duffy. His word was law. I never saw Harry with a hammer or paintbrush. I never saw him mow the lawn or clean the pool or weed the garden. I saw him give orders, and I saw them carried out, and I saw him laugh and drink and drink and drink. I was lucky, as children of alcoholics go. Some of us tiptoe through child-hood, holding little fingers in the air to gauge the weather in the house. Will Dad be happy or morose? Will he be loving or violent? Will he beat me today, or will he beat my mother? And the child must break the codes of behavior, know when to hide or stay at friends'. Learn how to keep secrets. This is the slow, careful, sad dance they learn.

My dance was different. I danced to keep my balance in the cyclone of wild gaiety and laughter that rang through the house. It was a dance of spinning and jumping and shouting. It kept me at the eye of the storm, the center of attention. I knew if I sat still, for even a moment, I'd be lost, and I'd be blown away. I had to forget myself, ignore my exhaustion, and keep up with Harry Duffy.

And oh, how I loved Harry Duffy.

I didn't mind the smell of liquor on Harry's breath. It was always there, but unlike my mother, he wasn't prone to depression. The liquor didn't make him moody or sloppy. He was affectionate and always happy. My first memory of his face is brief. He's tossing me in the air. I am still small, and he's enormous and strong. He's laughing, and I'm laughing. In my next memory of him, we are sitting in an elegant restaurant. We're dining, and he's drinking, and all the other grownups in the restaurant stop by and sit for a moment, he orders them drinks, and he introduces me as his little princess. He's the king. He's the master of his universe.

Thinking back, I believe I had a crush on my father. It wasn't a child's love. No, I think it was the kind of love you feel for someone you don't really know, whom you ache to know better. At the time, I only knew I loved him, wanted to always be with him. Now I understand my feelings for him. Misguided feelings. As I entered my teenage years, I suppose that I wanted to fuck him. And my mother, his wife, this beautiful other woman whom I wasn't terribly fond of in the first place, was always getting in my way.

Horrid

Harry Duffy's father was a railroad man. His mother was heiress to a lumber fortune. Harry worked for his father-in-law briefly before moving my mother and me to Anoka, a small blue-collar town located just north of Minneapolis. Here, he, his father, and his brother, Patrick, opened Duffy Lumber in the early 1940s.

I'm not sure what kept Harry out of the military service. Flat feet, maybe, or bad kidneys. I do know that World War II touched the Duffy home only superficially. We always had cigarettes doled out by the Red Cross (Harry and Jane were volunteers), and the maids recycled balls of tinfoil in the spirit of wartime conservation. Grandma Mamie was saddened by the 1945 death of Franklin Delano Roosevelt, while the event generated something less than grief in the Republican quarters of the Duffy clan. The war had made us rich. Duffy Lumber boomed along with the rest of the nation throughout the 1940s and 1950s, and the Duffys were hardly shy about celebrating their good fortune.

When you were a big shot in Anoka, you lived down on the Mississippi River, and the back lawn of our three-story, five-bedroom Colonial rolled right into the water. Jane and Harry went out five or six nights a week, leaving me to my reign of terror over a largely unhappy succession of housekeepers and baby-sitters. When Harry and Jane did stay home, the party came to them. To me, it seemed that the house was always full of people. I liked the decibel level. I

9

liked the energy. I liked the chaos—all of which I would duplicate years later in my own home.

I think back on our home in Anoka as a battleground where everyone was dying and nobody knew it. A stalwart soldier was I—precocious and arrogant and difficult and willful and smart enough to figure out early that nice girls don't count. By the age of six months, I had blossomed to a healthy twenty-six pounds and growing. I was the first grandchild and spoiled rotten by everyone, especially by my paternal grandparents, Mamie and P.J. My every wish was Mamie's command. I was her star, her love, her reason for existence. She told me that had I been a boy, I would have been the messiah and she indulged my sweet tooth with graham crackers slathered in heavy cream and powdered sugar.

What a defiant little bitch I was. I couldn't eat white bread because of allergies, and when my mother withheld it, I sneaked it upstairs and ate loaf after loaf. The allergic reaction to the stolen bread exacerbated the eczema and asthma that I suffered as a child (and that I still suffer sometimes as an adult). In itching fits, I rubbed my face raw. Allergy fits always worked. It brought my mother running, got me noticed, restored me to the eye of the storm. A girl's beauty is a very important part of her demeanor. You learn this when you are beautiful. You learn it the hard way when you are homely or heavy, and then you learn to get your second looks any way you can.

So I hated it when my little brother George arrived when I was two and staked his claim to his share of the spotlight. I put cement in his diaper and dropped him down the second-floor laundry chute. (He survived.) When Nana and Daddy Doc redecorated their master bedroom in fancy 1940s piss-elegant style, I enhanced the color scheme on the walls and fabrics with a tube of Nana's red lipstick.

The neighbors' children loved to play at our house, and

as the hostess, it was my job to make their stay exciting. We formed clubs and secret societies. I was invariably president, presiding over the proceedings. I enjoyed giving orders. It was my best friend Suzie's job, for example, to keep up with my asthma inhaler.

At a very early age, I became curious about the nether regions of the ice-show skaters who twirled around in those little orange skirts, so I decided that my friends Suzie and her sister Molly should play doctor with me. We spent years looking up each other's snatches, and when we began to sprout pubic hair, we divided into secret teams called Mahogany and Blond. I was never modest, I suppose because nudity was never a big issue in our family. Even when my breasts were just beginning to appear, I frolicked around the house wearing only a pair of baroque ruffled bloomers that my grandmother Mamie sewed for me out of bedsheets.

We were a close family, as far as the outside world was concerned. We boarded the Cadillac or cruise ship and took off on vacations every winter, and each fall (Harry and Jane never thought school should get in the way of a good time), we visited Nana and Daddy Doc in Mitchell, South Dakota, for Corn Palace Week. Now that was *something*.

When he was only in his twenties, Daddy Doc was one of the artists charged with decorating the Corn Palace, an elaborate convention center that was built in 1892 to accomodate the annual Corn Belt exposition. Each year artists still decorate the outside of the Corn Palace with scenes, portraits, and pictures, all rendered in jillions of kernels of corn. Daddy Doc was the first Corn Palace artist to add electric lights to the outside of the building, and his contribution made him a Mitchell legend. In 1942, the year I turned four, "Allied Victory" was the theme. Big corn American doughboys with bayonets stood guard on either side of the

Corn Palace entrance. I still remember the brilliant lights of red, white, and blue.

A month or so following Corn Palace Week, we always celebrated October 31 with great gusto in Anoka, the self-proclaimed Halloween Capital of the World. Each year the town staged a monstrous Halloween celebration for the kids, who came from all over the state in search of treats and prize money. Prizes of $25, $15, and $10 were given to those clubs and organizations with the best floats and marching bands. I always wanted to go to the celebration as a fairy princess, with gold threads in my dress and Shirley Temple curls. Jane ignored my pleas and dressed me as that bitch, the Queen of Hearts. Another time I went as the Bird in the Gilded Cage, in a costume complete with dyed red underwear. Harry served as one of the finance chairmen, and we always attended a high school football game called the Pumpkin Bowl. It was a very big to-do: A trip to Anoka's Halloween blowout was once given as a prize on *The Dating Game*.

I don't remember why I ran away from home at the age of three, but I remember what I wore: a camel hair coat, which matched that of my best friend and running mate, Leslie Johnson. (We made it two blocks, I think, before they caught us.) Throughout my life, even as my memory has grown feeble with alcohol and age and survival, I have an uncanny recall for what I wore during important events. For my first day of school, I chose a black watch plaid jumper and festooned my hair with pigtails.

I wore an adorable flannel nightgown the first time I saw my father's penis.

I was six or seven, and in bed with my mother, when Harry came out of the bathroom in a robe. He wanted to show Jane something—crabs, maybe, or a sore.

"Barbara," he said, "turn over."

So I went on my tummy and put my head in my hands,

and while she was examining him, I peeked. It was simply fabulous. The only penis I had seen up to this point was my little brother's, which was teeny. This one was big and sort of purple and had a head on it. I saw it a few times after that, on mornings when he sat on the sofa in the living room in his bathrobe, nursing a hangover, sipping a Bloody Mary, crossing and uncrossing his legs. He may or may not have known I was looking.

That was my first important penis. There would, of course, be more.

3

Breaking Down

We lie on therapists' sofas and talk about our parents. We do it to blame them at first, then we try to forgive, and finally, if we are very, very lucky, we realize that none of that matters, because they did the best they could. We learn that our parents are not us, and we don't *have* to be them, and a great burden is lifted. What's done is done, and we don't have to know them before we can know ourselves. Struggling through this process, I have learned to love my mother, and for that reason, I want to understand her. So I think about her a lot. I think about her past. That clears the way for love, and blows away the blame.

When she was a teenager, a doctor told her she was pregnant. She wasn't married and she was very scared. She was found in the street, going mad, beating her head against a cement curb.

My mother never told me much more than that, about this incident in her life, but before she died in 1990, after I had taken a strong pro-choice stand during my tenure on the Minneapolis City Council, my mother told me that she had terminated the pregnancy. I pressed her on one detail.

"Did Daddy Doc perform the abortion?" I asked her.

Jane wouldn't answer. She didn't have to. My mother's father did absolutely everything for his family. Daddy Doc hired the help, took Nana shopping, delivered his daughter's children, watched over the menus, and made sure the serving silver was in order. Why *wouldn't* he have performed the abortion?

After Daddy Doc delivered me, he brought my brother George into the world, and when I was six or seven, he agreed to deliver Harry and Jane's third child. Harry and Jane left for Mitchell shortly before the baby was due, while George and I stayed behind in the care of my doting grandparents, Mamie and P.J.

"Will it be a brother or a sister?" I demanded to know, for I needed to start devising this kid's torture as soon as possible. A day or two later the phone call came: I was going to have a sister, and her name would be Susan. But I would never meet her. She was born dead, strangled by her own umbilical cord.

Soon after that phone call, my mother and father returned from Daddy Doc's, and we never spoke of little Susan again. I wonder if my mother wanted to talk about Susan, but that Harry wouldn't let her, thinking that way was best. I still wonder how Daddy Doc must have felt, having his own granddaughter die in his arms in his delivery room. I do know that he never delivered another grandchild again. In 1948, Jane stayed in Minnesota for the birth of her last child, Bruce.

Jane began hemorrhaging during the delivery. By the time Daddy Doc and Nana drove up from Mitchell, they were told that Mother was dying, but that the baby would live. Bruce was removed by cesarean section, and my mother was thrown back together. The blood transfusions kept coming, but since the doctors had all but given up on her, her insides were thrown back in haphazardly. They taped her together and waited for her to die, blasting her body with painkillers.

Her insides were a wreck, physical and emotional ailments would hound her the rest of her life, and she had taken an unfortunate liking to Demerol.

My mother was probably an alcoholic even before she went into the hospital. She returned from the hospital an alcoholic, a drug addict, and a raging hypochondriac with real medical problems. She had become a creature to be reckoned with.

For the next thirty years, she coped as best she could, which meant she favored doctors who would double as dealers. She got uppers and downers and painkillers of every hue from every kind of doctor, including her brother and father, who were both physicians. They all thought she was darling and in terrible pain, and so of course they did what she asked. As a young girl, I couldn't begin to understand what she had gone through in that delivery room. Still, I never thought she was darling.

My mother was hospitalized for at least six months of every year. At home she was demanding and petulant. I remember her weeping and moaning and screaming at her children and servants. The doctors would come with shots and pills, and only then would she be quiet. I liked her better on Demerol.

Jane and Harry still went out, and the house still chimed with the sound of cocktail glasses and adult laughter, though now Jane often celebrated in her room with her scotch while a party raged downstairs. The mother I recall from my adolescence spent most of her time in bed, sipping a highball, reading, smoking, and watching TV. She watched a *lot* of television. *I Love Lucy*, game shows, soap operas, everything. Harry bought her big TVs, little TVs, TVs for the bathroom, for the bedroom, for the porch. I suppose she was addicted to TV, too.

I can't remember, much less count, all of Jane's suicide

attempts over the years. Usually she would be found conked out in bed next to a bottle of sleeping pills. Her stomach was pumped routinely. And to the Duffy children, visiting her in the loony bin became as normal as attending mass. Duffy women were supposed to throw parties and look great and play bridge. If they broke down, Harry Duffy sent them off for repairs, like last year's Cadillac.

Two years ago, Bruce told me that Harry had many, many affairs while we were growing up, in particular with a waitress from Greenhaven Country Club. I was livid when I found out. I couldn't believe that another woman had had my father, whom I had kept on a pedestel for so long. Why was I surprised? *I've* certainly had affairs, and I was an alcoholic. Why would my father be any different?

"It doesn't matter where he roams," Jane used to say when Harry wasn't home for dinner. "As long as he comes home to me." How sad. Now I know what she meant.

With Jane in bed or hospitalized, with Harry out drinking, working or fucking waitresses, I was left in charge of the house. If I couldn't have my parents, then goddammit, at least I would get my own way, and I would get it no matter what the body count. By the age of twelve, when I entered seventh grade, I was screaming at the maids if my collars weren't correctly starched. If the scrambled eggs were runny, the cook would be scraping them off the wall. I mouthed off. I ranted. I raved. The maids were dropping quicker than ever. I was a holy terror, hardly a proper Duffy woman. So Harry decided that it was time to send his daughter off for repairs, as well. Before I knew it, I was packed and ready to register at the Villa Maria Academy, a Catholic girls' boarding school in Frontenac, Minnesota. I was pissed. My one thought was, "By God, how those nice nuns are going to suffer for Harry's sin against me."

Madame Pompadour

On June 21, 1951, the day I turned thirteen, a *New York Times* headline announced: PSYCHIATRY URGED FOR YOUNG ADDICTS.

Prescient, was it not? There was also a chance of rain in the forecast that day, but I dared the weather to dampen my birthday party by inviting a few dozen of my closest friends for horseback riding at the stables outside town.

For 35 cents every Friday evening we would watch movie westerns starring Dale Evans, Roy Rodgers, and Hopalong Cassidy. On my birthday, I decided as I mounted Trigger— or whatever the hell the horse's name was—that I would show my friends that Hopalong had nothing on Barbara Jane Duffy. I saw a tree in the distance. Riding as if on the wind, I envisioned how I would take hold of one of the tree's lower branches, lift myself off Trigger's back, then drop gracefully on my feet as he galloped into the distance with his empty saddle. Well, at least that was the plan.

I jumped on my horse and gave him a good goosing. He followed instructions beautifully. We must have been doing a hundred by the time I got to the branch. And that's the last thing I remember.

For my thirteenth birthday, I gave myself a broken collarbone and a brain concussion. Most humiliating of all, when I got knocked out, I peed my pants in front of all my friends. I decided to blame the horse. I hope he's glue now.

By the grace of a benevolent God, I had recuperated and was done with the neck brace by the time eighth grade arrived. My parents dropped me off for some fine-tuning at the Villa Maria Academy. You will not be surprised to learn that Catholic school did not work the miracle that Harry and Jane had hoped. I hated boarding school. I didn't like the nuns telling me what to do, and I didn't like the discipline, and I didn't like going to class on Saturdays.

My first clash of wills with the sisters took place over a rip in my dull blue jumper, the school uniform, and I won. The rip had been there a few days before a sister noticed it in the hallway.

"You must sew that up, dear," she said, and would have gladly taught me how to patch my garment if only I had asked. I looked her right in the eye.

"Over my dead body," I said. This would not be the last time I left a nun speechless. I saw that rip as a merit badge and proudly wore it for another six months.

Studying was not something that fit into my schedule the first semester, but that doesn't mean I didn't learn anything. I met my first lesbian at Villa Maria. She asked me to crawl into her bed one night. I didn't know exactly what she had in mind, but I understood enough to answer, "Absolutely not." And that was the end of that.

I also learned the true beauty of the words, "Charge it, please." I had uttered these words before, but never so often and so bountifully as I did at Villa Maria. With abandon, I charged poodle skirts and records to Harry and made sure my girlfriends never went hungry. I was a very popular kid.

But when I think back on being thirteen, my mind doesn't immediately turn to boarding school and spending sprees and lesbians and exasperated nuns. Age thirteen is when I took my first drink.

This pivotal moment in my life occurred at the Duffy Thanksgiving celebration, which featured Madame Pompadours in Mamie's great silver punch bowl. Brandy, sliced oranges, maraschino cherries, and champagne—now tell me a soul, a living soul in this world, who could resist it. It was fabulous, and by the fourth glass, *I* was fabulous. I was wild, giggly, fearless, flying high on my very first drunk, and I loved it. By the time the adults sat down for dinner with their martinis, bourbon and wine, they had long since left behind their ability to notice that the thirteen-year-old was nearly single-handedly draining the punch bowl.

The next day wasn't so fabulous. If someone had told me that the Anoka Sanitation Department had dispatched garbage trucks into my head, it wouldn't have surprised me. My eyes could not focus. I only left my bed to vomit in the toilet across the hall. And yet, in spite of the agony, I knew that I had loved the taste of that brandy and champagne. I could not forget the dandy out-of-control feeling it gave me. I planned to get some more of it just as soon as I could keep anything down.

I was an alcoholic.

4

Orangutans

A chemical dependency therapist once told me that ignoring alcoholism in a family is like ignoring the orangutan in the living room. Well, let me tell you: The Duffys were keeping an entire fucking zoo. Everything we did revolved around drinking. You didn't relax without a beer or glass of wine. The real drinking started at five o'clock sharp—cocktail hour—when Harry got home from the lumberyard, usually still buzzed from his four-martini lunch. Even mornings after a party were a special time for the Duffy family. In the kitchen, Harry and Jane nursed their hangovers with brandy Alexanders, offering sips to little Bruce ("Tastes like a milk-shake," he would say), while George and I were in the living room, enjoying the dregs of leftover highballs.

Like my father, I was a delightful drunk, a tipsy teen who was never sullen and always outrageous. The alcohol kept my inner demons at bay. Harry Duffy didn't lose a girl to alcoholism. He gained a drinking buddy.

I was there to keep him company in 1952, when Jane spent the better part of spring recuperating in the Milwaukee Sanitorium in Wawatosa, Wisconsin. I can't remember what Jane had done; whether she had tried to kill herself or was found singing naked in the garage. But one day my father picked me up at Villa Maria, and we took the train to visit her. He took her a dozen roses, made polite conversation with the mother of his children, and then whisked me off to Chicago for dinner at Trader Vic's.

I was wearing a black silk dress that he had purchased for me on one of our shopping trips.

How wonderful, I thought, to go to Chicago just for dinner. Not yet fourteen and sitting here sipping a mai tai. In Jane's absence, I was playing Harry's wife—just the role I'd always wanted. When I returned to Anoka following my first and only year at Villa Maria, I took over hostess duties from my mother, as well. I attended ninth grade at public school and lived at home. While the real Mrs. Duffy was alone upstairs watching TV in bed, I was making sandwiches for Harry's card games in the den. When he built a pool the following summer, I mixed drinks for his pool parties. I kept the glasses filled during cocktail hour and often took my mother's place at Harry's regular table at Charlie's Cafe Exceptionale.

How I loved going to Charlie's. To a teenage girl, Charlie's was the epitome of glamour, even though we had been regulars for years. Bob Hope and Arthur Godfrey and Jayne Mansfield and Esther Williams all ate there when they passed through town. The owner, Charlie Saunders, patterned the restaurant after the 21 Club in New York. There was one room after another, paneled in oak, and a sweeping mahogany bar. There were enormous murals of hunting scenes in the entrance hall and Vikings in the Nordic Room. A life-size bronze nude classic statue named Harriet had been placed at the entrance in 1948. This installation riled the pastor of the First Covenant Church of Minneapolis, who wrote Saunders that the nudity would "offend the moral sense of masses of our Minneapolis citizens." As it turned out, the masses didn't give a damn, and Harriet stayed there, snatch to the wind, until the restaurant closed in 1982.

Henry, the maître d', always escorted us to Harry's regular table in one of the small dining rooms. My father would eat steaks, while I put away Charlie's legendary potato salad and the New York sandwich—sliced Virginia ham and breast of chicken smothered in cheese sauce. This was not a kind diet to a girl prone to chubbiness. Prior to my teen years, growing spurts had kept my weight in check. Now that I was older, taking Jane's place at Charlie's and drinking every night, I quickly swelled to 145 pounds.

"I like my women thin," Harry told me, and so I began a pattern of crash dieting and binging that would continue for the rest of my life. As a teen blossom, however, I managed to control my weight, like so many girls of the 1950s, with Dexedrine tablets.

"Let us control your appetite, young lady," these little amphetamine devils promised. Bullshit. They were uppers, and they screwed up my metabolism, always giving me a nice jolt.

But more importantly, they kept me thin for Harry Duffy.

Sandra

My first fur coat was a short, blue-gray beaver jacket. Oh, how soft and wonderful it was. Harry bought it for me when I was in ninth grade, and I have been proudly, defiantly, politically incorrect on the issue of fur ever since. I often invite representatives from the People for the Ethical Treatment of Animals on my talk show, and I tell them they're nuts.

"If a mink can wear mink, so can I," say I. "*You* wear plastic, which is going to stay in the landfill for years and years and years and years and never break down. God made the little furry creatures for me to be warm."

A couple of years ago I announced on the air that a furrier

in Minneapolis was going to make me a coat out of the raccoons that were taking over my neighborhood. They were huge. They knocked over garbage cans and lived in the sewers. We were going to catch them, and I was going to have a new fur coat. But it never happened. The station manager refused to let us kill them on the station property, and, besides, we had a devil of a time deciding how to do the little bastards in. Oh well, the best laid plans of mink and men . . .

My pool parties were a hot ticket in Anoka the summer I turned fifteen, and when Harry and Jane left town for a few days, a hundred or so of my friends moved in. We must have killed a maid or done something just as horrible that skips my mind, because I found myself back in boarding school that fall. This time I was enrolled in the Convent of the Visitation in St. Paul.

However, I did not suffer a sense of dread as I packed for my sophomore year away from home. Public school, I discovered, was much too crowded, and there were too many lines to stand in. Plus, this time, I was taking to boarding school with me a great new friend: the Bottle. As a result, my memories from this point through high school graduation three years later are foggy. I know I smuggled vodka into the boarding house, where I lived with a dozen other Visitation girls, and that's just about the last thing I remember.

It was clear right away that this sophomore was not on her way to a Rhodes scholarship, but the nuns were stuck with me as long as Harry Duffy could afford to pay the freight. They must have been thrilled. During my first week in class, I was assigned a current events report. Of course, I was too busy planning clandestine cocktail parties to make it to the library. So I plumbed my report from my new issue of *Confidential,* one of those 1950s *National Enquirer* precursors. I can't remember what article I chose, though chances are, I got up and told the nun and all these sweet little girls some story about the new gangster Lana Turner was allegedly screwing. I don't recall being chastised for this; I suppose the nuns thought I would grow out of such behavior.

After our sophomore year, my dorm mates and I graduated to another large house next door and spent a lot of time and energy decorating it. We papered the walls, hung white curtains, and put matching blue silky comforters on our twin beds. And my goodness, how we ate. When they measured Visitation girls for uniforms at the beginning of the year, they always allowed for two extra inches for the weight gain that was to come. They would have had to allow for at least eight inches, had it not been for the Dexedrine. All the girls popped it constantly, and we hummed with energy.

Sandra Peterson, who had come from Anoka to Visitation with me, was my best friend. She was perfect. I have always been attracted to opposites when choosing close friends and lovers, a trend that began with Sandra. I was always losing my pumps or wearing blue jeans and looking like hell. Meanwhile, there was Sandra, beside me, looking so dignified in one of her immaculately starched white blouses. She was an only child and the daughter of an alcoholic father. She had spent her first fifteen years on this earth helping her mother run the shoe store they owned and caring for her dad when he wasn't in the bin. Like so many children of alcoholics, she thought it was her lot in life to take care of drunks. It didn't take her long to find me.

Without complaint, Sandra was forever driving me home and putting me to bed. I can remember feeling sick on gin, just *reeling*, after one of our picnics out by a lake had evolved into a late-night toot. My friends were leaving, the bonfire was dying down, and Sandra was trying her damnedest to get me home.

"Turn like a top," I can remember her saying, as she tried to gently force my fat unwieldy ass into the car. I'm sure I threw up on Sandra more than once. To this day, she's too nice to mention it.

Had it not been for Sandra, I'm sure I would have burned down our dormitory. By age sixteen, I was smoking two packs of Winstons a day, keeping about a half-dozen cigarettes burning at any given time. Sandra followed me from room to room, patiently mashing burning butts into the ashtrays. Daddy Doc, who was ahead of his time on the smoking issue, frowned on the habit. (He also insisted that his family install seat belts in their cars in the 1950s, long before belts were mandatory). During a visit to Mitchell one weekend, I sneaked off to an upstairs bathroom for a puff or two, got carried away, and wound up having an asthma attack. I fainted, but somehow before I lost all consciousness, I managed to flush the cigarettes down the toilet, so no one knew *what* was wrong with me. Daddy Doc and Nana rushed me to the hospital.

"Were you smoking?" asked the attending physician in the emergency room, certain he had found the problem. He must have smelled the smoke on my breath.

"Of course not," I told him. I stuck to my story and spent the next two days in the hospital undergoing tests.

When Visitation shut down for the summer, I moved back to Anoka and tried working for Harry at the lumberyard as a secretary. I would arrive at work late, leave for lunch early, and call in sick frequently. After two weeks, I stopped showing up at all. For Heaven's sake, there was a pool at home and parties to plan. Little did Harry and Jane know that their darling daughter also had quite a night life going. My bedroom had a sundeck, and just after dusk, I would prop a ladder against the house. Around eleven P.M., as Harry and Jane turned in, my performance would begin. I put my hair in curlers, smeared white zinc oxide on my face, and put on a nightgown. I dutifully kissed Harry and Jane good night, disappeared back into my room with a book, and waited. As soon as the light in their bedroom went out, the curlers came out and the cream came off. I pulled off the nightgown, revealing jeans underneath, crawled out the window, and climbed down the ladder. The freedom machine was my red and white Chevy convertible.

I was usually sneaking out to play with my girlfriends or make out with my boyfriends, Bob or Jack, both of whom I met in high school, and both of whom strutted in and out of my life for a few years. Bob was a nice enough kid, but Harry and Jane hated Jack. He looked like a hood, complete with slicked-back hair and a black leather jacket. I found him absolutely gorgeous. We called him Cadillac Jack, after his love for flashy cars. We called his mother "Oh My God Honey," because this was her favorite expression.

So besides Harry there were other men in my life, but other than some heavy petting, sex was not a part of my adolescence. This was the 1950s, and an unwanted pregnancy was a Holocaust for a Catholic teenage girl. Occasionally good Catholic girls would begin to put on weight, then disappear for six months, no explanation offered. Of course, everyone knew they had been shipped off to their grandmother's house in Florida or New York or Seattle or wherever to have the kid and sign it over to the adoption agency. They always came back home eventually, their spirits broken, no questions asked.

"There but for the grace of God . . . ," I said when they disappeared. I remember sitting on the toilet at the end of every month, praying that one of those little sperm hadn't somehow escaped through Cadillac Jack's zipper and journeyed down through my waistband.

"Please, dear God and the Virgin Mary and all the saints in Heaven! Come, period! Come!" This was my mantra.

In June of 1956, just before my eighteenth birthday, we celebrated my graduation from Visitation with an opulent black-tie dinner at home in Anoka. All the girls wore beautiful organdy dresses, Harry hired a band, and we danced by the pool. I felt euphoric and sad. I was sad to say good-bye to the nuns, whom I had come to appreciate in a begrudging sort of way (they were mostly kind and the closest things to parents I had ever known), and sad to know that Sandra would be leaving Anoka soon for college, while I would be living at home. I washed down the sadness with one gin and tonic after another. It was the last time, if I remember correctly—and I probably don't—that Sandra put me to bed.

Forty years later in October 1994, I was driving home from the radio station in Minneapolis when my car veered toward Anoka. I didn't know why, but I had to go back home, and something was telling me I had to see Sandra. Though not estranged, we had spent our adult lives apart. She had married a shoe salesman named Jack Purtle, whom I didn't like very much. I thought he was an opportunist. He thought I was a bitch. I thought he drank too much. He thought I talked too much.

I stopped by to visit Sandra at her family's shoe store, which she still owns. She told me that it was Jack's birthday and asked me to join them for dinner at a restaurant that evening. Strangely, I said yes, and even more strangely, Jack seemed happy to see me.

He didn't drink that night, and there was a peace about him that I had never seen. When Jack and I were alone, he spoke to me about how much he loved Sandra. He told me how proud he was of their three grown children. I wondered if he had ever told them these things himself and why in the world he was telling me.

A few weeks later, Jack Purtle died of a heart attack. At his funeral, I repeated to Sandra, his daughter, and his two sons all the wonderful things he had said about them. Then I realized why my car had turned toward Anoka that day. I really believe that some part of Jack, the part that was preparing to die, had chosen me as a messenger. Since then Sandra and I have resumed a friendship that lay dormant for four decades. She spent her first New Year's Eve without Jack in the room I fixed up for her at my lake house.

Now, I believe, it's my turn to take care of her.

5

Trapeze

The first time I ever let a man touch my tits, I wore a blue and white dress. It happened at the Starlight Drive-in during *Trapeze,* starring Burt Lancaster, Tony Curtis, and Gina Lollobrigida. Burt wore white tights that revealed a big smooth lump in his crotch.

Burt fell from his trapeze just before the opening credits. I cringed, scooted closer to Cadillac Jack, and let him put his right arm around my shoulders. Halfway through the movie, as Burt was emoting, Tony was swinging here and yon, and Gina was doing whatever the hell she did, Jack's left hand floated slowly over the gearshift and landed gently on my right breast.

"Finally," I thought with relief, as I sacrificed my virginal eighteen-year-old orbs to Cadillac Jack. "Now, is this all there is?"

I can still see my reflection in the car's side mirror. I am smiling at me.

I'm fairly sure that my affection for Cadillac Jack owed a great deal to the fact that Jane had so much animosity for him. Even as a young adult I remained hell-bent on driving the poor old girl out of her mind. When Jack proposed, Jane vowed that no daughter of hers would ever marry him. Privately, I told Jack that it would never work out; I wasn't in love, but we decided to keep dating. However, to give Jane a fit, I bought a wedding dress and told her to start planning a wedding. For a couple of weeks she tried to forbid me from leaving the house.

"Where the hell are you going?" she hollered from her bedroom one evening.

"Out."

"Out where?"

"Out with Jack."

"No, Barbara, you're not," she said. "You are *not* going out with that creep."

"I don't care what you want. I'm going." I took off down the stairs and reached for my purse in the front hall.

Suddenly, Jane appeared at the top of the staircase in her nightgown. She was shaking, loaded on scotch and Demerol, and clumsily cocking a double-barreled shotgun. It must have been twice her size, and it was aimed directly at me.

"You take one more step, and I'm going to blow you away," she slurred.

I held my purse, and I stared up into the barrels. I don't recall fear or shock. I was probably aware that in her stupor she couldn't hit the damn swimming pool, much less a moving target. I think I rolled my eyes.

"Adios," I said coolly, and slammed the door on my way out.

I spent the evening with Jack, had a lovely time, then on my way home began wondering if Jane might still be standing behind the door with the shotgun. I pulled off the road and spent the night alone in a cheap motel, making sure that Jane had time to cool down by the time I returned home. When I walked in the door the next day, not knowing *what* to expect, Jane had sobered up and seemed calm. We never discussed the shotgun incident, probably because she didn't remember it. Or maybe because amid the chaos of the Duffy household, pulling a gun on one's daughter just didn't seem to be that far out of line. I found out much later that she had reported me missing that night. I took that as a nice display of affection.

Queen of All the Acrobats

When I wasn't blazing toward second base with Jack, I spent the summer of 1956 trying to choose my place of higher education. If I chose the University of Colorado, I could learn to ski. At the University of Miami, I could maintain a gorgeous suntan. New York University would put me right in the heart of Manhattan, the center of the universe. I considered all the possibilities.

What I did *not* consider was taking one of those aptitude tests, the scores of which colleges are so fond of having on their students' applications. This altered my options drastically. So, that fall, after Harry made a phone call to one of his buddies in the administration building, I began attending freshman classes at the University of Minnesota.

I spent most of my hours at the V—the Varsity Cafe— where we smoked and gossiped and ate. It was there that my capacity for alcohol rapidly increased to Faulknerian dimensions.

When I began failing all of my classes, Harry decided that I must be having some kind of mental breakdown. Psychiatric tests were ordered. "There's no reason this kid is not doing 'A' work," one of the psychiatrists told him. Of course, I wasn't telling anyone that I was drinking all the time and skipping class. Harry and Jane had no idea *what* was wrong. Sure Barbara drank, but didn't everybody? So I ended my freshman year undergoing evaluation at the Milwaukee Sanitarium, the same funny farm where Harry and I had visited Jane years before.

Being the daughter of Jane Duffy, I didn't consider going to a sanitarium any big deal. I just thought it was something women *did*. And this was not my first experience with psychotherapy. I saw my first shrink at the age of six. Why, I don't know—perhaps I had tried to kill my brother. I remember pictures of Dumbo and Cinderella on the wallpaper. I remember taking one of the doctor's medical books from the shelf, sitting in his lap, and discussing how babies were born.

The Milwaukee Sanitarium must have been a happy experience because, like a true Duffy woman, I took to therapy and decided that mental hospitals provided a wonderful retreat from responsibility. The worse you act, the more petulant you become, the more you fit in. Plus, they never asked me about my drinking, and I would return to the sanitarium drunk after dinners out. So there I was, enjoying the luxuries of treatment and getting to drink at the same time. Fabulous. From the ages of eighteen to twenty-three, I was shipped off to the loony bin four times. Of all the funny farms I have known and loved, Milwaukee would have to be the best. The staff set the table in the finest linens. We dressed for dinner. No wonder Jane loved it! I got massages and hydrotherapy. Other patients were given shock and insulin treatments. They'd be all dressed up for dinner, but couldn't remember a damn thing.

Harry visited and took me shopping. He bought me beautiful clothes from the finest stores in Milwaukee. Jane visited once and got drunk on scotch and milk—that's right, scotch and milk—during dinner. I put away a few drinks myself, and we ended the evening with a shouting match. After that, she never visited again.

Well fed and well rested, I was released from Milwaukee after a couple of months. I got home, went to lunch with a friend, and drove back to the house drunk.

In my absence, Harry and Jane had decided that I should try holding a job for a while, instead of wasting their money at the university. So Harry got me a position in the sportswear department of Harold's, a wonderful specialty shop on Nicollet Avenue. While my friends were hitchhiking through Europe during the summer and getting pinned and going to football games at the university in the fall, I toiled at Harold's selling clothes by B. H. Wraggee and Pauline Trigere and lived at home. But I did not want for a social life. All my college buddies came to Chez Duffy, where I played hostess with the mostest. I had seen the movie *Call Me Madam* several times and decided that Ethel Merman was as good a role model as any.

There was the Harry-and-Jane-Go-to-the-Kentucky-Derby Party, and the Harry-and-Jane-Spend-February-in-Florida Party, traditions that I had begun back in high school. Friends moved in for days at a time, and my youngest brother, Bruce, played bartender. George, whose athletic prowess, good grades, and sobriety made him an anomaly in the Duffy family, had escaped to Harvard by this time.

The parties officially peaked with my rendition of a ditty called "Mary Ann Barnes," which I sang in a nightgown, nothing underneath, on the grand piano, while holding a candelabra:

Mary Ann Barnes was the queen of all the acrobats.
She could do tricks that would give a cat the shits.
She could shoot green peas from her fundamental
   orifice,
Do a double somersault and catch them on her tits. . . .

Blood

At some point, I lost my virginity. I like to *think* it was with Bob or Cadillac Jack, but the claiming of my cherry has remained one of the great mysteries of my life. I have even beseeched my radio listeners for help, inviting "the man who took my maidenhood in his stride" to call up and confess. So far, no response.

Yet, I am afraid I do know exactly how my virginity was taken.

It came to me in 1983, just before New Year's Eve, during my second year on the Minneapolis City Council. We were facing a vote on an antipornography ordinance that would have defined certain sexually explicit material as a violation of women's civil rights. The ordinance made national news, and Minneapolis became a rallying ground for the radical feminist front. The scholar and attorney Catherine MacKinnon had written the ordinance, and she came to town to fight for it, as did the feminist writer Andrea Dworkin.

The most effective proponents of the ordinance were, in fact, rape victims, who thought that certain kinds of pornography lead to violence against women. For me, however, it became a First Amendment issue, and I viewed it as a threat to my freedom of choice. My life then, as it is now, was based on choice, on decisions for which I am solely responsible and am, for the most part, proud. I wake up every day and make the decision to repair my relationships with my children, to do my best at my job, and to forego alcohol for one more day. The idea of choice was extremely important to me when the ordinance was being discussed, and it was a very emotional issue for everyone involved.

The day before the vote I was having lunch with a friend. Although it was totally unrelated to the conversation at hand,

I blurted out that I had been raped. I immediately returned to whatever we were discussing, as though I had never said it. My friend let it slide, too, not knowing exactly how to respond.

It was the strangest thing. I had never remembered being raped until then. Imagine my surprise. That afternoon, I was in a meeting with Dr. Sharon Satterfield, who was then head of the Department of Human Sexuality at the University of Minnesota. She was opposed to the ordinance, asserting that pornography didn't lead to violence against women and that, in fact, pornography could provide a beneficial service in training programs for counselors. Martha Allen, a friend and newspaper reporter, was there to give me both public and private support; so was Bob Knight, a good friend who worked in the mayor's office. These people provided a comfortable environment in which to talk about the rape, and I did. As the afternoon unfolded, so did my memory of the rape, one horrible detail after another.

I was twenty, maybe nineteen. It was one of those evenings when I felt beautiful. You know the feeling, when every man notices you. I looked wonderful and felt divine. I was thin and draped in a magnificent blue satin dress, and I wore matching satin pumps. I attended a ball at the country club with a man named Bill, who was a dear friend. I remember looking across the room and seeing another man, whom I didn't know. He was tall and handsome. He was there with his own date, but we talked for a few minutes. We laughed and drank and made a date for Sunday evening.

I met him at a bar and ordered a bourbon, which I have never been able to drink since, probably because my subconscious remembered what happened later. I remember a motel and a bottle of liquor on a table between two plastic chairs. This much came back to me; the rape that followed remains lost to what must have been an alcohol blackout. The next thing that came back to me, though, was waking up the next morning and *knowing* that I had been raped. I wondered where I was for a moment and then noticed blood on the headboard and a few streaks, beginning to turn brown, smeared on the wall. I hadn't been hurt or mutilated; so I believe the blood was there because it was the first time I had been penetrated.

I was alone and stunned. Silent, dry-eyed, and stoic, I stumbled to the bathroom, eased my body into the tub, and closed my eyes and turned off my brain. After I had soaked for a while and cleaned up, I dressed and drove to Harold's to report for work. Somewhere between the motel and work, I buried the rape and surrounding events deep inside my memory. For years, I would not think of them again.

I repressed the memory in a cloak of guilt. I assumed the responsibility for not only drinking and for going to a motel room with this man, but in my heart of hearts, I believed that I deserved to be raped. I suppose I still do, and it's terrible to think about it. I was there, wasn't I? I had put myself in that very precarious position. I was simply unable to cope with the pain, humiliation, and the sight of blood on the sheets.

I think God works in protective ways. Many times we only recall the pain when we are able to bear it and face it. If I had tried to deal with the rage inflicted on me by that rape, I probably would have failed. I'm almost certain I would have ended my life. Throughout our meeting that afternoon, I wept. Sharon held my hand as I recalled what had happened to me. That night I went home to my husband, Pete, whom I had been married to for only six months, and I cried in his arms some more.

The next day, I gave a statement to reporters concerning the antipornography ordinance. "I know that my rape wasn't caused by pornography, but by alcohol," I said. "I've worked hard to get well. I've fought alcoholism and other terrible family traumas. I've really struggled, and now they want to take a choice away from me. I've never been so emotional about an issue before. I'll fight this every inch of the way. This ordinance is a stronger violation of me and my rights than that rape."

Mayor Don Fraser would later veto the ordinance, but soon after I spoke, the council passed it by one vote.

6

Shoes

While working at Harold's, I realized that I had absorbed Jane's taste and knowledge about fine fabrics and colors and prints. Even more importantly, I learned that I was a born salesman, and I spent two years at Harold's climbing the merchandising ladder. The summer I turned twenty-one, Mrs. Dredge, the doyenne of sportswear, decided I should start accompanying her on buying trips. We landed in New York City on a warm afternoon in early June.

This was my first voyage to New York sans parents, so naturally I couldn't wait to carouse in the Big Apple. I hit the bars with my good friend Ann Fankhanel, my former college roommate who lived in Manhattan, and her date, a man named Dick. I wore a black dress and pearls and a pair of very expensive black patent leather pumps with brown trim. They cost me $35, a week's salary, and were worth every penny.

By the time we got to the Whaler Bar in Manhattan, I was feeling warm, cozy, and a touch lonely. In addition, Dick was not too happy to have me tagging along. He needed all his concentration to seduce Ann. I saw another man sitting at the bar. He was thirtysomething and gorgeous. He was tall, with dark hair and tortoiseshell eyeglasses, a true preppy in that Brooks Brothers way. I wanted him.

"Dick," I said conspiratorially. "See that man sitting over there? Go get him for me."

Dick eagerly did as he was told.

"You're not going to believe this," he said to the stranger, "but I really want to spend time with my date, and she's got this loud friend from out of town. Would you be nice enough to come over and have a drink with her?"

The man came to our table and introduced himself as Lou. We began talking, and I quickly got all of his vital statistics from him. He was an executive. Separated from his wife. Living at the Yale Club. We drank and talked and laughed, and I fell hat over pumps for this man. I thought he was Heaven-sent, and, oh, how he made me laugh. When we took a moment to look around, we found that Dick and Ann were gone. Lou and I walked to Michael's Pub, where we drank more and listened to Jonah Jones. I hummed along quietly as he played "Please Be Kind" on his golden trumpet.

Later, we danced in the fountain in front of the Plaza Hotel. In the small hours of the morning, I found myself in Lou's arms in a horse-drawn carriage circling through Central Park. I succumbed to his kiss and then some. As I stepped out of the carriage, I discovered that one of my pumps was missing. It had fallen out during the ride, lost in the green of the park. I didn't care.

I spent every extra moment with Lou that trip. He took me to all his favorite haunts among the chic boutiques of Park Avenue and along the tree-lined streets of Greenwich Village. We dined together every night, and he took me to see *West Side Story* on Broadway. Even now, I can't hear "Somewhere" without tearing up. We talked of marriage, and I began to plan my future. I named the children I envisioned that I would have with him. I was his to do with as he wished, but he told me he wasn't ready to make love. I think he knew even during our blissful week that his marriage was not over. I knew only one thing at that time. The affair with the love of my life had begun.

Good Housekeeping

Leaving Lou in New York, I landed in Minneapolis distraught and tear-streaked and determined to run back into his waiting arms. I resigned from Harold's soon after and convinced my parents that I should move to New York to advance my merchandising career. Ann said I could live with her at the London Terrace apartments. I knew that my future would be filled with love, happiness, marriage, and children.

I downplayed one teensy weensy detail in this equation. Lou, with a wife and three children, had not yet agreed to any of it.

After plans were made, trunks were packed (I do not travel lightly) and adieus were bid, I called the Yale Club to give Lou the good news that I was coming to join him in New York. He was no longer living at the club, they informed me. I feared the worst, and when I called his office the next day, he justified my fears. He had gone back to his wife.

I was devastated. I bawled for the next fourteen hours at my old friend Sandra's house. Then I decided stubbornly to seek my destiny in New York anyway, hoping that I'd get Lou back in the process. So began one of the strangest summers of my life. I went to New York and got a job in the buying office of the Allied Stores Corp. It lasted about a week.

I was in no condition to work. I was too busy trying to figure out a way to get Lou back. But I saw him only once that summer. He came down from his Park Avenue office to have lunch with me at our favorite café in the Village. I looked spectacular, thin (gaunt, really) from weeks of crying hours each day. I'm telling you, Ophelia was my middle name.

I dressed for lunch in a big wonderful hat with a veil, flowers, and feathers. It was all to no avail. I could not take my eyes off him. All I wanted to do was touch him. I wanted to bring back every feeling and memory of that magnificent week in June. But he spoke of obligations, of his children. My heart was in pieces. I wanted to nuzzle, he wanted to be practical. I thought if only I were pretty enough, nice enough, sexy enough, warm enough, or loving enough, he would be mine again. As he left me in the cab outside his office after lunch, he leaned over and kissed me and said, "I know this is not going to make any difference to you, but I will always love you."

So ended my second tearful good-bye to Lou. This time, I wouldn't see him again for years.

But here I was, young and in Manhattan, broken hearted and broke. I seldom left London Terrace, my apartment building. I sat home eating Velveeta cheese sandwiches, drinking root beer, and consuming a novel a day. I've been through several novel-a-day periods in my life, trying to fight off depression.

I never told Harry I wasn't working, afraid he would make me come home. Fortunately, I made enough money to live by playing gin rummy with an eighty-five-year-old count on the weekends at the estate of Gordon and Vivian Fawcett in Greenwich, Connecticut. Mr. Fawcett had been one of Harry's Sigma Chi fraternity brothers at the University of Minnesota, and one of the heirs of the Fawcett publishing fortune.

The count was always there, and I spent each Sunday afternoon with him playing cards and drinking gin and tonics. He was absolutely adorable, a good sport, and a dreadful card player. So when I boarded the 8 P.M. train back to Manhattan, I always took with me enough of the count's cash to survive another week. I don't know what would have happened had I ever lost.

One week during this long, hot summer, I flew to Chicago to meet Cadillac Jack. We drove back to New York via Niagara Falls. Our affair had stopped and started several times over the years. I was lonely and thought perhaps the Falls would work their magic for us. They did not. We went back to Manhattan, Jack stayed with my roommate and me in the apartment for a few days, and I woke up one night to find him screwing an old friend of mine in the next bed.

I can't say I was surprised. He was irresistible and sexy, and I knew that Jack would screw anything that wasn't nailed down—and maybe even that. Once, after he fell four stories from a building while working on a construction site, he managed to seduce his nurse while laid up in the hospital with a broken back. He had her right there in his hospital bed.

At the end of the summer, when I had consumed my last grilled cheese, drunk my last root beer, and exhausted my gin rummy winnings, I decided I might as well be devastated in Anoka. At least there I could be closer to Daddy and his credit cards.

Back I went to Anoka, and despite my promise in the field, sportswear was clearly not my destiny. I returned to the University in the fall of 1959 to study art. I was still absolutely distraught after my Lou-less summer.

But a broken heart is a wonderful excuse to drink. Once again, by spring I was failing all my classes, and Harry decided that a stint in the loony bin might remedy my academic malaise. So on March 16, 1960, I was admitted to St. Mary's Hospital in Minneapolis. Fifteen years later, St. Mary's alcohol rehabilitation center would give me back my life. This first trip out did not go so well.

First of all, it was not the country club that Milwaukee Sanitarium had been. My records show that I was a sullen bitch, a terrible snob, and was not a good worker in group therapy. I went to bed early, got up late, and watched TV alone. I met a woman there who had six children. She told me she couldn't handle the stress of motherhood, that she worried about money. I told her that if she simply followed the recipes in *Good Housekeeping,* she'd be fine, and to stop complaining. I made a nurse cry when she presumed to call me Barbara.

"You may call me Miss Duffy," I hissed.

I was furious to be at St. Mary's on St. Patrick's Day and not out drinking with my friends. Really—an alcoholic missing St. Patrick's Day is like a four-year-old sleeping through Christmas. I heard later that on this particular St. Patty's, down at the University Club in St. Paul, my friend Mary took a spill while dancing on the bar and broke her arm. God, how I *hated* missing things like that. I would have gladly suffered a broken limb of my own to have been there.

According to my records, the diagnosis at St. Mary's was "acute depressive reaction in an emotionally unstable personality." No! *I was drunk!* I just refused to tell them how *much* I was drinking, so they didn't know what the source of my problem was. Then again, I don't know how they failed to figure it out on their own. The records also show that during my month-long visit I constantly talked about drinking, requested only medication that could mix with alcohol, and insisted on leaving the grounds during the day so I could down a couple of scotch-and-waters at lunch.

One afternoon, after I returned from an especially long lunch with my father at Charlie's, the staff found me in a utility closet, passed out in the sink, my mink stole drenched by the dripping faucet.

I still don't know why St. Mary's decided that I was fit company for the outside world, but on April 13 I was released. And I managed just fine, at least until I tried to kill myself.

I decided to end it all because my father ignored my twenty-second birthday. We were both born on June 21, so it seemed strange that he would forget it. Maybe he didn't forget, but he sure as hell wasn't there. He was out playing golf with his buddies. As the day wore on, I began feeling hurt that he hadn't made any plans to take me to dinner. So I lay by the pool and sulked in the company of Budweiser. By late afternoon, I was piss drunk and pissed off. So I did what any healthy young whacko would do: I went upstairs to the bathroom and slashed my wrists. Then I went downstairs and found Jane in the kitchen.

"Mother," I said, standing in the doorway, "I've just slashed my wrists."

She turned and saw me oozing blood. I was strangely calm, maybe because I'd been in enough loony bins by this point to know that slit wrists were hardly a death sentence. This was just a way of giving my parents everything they deserved. Jane remained perfectly cool. She wrapped dish towels around my wrists as she carefully led me out to the car. If Jane knew anything, it was how to get to the hospital.

I don't remember much about the trip to the emergency room, but I must not have done much damage. I do recall having lunch the following day at the Viking Room, a wood-paneled watering hole in the downtown Radisson Hotel. I was proudly showing off my bandages to all my friends.

"Of course," my effete friend Michael responded. "Everyone who's anyone should slash her wrists, especially when she can't find a fourth for bridge." I'm still not quite sure what the hell he was talking about.

I Spent the Evening with
a Cheap, Drunk Broad

Some people have lost weekends. I have a lost decade. Well, half a decade. My lost years lie between the time I met Lou around my twenty-first birthday (1959) and my marriage to Arne Carlson just before I turned twenty-seven (1965). I resumed my career in merchandising, working sporadically at the Oval Room and as the accessories buyer for Jaffees, an upscale shoe store in Minneapolis. Since Harry was supporting me, though, I thought nothing of taking long unpaid vacations and entire summers off.

Really, I did nothing except drink and sleep with married men. I was *not* an asset to society. Why married men? They were the perfect partners. I got laid and stayed away from commitments, remaining available to Lou. I had no doubt that he would soon give up that silly family of his and ride into town on his white horse to fetch me. Well, the horse never showed up.

What I recall most vividly from the early sixties is having lunch. I did a *lot* of lunch, often with Harry. Many of these were liquid lunches, of course, hence the lost aspect of these years. When I wasn't lunching with dad, Sally Kinnard and I were noon regulars at the Viking Room. Sally's a petite blond bombshell who has always left men lying crying in her wake. (This includes three husbands and a stud farm's worth of lovers.)

We always drank well into the afternoon and charged it to our fathers' accounts. Sally's father, John Kinnard, was gorgeous and owned a tremendously successful brokerage firm. Like my own father, he was notorious for chasing women and doted faithfully on his daughter. If and when they questioned the bills, we told our daddies that we were downtown "job hunting." We pretended to job hunt for years on end—even when we were working. One afternoon, as the waiter at the Viking cleared the glasses away, I decided it would be a wonderful idea to go up to the pet department at Dayton's and charge up a guinea pig.

I picked out a furry little fellow and named him Mort. My new little friend would need a home, so I promptly called Duffy Lumber.

"Hi, it's Barbara Duffy," I said to the unlucky employee who answered the phone. "I need a cage for my guinea pig, so build it and I'll come pick it up later this afternoon." Click.

While we waited for the cage to be built, we drank some more in the Viking Room, which of course had a no-pet policy. I stuffed Mort in my wonderful gray wool suit with the chinchilla collar and let him crawl around. The nice ladies at the next table tried not to stare at my traveling hump. After a while Mort fell asleep, and I forgot about him. I honestly *forgot* about the guinea pig napping between my tits. All of a sudden he woke up and made a beeline for my pearls. His little head popped out, I screamed, and cleared four highballs off the table trying to push the little fucker back in.

My friend Barbie McConagha was there during my lost years matching me stunt for stunt. Barbie is a Jewish princess tightly wound—a gorgeous, rail-thin, electric wire of anger and humor. She was adored by her father and physically abused by her mother.

"I fell down the stairs," she used to say when someone asked about her black eye, and my heart would just shatter.

Sometime in the early sixties, Barbie decided that she wanted to meet Mort Sahl, the comedian, who was in town performing. Through various connections, she was able to invite him to a party at her parents' house, and he agreed to attend. I wanted to meet the guest of honor and make sure there was some attention paid to me, as well. As the scotch flowed, my demeanor changed. I was no longer the polite young lady from Anoka. I was beginning to slur my words and scowl.

"Mr. Sahl," I said through my teeth. "How can you possibly make as much money as you do for the trite way you perform?"

He ignored me.

"Mr. Sahl," I said more assertively. "Please share with the room how you can get paid for being such an asshole."

My dear old friend Larry Walsh whispered to me, "Sweetums, I think it's time to shut your mouth."

But I persisted. "Mr. Sahl . . ."

This time he cut me off. "Tomorrow morning, you will wake up and say, 'I spent the evening with the great Mort Sahl,'" he said in a voice filled with disdain, his beady eyes shooting darts into my head. "Tomorrow morning, *I* will awake and say, 'I spent the evening with a cheap, drunk broad.'"

7

King George

George Duffy, the older of my little brothers, was the golden boy. He excelled in sports. He excelled in school. He went to Harvard. My God, is it any wonder that I threw him down the laundry chute? He was a good kid, and he drove me nuts. My ego could not bear to watch him graduate valedictorian of his high school class when I was nineteen. I dared my friend Colleen to dump a bag of flour on my head just before we left the house for the ceremony, and there wasn't time for me to clean up and get to the event on time. It was one of the few occasions I've seen Harry genuinely angry with me.

We always said George was the sober one in the family, but I think he's addicted to religion like the rest of us were addicted to booze. He is extremely committed to his church. He's a wonderful husband and father. In other words, he's *still* good, and he still drives me nuts. He lives in Virginia, and he sorely tested my love for him in 1994 by voting for Ollie North during the U.S. Senate race.

Yet no matter how errant his politics, my big-sisterly love for George endured. While he was at Harvard, I was a college dropout, a drunk living at home, utterly irresponsible (I lost that guinea pig, for chrissakes, and have no idea what happened to it). Bruce was playing hooky from school and clearly not headed for the Ivy League. So George alone shouldered the burden of being the Great White Hope. Harry wanted George to come back home with a Harvard law degree and run the lumber company. Then in 1961, while he was still an undergraduate, George announced his plans to marry Diana Wennerlund, whom he had met in high school, and make a career of the Army rather than return to the warm, comforting bosom of his inebriated family. Marriage to Diana did not fit into Harry's plans for his son, and he made his objections known.

Religion became the battlefield. Harry said he didn't want George to get married in Diana's Lutheran church and raised quite a stink. But George and Diana refused to let him control the situation. They stood firm and eventually married in Boston. The marriage has lasted now more than three decades, and they've got three great kids. They showed us. But I think my blind willingness to take Harry's side in the argument and my coldness toward Diana in the beginning of their marriage has frayed my relationship with George. I can honestly say that he's the only Ollie North Republican whom I wish I knew better.

Spit Curls and Glue

More Lou.

Around the time Harry was putting up obstacles in front of George and Diana, he scheduled a trip to New York with my mother and invited me to go along. I went for one reason, and his name was—you guessed it.

I knew that Lou had moved his family to England, but I also knew that he spent some time in his firm's New York office. Before my parents and I departed from Anoka, I crossed my fingers, lit candles, chanted, and prayed that my path would cross Lou's during the trip. A couple of days before we got there I found that Yes! Lou would be in New York, and he wanted to see me.

On our first night in town, I left my parents' hotel to meet Lou in a bar on Park Avenue. Harry and Jane knew he was a married man but didn't try to stop me. They understood the depth of my feelings for him. Jesus, how difficult it must have been for them to watch me leave that night, knowing their daughter was bound to return with her heart shattered once again.

None of this occurred to me, of course. I couldn't have been happier. I was a vision, an absolute vision in my new, very expensive, black Christian Dior suit. For a femme fatale effect, I put on a blond wig, glued perfect little spit curls to each cheek, and topped it all with a generous chapeau angled seductively over my brow. I sat at the bar alone for a few minutes and watched Lou step out of his cab. We nestled into the banquette and cooed for hours. He was still unhappy in his marriage. He still cared for me.

"I'm still in love," I told him.

He finished his umpteenth martini and pledged his own undying love. Then he had the bright idea of going to my parents' hotel to tell *them* how much he loved me. Thank God they weren't there. We sat outside their door in the hallway for a while, sharing a bottle of scotch and waiting for their return. Finally we gave up, and I accompanied Lou to his hotel.

I was too drunk to think to leave a note informing Harry and Jane that I would be staying at Lou's that night. When I returned to the hotel the next day, they were understandably frantic. I couldn't be bothered with their concern. I packed my things and told my parents I'd be at Lou's hotel for the rest of our stay.

As the next forty-eight hours unfolded and Lou's impending flight back to London drew closer, I grew more depressed. For the sake of our lovemaking, I was shaving my legs and armpits at every opportunity. When I accidentally cut my finger with the razor in the tub, Lou began to fear that I was becoming suicidal. I told him I had no intention of killing myself, but out of concern he persuaded a friend of his to drive in from Long Island in a snowstorm. Lou told him to keep an eye on me after he had left town.

When it was time for Lou to leave, he and his friend and I had a farewell drink at his hotel bar.

"I'll be in the air at one A.M. New York time," he told me. "Let's toast each other then."

He kissed me good-bye and left me in a veil of tears. His friend—a nice man whose face and name I will never remember—took me to the Oak Bar at the Plaza Hotel, tried his best to console me, gave up, and dropped me off in the care of my parents. I was in a shambles. Jane woke me that night at one so I could toast Lou, and Harry took me to an opulent lunch at the Four Seasons the next day, hoping it would make me feel better. I was sobbing so steadily, I could not eat.

Within a very short period of time, my parents' golden boy had defied their wishes to cancel his engagement, and their only daughter seemed headed toward a nervous breakdown over a married man. Harry and Jane must have wondered where on earth they had gone wrong.

Rats

"Goddammit, *what* did I do with my glasses?"

I have said this many, many times in my life, and one day in 1964 I said it again. I had left my office at Jaffees to make deliveries for the store. Without my glasses I couldn't read the addresses, but I finally got the job done in spite of my partial blindness, and by the time I met my friends at the University Club, I needed a drink.

I was wearing a green linen suit.

On the way downstairs to the bar, accompanied by my friends Larry Walsh, Byron Webster, and Jimmy Moore, I passed a shortish, businesslike blond man going up the stairs. "Arne," one of my friends said to the young man, "this is Barbara Duffy."

"Hello," he said.

"Hello," I said.

My relationship with Arne Carlson began. He had just finished a game of squash and was going upstairs to read *U.S. News and World Report* in the library. I was on my way downstairs to down a glass of scotch. Opposite directions. The story of our lives.

Arne Carlson came from a world I could not imagine, and grew into a man whom I could not understand, comfort, or reach. He was born on September 24, 1934, the son of Swedish immigrants. When he was four years old, he watched his pregnant mother and older brother Sten go around their Chicago basement apartment killing rats with sticks, so they wouldn't eat the new baby. Arne's mother, whom we always called Mama, delivered Arne's little brother, Lars, on an ironing board. Mama was too proud to go on welfare, so she scooped flour out of trash cans on the street and burned it for fuel. It's a wonder the family didn't burn alive.

When Arne was still a child, the Carlsons moved to New York City, took up residence in a Lower East Side tenement, and slept on beds made with newspapers. Fearing that the landlord wouldn't rent to a family with three rowdy boys, Mama claimed they had only two sons. She kept Arne, who was the quietest of the bunch, hidden for three months by sending him to school two hours early and parking him in a booth at the diner where she worked in the evenings.

Papa, Arne's father, worked as a janitor and building superintendent, but fancied himself an impresario. He insisted his sons talk of world events around the dinner table, even if the dinner table was a recycled orange crate. Papa saved his pennies and went to the opera, which provided an outlet for his passion and temper, both of which made him a very difficult man to live with. Mama and Papa Carlson divorced after the children were grown.

As a child, Arne learned to stoically endure beatings by Papa. He developed a severe stutter—often he could not finish a sentence—and he might have come out of his childhood broken, had it not been for a New York City social worker. The social worker got Arne's older brother, Sten, into a fresh-air camp, which led to a prep school scholarship at Choate, the camp's sponsor, and finally to Yale.

Arne decided that he should go to Choate, too.

"Don't be foolish," Papa told him. "You're not smart enough. You'll work with your hands and be a carpenter."

Mama stood up to him on Arne's behalf. "If he wants to go, I'm going to help him," she said. She worked three shifts a day as a waitress, six A.M. to midnight, in order to raise money for his education. Every day before she left for work, Arne devoured the *Encyclopedia Britannica.* Somehow Arne got a scholarship, but had to leave part of the entrance exam blank. He had never heard the words "algebra" or "grammar" in public school.

During Arne's freshman year, each student was required to stand in front of the others, give his name, and sing the school song alone. Arne stood before his class, stammering and horrified. He couldn't get his name out. A professor wearing a black cloak approached him from the back of the room. Arne had never known such fear. But the man put a gentle hand on his shoulder.

"My son," he said. "I'm going to make a championship debater out of you."

Arne excelled academically, well enough to earn a scholarship at Williams College, where he competed in freshman football and wrestling and edited the school newspaper.

I don't think that Arne ever gave serious thought to any career other than politics. After graduate school, he worked on Hubert Humphrey's Democratic campaign for president, edited a newsletter for the Republican governor of Minnesota, and campaigned in San Francisco for an alderman. By the time we met, Arne was managing the congressional campaign of Republican John Johnson and considering his own bid for the Minneapolis City Council.

Sparks did not fly during our first meeting at the University Club, but a few days later he surprised me by calling and asking me to accompany him to a political rally for Johnson at Republican headquarters. Arne was scheduled to give a three-minute speech. We sat in the back of the room until his time came. Then I watched him as he stepped up to the podium. It was as if Superman had come flying out of a phone booth. I was mesmerized, absolutely entranced by this little man's ability to hold his audience, the way he hammered each concise point with a voice that resonated. This from a man who had overcome a debilitating stutter. From then on, when he was at the podium, whenever I heard him speak, that is when I loved him most.

We slept together on our first date. I had hoped that sex with Arne would make me forget Lou. It didn't. My physical attraction to Arne wasn't as strong as what I felt for Lou. There was less tenderness with Arne, no foreplay. But I must say this for little Arne: He could last forever.

I liked him. He was smart, more ambitious than the men

I drank with, and Lou wasn't knocking on my door, so I continued to date Arne and got involved in the Johnson campaign. It was the only way I could see him. I discovered I loved Arne's mind and enthusiasm, and that I loved politics just as much. I loved the gamble of it and the strong, opinionated people involved. I thought it was just dynamite that I was twenty-five years old and getting invited to the same cocktail party as Governor Anderson. Although Johnson would continue for awhile in politics, he lost that 1964 campaign. I was terribly upset. I thought that if you worked hard enough, you were supposed to win. Actually, I still believe that.

A therapist once asked me why I married Arne. I said, "He went to the right schools." I also believe I began to love him—or to tell myself I loved him—when he started discussing running for alderman on the Minneapolis City Council. My friends had all graduated from college, they were working, getting married and having babies. It was time for me to get my own life, and a life in politics didn't sound bad.

Arne was convinced that he could beat the incumbent in Minneapolis's 12th ward, so he rented an apartment there, and I helped him move in. I helped him knock on doors. I helped him raise money, and I introduced him to all the right people at parties that my parents threw in Anoka. Arne adored and admired Harry. And he was able to tell himself that he loved me, at least for a while.

In September of 1964, I flew to New York on a buying trip for Jaffees. Lou was in town, and I had another genius plan. Since my vacation with Harry and Jane, I had seen him a few times during my buying trips. I could sense that he had decided the affair had dragged on long enough.

"I want to meet you for a drink," I told him when I called his office.

He was curt. But I insisted, and he met me in our regular banquette in a bar on Park Avenue. We ordered drinks, and I set my plan in motion.

"I'm getting married," I told him.

Lou didn't flinch.

"Congratulations," he said flatly. "Tell me about the man you want to marry."

"He's a graduate of Choate and Williams College," I said. He looked at me aghast.

"I didn't ask where the hell he went to school," he barked. "I asked you about the man you are considering spending the rest of your life with!"

"His name is Arne Carlson," I said, confident my plan was working. I was getting to him.

Lou calmed down immediately, shook his head, placed money on the table, said "Congratulations" again, and left.

I sat there stunned and hopelessly alone. This was *not* the way it was supposed to happen. Suddenly I was thirteen again, tasting that tree limb.

I ordered two glasses of scotch to be delivered simultaneously, gulped them down, and returned to my hotel. In my room, I wept and I cried and carried on. I couldn't sleep, so I drank all night and ate club sandwiches from room service. I remember watching *The Man From U.N.C.L.E.* on TV.

I did not look my best when I showed up at Lou's office the next day.

"I'm here to see Lou," I told his receptionist.

Lou heard me, walked calmly out of his office, and took my arm. "I can't talk to you now, Barbara," he said as he walked me toward the elevator.

Once again, I could hardly speak. Nor could I cry or make any noise at all. What had I done? What could I do? I got in the elevator, and it carried me down to the street, away from my great love.

When I got back to Minneapolis, after a rather grueling and elaborate display of grief on the return plane ride (I think the flight attendants on the Kennedy-Minneapolis flight were beginning to recognize me), I was thinking with the clear head of a woman scorned. "Shoot," I thought. "I don't have any better prospects. Maybe I *will* marry Arne Carlson."

Of course, there was just one small problem. Arne hadn't proposed yet.

8
$\mathscr{P}$romises, $\mathscr{P}$romises

Sometime after my ill-advised trip to New York, where I had made up my mind to marry him, Arne was advised by a campaign supporter that he could not win his ward without being married. I was his most likely prospect. I was socially acceptable, despite my outrageous behavior. He could take me anywhere. I honestly don't think he ever stopped to consider whether he was in love. One night, while I slept, Arne sought advice from an old chaplain he knew, and Dr. Taylor, after copious quantities of booze, gave him his blessing to make Barbara Duffy an honest woman.

Dr. Taylor (not his real name) was married, but he loved to hit on women and adored talking about sex. I adored him, and Arne and I were always happy to accompany him on his girl hunts. So one evening in January of 1965, still empty-handed after our bar-hopping, he returned to Arne's apartment with us. I went to sleep in the bedroom, while he and Arne stayed up talking. At three A.M., after Dr. Taylor's departure, Arne woke me up. "Barbara, I want to talk to you," he said in a businesslike whisper.

"What?" I asked with a note of panic. Of course I thought someone had died.

"Let's get married," he said.

Wait a minute. This was not the way they proposed in the movies.

"Arne, how can I marry you when you haven't even told me that you love me?"

"All right," he said impatiently. "I love you. Now will you marry me?"

"Okay," I said. We both went back to sleep.

I woke up the next morning engaged to be married. Like a wind-up, bride-to-be doll, I resigned from my job at Jaffees so I could plan the wedding and concentrate on Arne's all-consuming campaign. We set the date for May 1. May Day.

Some of my friends warned me about Arne's coldness. I wouldn't listen, and partially out of defiance, I stuck with my decision to marry him. I knew there was no passion between us. He never kissed me, except once, on the first night we slept together. I had been in love before—I still am in love with Lou—so I knew what love was supposed to feel like. I also assumed that love, at least for me, was unattainable. I married Arne because it was time to get married. He married me to win an election.

Midway through the engagement, however, I met Arne's brother, Lars, who came to town to help on the campaign. Lars and I took an immediate dislike to each other, and Arne's feet chilled. Once again my stubbornness reared its head. That sonofabitch Lars was *not* going to wreck my up-coming nuptials. So I asked Harry to fix it. Harry fixed everything.

He took Arne to Michael's, one of his old drinking haunts, plied Arne and himself with stingers, and made some promises.

"Arne," he began, "I know you're concerned about Barbara's messiness."

Harry promised Arne that I would be neat and tidy. He promised him that I would never gain weight. He sold me like a two-by-four, and Arne bought it. For the rest of his life, Harry would boast that it was his greatest selling job ever. The engagement resumed, and I began spending all my time at Arne's little one-bedroom apartment. Lars slept on the living room sofa, so the lovely stench of tension always hung in the air.

Tension was, in fact, epidemic among the wedding party. When Arne told his father that he was getting married, Papa asked, "What's her name?"

"Barbara Duffy," he answered.

"If her name is Duffy, then she must be Irish," Papa growled. "If she's Irish, she must be Catholic. And if she's Catholic, I'm not coming."

To appease Papa, Arne refused to have our ceremony in the Catholic church and insisted it be held on his own turf— the nontraditional, nonhierarchical Congregational church. My brother George had been forced to get married in Boston, rather than embarrass his family by having a non-Catholic ceremony in Anoka. Imagine how George must have felt when Harry gave Arne his blessing to get married wherever the hell he wanted.

I bought the most elegant, cream linen bridal dress with heavy lace sleeves. For my bridesmaids, I had my friend Shannon Murphy fly to New York. She found shift designer dresses in a mustard color with bands of white lace around the bottom, and jolts of orange, turquoise, and olive green thread. Of course I chose some lovely matching pillbox hats as well. My bridesmaids all hated the dresses and bitched about how much they cost. But they were the only dresses that came in the right variety of sizes. These bridesmaids looked like a bunch of melted candles—short, tall, fat, thin. Suzy Maurer, my maid of honor, had just given birth to a daughter by C-section one week before. She could barely stand up, she was in so much pain. Then, when Sally Kinnard's father found out that she would be walking down the aisle with Frank Kent, a black groomsman, he threatened to disinherit her.

Now, for the record, Sally ended up walking with Frank, who went on to become the first human rights commissioner in Minnesota, and Papa ended up attending the wedding.

The bridal dinner on the eve of the ceremony, however, did not have such a happy ending. Shortly after I boarded the grand piano, I serenaded the guests with my trademark dirty ditty "Mary Ann Barnes," and then I passed out, loaded. Arne carried me upstairs—I was still thin—and put me on my mother's bed. I came to and looked up into his cold blue eyes.

"I hate you," I screamed. "I never want to see you as long as I live." I can't recall what prompted that outburst. Maybe I wanted to go back down to the party, and he wanted to put me to bed. Maybe I was blaming him for the lack of real affection between us. Maybe I was screaming for help. Whatever the reason, the next day I became Mrs. Arne H. Carlson.

Pajamas

The wedding was your typical, high-collar drunken to-do with a few religious rites in the middle. I don't think we ever got a picture of all nine bridesmaids together before or after the wedding ceremony; most of them were so hungover from the bridal dinner that at any given time at least one of them was in the ladies' room sick. I had no engagement ring, since all of Arne's money was going into the campaign. The honeymoon we had planned was a night at a motel outside Anoka, where the out-of-town wedding guests were staying. I didn't mind this no-frills aspect of marrying Arne. It was my wedding day, and I was happy. For a while.

Arne and I held our reception at my parents' home, and later spent the evening chatting with his relatives around the indoor pool at the motel. When we retired to our room, I slipped into a sexy negligee I had purchased for the occasion and waited for him to come out of the bathroom. I was excited, a blushing bride ready for action.

Arne appeared in pajamas.

Not *just* pajamas—these were the knit, crew-neck, little-boy kind with maroon elastic cuffs on the sleeves and bottoms. He must have had them since prep school; they had faded to a dingy gray. I will never forget them. He got into bed and turned out the light. He didn't even say good night.

"Um ... Arne?" I said, tapping him on his shoulder.

"Hmm?"

"Have you forgotten something?"

He lifted his head. "Do you really want to do it?" he whined.

"Well, it might be a nice gesture to consummate our marriage," I said. I did my best to suppress my shock. *It was our wedding night!*

Without bothering to remove his shirt, he pulled his pajama bottoms down to his knees and climbed on top of me. I must say this for Arne, even when his heart wasn't in it, and it never was, he always kept going for as long as I needed. If not a romantic, he was at least a gentleman. That night, I had my first orgasm. I assume I was able to because I could finally relax during intercourse. I was so happy to be married and never again to have to worry about getting pregnant.

The afterglow faded quickly. When we were done, he rolled over and went to sleep. When you love someone, you watch him sleep and listen to the music of his breathing. All

I saw when I looked at him were those damn pajamas. I stared out the window at a street light until nearly sunrise. "What the hell have I done?" I kept thinking. I cannot describe the desperate loneliness I felt lying in bed with Arne Carlson. But I was there. And I was married.

Potholes

Late one evening soon after our wedding, Arne and I sat in our living room reading good books and listening to classical music. I went out to the kitchen and returned with my fourth glass of sherry.

"Barbara, *please*," he begged, "you have got to slow down."

"Mind your own business," I snapped. I grabbed my book and raced to our bedroom to read and drink alone.

On June 8, 1965, one month after our wedding, Arne Carlson, thirty, won his first election. He beat the twelfth-ward incumbent, Richard Franson, 5,482 to 4,846. The following week, the first newspaper story about Barbara Carlson, twenty-six, appeared under the headline, "Alderman's Bride Starts House Work."

The story told of our whirlwind romance on the campaign trail and how we were strained financially. It mentioned our hope that we could someday buy a home in the twelfth ward and ended on this charming note, "Mrs. Carlson plans to settle down to homemaking chores now." So much for accuracy.

But a little postage-stamp size photo of me that ran with the article spoke louder than the words. I seemed to be smiling through panic. I had big, dark circles under my eyes.

Jesus, I looked possessed. The reporter also noted halfway through the piece that I was chain-smoking in what I jokingly referred to as "the postelection depression"—a depression that soon would bloom into all-out devastation.

After Arne won, Richard Franson sued Arne for violating the corrupt practices act of the Minnesota election laws. At issue was a piece of Carlson campaign literature that looked exactly like a real estate tax assessment from the city. It was designed to alert voters that their taxes on a 40-foot lot would increase by $200 under Franson. I thought the literature was quite clever. But not everyone agreed.

On July 16, Hennepin County District Judge Luther Sletten ruled in Franson's favor. The judge agreed with Sletten that the statement was intended to mislead voters and done "deliberately and designed to gain attention."

Well, of course it was supposed to gain attention! Why else would you send out campaign literature? But the court had made its decision, and Arne was ordered removed from office.

I was in a state of shock. I couldn't believe Sletten had ruled against him. I was devastated for Arne—and for me. Part of marrying Arne was the excitement of his political career, and here he was, accused of corrupt practices.

The scandal played out in the headlines all summer. When Arne took his seat in the council chamber awaiting his Supreme Court appeal, the Democrats on the council stormed out in protest. With Arne, the Republicans—or Independents as they were called at the time—had seven seats on the council, while the Liberals had only six. When Arne stopped attending meetings for the sake of civic peace, the city council was deadlocked. Minneapolis politics screeched to an uncertain stop.

There was nothing for Arne to do until September when the Supreme Court would hear the case. We spent the entire summer gong to movies, sometimes as many as two or three a day. We watched *My Fair Lady, The Sound of Music, What's New Pussycat?* and everything else in release that summer. We also spent a lot of time looking for potholes. Arne always felt that repairing potholes was an important part of constituent service, and between movies he drove up and down the streets of the 12th ward, dictating to me notations about the size and location of potholes. Movies and potholes. Married life was turning out to be a barrel of monkeys.

We went to court on September 23. Throughout the tedious proceedings, I kept myself entertained by focusing on the lawyers. Arne's attorney, Peter Dorsey, was one of Minneapolis' most attractive men. He was suave, charming, and impeccably groomed in his cuffed glen plaid suit. Then there was Irv Nemerov, Franson's attorney, who was bowed down with unruly hair. He wore a little poplin suit, and—no kidding—his *jacket* had sweat stains under the armpits! Franson never stood a chance.

A little more than a month later, the court reluctantly upheld Arne's election on a technicality. Franson had begun contest proceedings too early—on June 10, a day before the canvassing report on the election had been issued. Had it not been for Franson's impatience, Arne Carlson's political career might have ended that summer, and we'd still be going to the movies.

Ironically, the scandal that almost aborted Arne's political career turned out to be his lucky break. After four months in the headlines, he now held one of the keys to political success: name recognition. His supporters were already measuring his chances in the city's next mayoral race. To accomodate his strengthened profile, Arne and I moved to a bigger place—a two-bedroom duplex on 28th Avenue South. I covered the windows with drapes from Dayton's, the floors with Karastan carpets, and filled it with antiques borrowed from Jane.

As 1965 came to an end, I felt positive about life, about Arne's political future, and about our future together. We added a big, wonderful, floppy sheepdog named Professor into the mix. That winter I found out I was pregnant.

Were we the perfect couple, or what?

9

God's Littlest Angel

I adored being pregnant and couldn't wait to become a mommy.

It was an easy pregnancy. I vowed that I would not be one of those ridiculous mothers who frets constantly over her baby, worrying about every little spit and sneeze. I would be a sophisticated young mother. Arne and I argued about names. I suggested Gillis, my mother's maiden name, for either a boy or a girl. Arne hated the idea. I can't remember the boy's name he was considering, but I know he wanted the name Kristin for a girl. On a Sunday evening in September, 1966, my water broke while we were sleeping. I calmly took a shower, and Arne got me in the car. I remember putting a pad between my legs, in case of more water, and bouncing with joy all the way to St. Barnabus Hospital. Of course, I remember what I wore: a black sleeveless maternity dress with a little flat bow over my very big stomach, a string of pearls, and a turquoise pin. I can't remember the labor pains, only the excitement.

But there must have been pain, and it must have been excruciating. I wasn't dilating—I waited to do so in the labor room for more than forty-eight hours. Arne went home to sleep on the second night, leaving me fairly agitated and lonely.

A kind nurse came in to keep me company. "Let me read to you," she said.

I probably rolled my eyes and wondered how long I would have to suffer this lunacy. Well, she read poetry. I can't remember the words, only the soothing cadences of her voice that caressed me and her soft hand on my tummy. It was, I think, the most wonderful, sensual experience of my life. It was certainly one of the kindest things that anyone has ever done for me. The next day I still hadn't dilated. Dr. Tom Moehn, my physician and family friend, decided to take the baby by cesarean section.

I liked the idea, since I didn't think of it as surgery; to me it was high drama. As the hospital staff rolled me down the hallway on the operating table and the elevator doors opened, I looked up and saw Arne.

"Arne," I groaned. "If I die from giving birth to this baby, will you name it Gillis?"

"Absolutely not," he said.

The doors closed.

I could feel the incision. I wanted to watch, but they wouldn't let me. I could feel Dr. Moehn pushing the baby out. I heard a sputter and a loud, healthy cry.

"Barbara," Dr. Moehn said delightedly, "you have a beautiful baby daughter, and she looks just like Harry."

I stared at the baby as one of the nurses carried her to the nursery. "Well, she's a cute baby," I thought, in a strange detached way. I sensed my relief that she was okay. I sensed my affection for her. But I was not overcome by passion and love for this child, I did not feel the way I thought I was supposed to feel.

But I drank away the angst and had a fabulous time in the hospital. While I recovered from the C-section, I mixed martinis and poured champagne for my visitors. I remember standing in the hallway, viewing the babies. Kristin was the most beautiful baby there. She had a delicate dusting of blond hair, crystal blue eyes, luminous skin. After a week, I took her home.

Despite my initial doubts about my feelings for my little girl, Kristin grew on me. I took her everywhere. I visited friends with her, took her on errands, often drove with her out to Anoka to visit Harry and Jane. She could be cranky, but most of the time she was a placid, loving baby. I wanted to carry her always. I had become one of those ridiculous mothers I had always joked about, jumping to see to Kristin's every demand.

"Barbara," my doctor told me, "sometimes you just have to let them cry."

On October 2, 1966, Arne and I were watching *The Bridge Over the River Kwai* on TV. Since Kristin's nursery was in the den next to the living room, I worried that the noise would keep her awake. I took her to her car bed in our bedroom and placed her on her stomach. I turned out the light and returned to the movie. A few minutes later I heard her begin to cry.

I remembered my doctor's words. *"Barbara, sometimes you just have to let them cry."*

I continued watching the movie, and Kristin quieted down. I can remember joking to Arne, "Boy, she stopped crying quickly. I hope she's not dead."

I went in to check on her after the film. She lay face down, her little head butted up against the plastic.

I felt her body. She was still warm.

I picked her up, saw her face and I knew she was dead. She was pale and blood trickled down the side of her chin.

I put her down and ran downstairs for Mrs. Smith, our landlady. I was screaming, "I've killed my baby! I've killed my baby!"

She rushed up the stairs. Arne was there, and Kristin was

dead. Arne's brother Lars arrived. So did my pediatrician and Dr. Moehn and the paramedics.

"I've killed my baby!" I kept saying it. I had to tell them. I had to confess. I had killed her. I hadn't loved her enough. I knew it, and I felt as though they should lead me off in handcuffs.

Somewhere in the confusion, beneath the sirens, I heard Dr. Moehn say, "I wonder if this isn't crib death."

"This cannot be happening," I thought. It was horribly surreal. I stood in the front yard in my shorts and Arne's white dress shirt, pleading with God to change what had happened. At that point, someone came and told me what I already knew—my baby girl was dead. I wanted to go to her and hold her little body in my arms. They wouldn't let me.

After a while my brother Bruce and my father arrived to take Arne and me to Anoka. They did not want us to stay in our house alone after the trauma we had just gone through. I rode with my father. Arne rode with Bruce. The two cars idled at a stop sign, next to each other. I looked over at Arne in the next car.

"This is not right," I muttered. "We have just lost a child. We should be together." No one heard me say it.

In the guest room of my parents' home, Arne and I pushed the twin beds together. Our huge dog, Professor, climbed into bed with us and whined. I couldn't sleep. There was no one to talk to. Arne was lost in his own grief and lay with his back to me. Harry had had too much to drink before he got the news, so he was in bed. My mother was absent—probably off in a mental hospital somewhere. So I got dressed, got into the car, and drove to the home of Alice Kerns, the mother of my childhood friend Colleen. She held me while I cried and cried and cried.

Hours later she took me, exhausted by grief, back to my parents' house. Arne slept soundly as I got into bed. How I wanted him to hold me and share this incredible pain. But I didn't wake him. I was afraid that our embrace would be colder than lying alone. So I held myself, curled up in the fetal position, facing away from him, and cried myself to sleep.

The next thing I remember is the funeral. Oh God, the funeral. Lars, Arne's brother, had taken charge of making the arrangements. He had purchased a small, plain white casket that looked like it was made of Styrofoam. It looked like a beer cooler. There was a little plastic plaque on the end that said, "God's Littlest Angel." I knew that Lars had done the best he could, but how I hated that casket. When my sister, Susan, had died so many years before, she was buried in a casket of white cut velvet. Why was Kristin in Styrofoam? They opened the casket for me, and I looked at my beloved Kristin's face for the last time. I knew that I could not forget it, that this was my last memory of her. Save it, cherish it, I thought. There were so few memories. She was beautiful. I finally knew how much I really loved her.

Rain

Arthur Mampel, a close friend of ours, delivered the sermon at Kristin's service. He spoke of ownership, using the image of a drop of rain that lands in a stream. The stream rushes into the river, the river into the ocean, and finally a storm absorbs that drop back into the heavens. Each body of water considers that drop of rain its own—"This is mine. This drop of water is making me larger, making me more grand, making me whole, making me fulfilled." But the rain is theirs for such a short time.

Arthur said we do not own our children. They are gifts, and they all will return to God whether as tiny babies or old people, who become, in many ways, helpless like children at the end of their lives.

I don't know if Arne cried at the funeral. I saw Arne weep for his beautiful baby daughter only on the night of the funeral. While we had been staying in Anoka, our friends had gone to our apartment in Minneapolis and cleaned out every remnant and belonging of Kristin Duffy Carlson. When I returned home, it was as though she had never lived. There were no clues left that the house had just been home to a baby. They gave away her stuffed animals, her little clothes, her shoes, her tiny nightgowns, her crib, and her swing. My friends felt that they were helping me. They loved me, and I've always been grateful for their love and concern, but I missed going through my baby's belongings myself.

I did not want to forget her. I was desperately trying to grieve for Kristin. "Please let me hold my baby," I had begged. I never had the chance to say good-bye. At the funeral I had been in shock. I hadn't had a moment alone with her little body at the funeral. Her toys and clothes had been taken from me. So I sat up nights crying in my rocking chair, caressing her picture, holding my tummy, trying to cover the hurt of having her ripped from me again, wanting this dead child to forgive me for not loving her enough when she was alive. Guilt. Terrible, debilitating guilt.

"Sometimes you just have to let them cry...." I was haunted by the words.

"You have to stop this, Barbara, and come to bed," Arne said one night, but he didn't offer comfort. We couldn't comfort each other, we couldn't console each other, we couldn't speak of her to each other. The emotional chasm between us was so great that not even grief this far-reaching could bridge it. This depressed and angered me, but mostly it defeated me. Our baby was dead. Our marriage was over.

Kristin had succumbed to Sudden Infant Death Syndrome, which means we didn't really know *why* she died. We were both furious that there was so little help for parents like us who had suffered the loss of a child this way. We wanted to help other parents going through the devastating loss. So we met with the chief pathologist at the Hennepin County General Hospital and with the Minneapolis health commissioner, to talk about what they were doing in the field of SIDS. Today we still don't know a hell of a lot more about SIDS than we did in 1966. Maybe the child's immature respiratory system is the cause. Secondhand smoke could be a contributor. Every year in the United States, SIDS takes the lives of nearly eight thousand children.

The county pathologist sent Arne the names of families of children who had died unexpectedly and mysteriously. Arne wrote them all moving and beautiful letters. Through his letters we met the other parents and spoke to a couple we knew from our university days who had lost a child six months before Kristin died. A small group of us formed the Minnesota Sudden Infant Death Center, to offer families support and give them a voice. Today the SID Center has evolved into an enormous operation that provides bereavement services to about three hundred families a year and publishes a newsletter.

I'm astounded that Arne has never shared more with his constituency and his friends the magnificent work he did on behalf of children and babies. To me it was Arne's finest hour in public life. Maybe reaching out to others was his way of dealing with the loss of Kristin. I don't know, because we've never shared our feelings. Just as my own mother and father never discussed the loss of my little sister, Susan, Arne and I never spoke together of Kristin again.

Loss

After Kristin's death I decided to push myself into an activity to help me heal. I began volunteer work at a public facility for children with severe physical handicaps. The little boys in my group were amazing. Some could not speak, but they could smile. If they couldn't smile with their lips, their eyes would light up. They showed me love, they were so grateful for the time I spent with them, and made me realize that both love and grief are universal. Being with these courageous, strong kids, I could not feel sorry for myself. I realized through my work with them that there were many children who were still alive who needed help.

The following February, Arne announced his candidacy for mayor of Minneapolis. Politics and campaigning were the passions we could share. When I wasn't playing hostess at coffee parties, I was giving speeches and working hard at campaign headquarters with our friends.

Once again, Arne was taking on a Democratic incumbent. His platform this time around was getting tough on crime. In newspaper interviews, he accused Mayor Arthur Naftalin of ignoring an understaffed, overworked Police Department. At that time, the men in blue were always a popular campaign issue in Minneapolis mayoral races, since it was the only major city department under the mayor's direct jurisdiction.

Gary Franson, the brother of Arne's old nemesis, Richard Franson, and a maintenance worker in the sewer division of the Minneapolis Public Works Department, formed the Committee for Honesty in Government to remind voters of Arne's 1965 corrupt practices charge. After Gary was eliminated from the comptroller race during the primary, he and another Franson brother (who had lost his own bid for treasurer) spent a great deal of time distributing anti-Arne campaign literature recounting the scandal.

Arne confronted the Fransons and many other issues head on. He accused Naftalin's campaign of distributing the Franson literature. When he wasn't wrangling with them, he said the city was "sick" and that it had hit "rock bottom," citing all the boarded-up storefronts downtown. He reached out to young voters; Arne was good-looking, thirty-one, and they found him tremendously appealing. He encouraged them to call his office with ideas and get active in politics by letter-writing and campaigning. "It's not enough to demonstrate against Vietnam," he said. Shrewdly, he was establishing a base of young supporters who would grow, and grow old with him. He was a great politician and still is.

But at the time, the old-guard Republicans saw Arne as cocky. Consequently, Arne's campaign team simply side-stepped the old party pols, a strategy that cost him a lot of Republican wards. Even though Naftalin was a liberal, he had a solid track record and was a big cog in the local political machine, so voters were more comfortable with him than with this young cavalier.

On election night, I sat upstairs in a hospitality suite at the Sheraton-Ritz Hotel, watching the election returns on TV with Harry and Jane. When it became clear that Arne wasn't gong to win, I tried to numb the disappointment with booze. I couldn't seem to get drunk. I was already too depressed.

If it's possible to pinpoint the moment you grew up, I would have to say that this was mine. Until this moment, when I realized Arne had lost, I had believed that everything was possible with diligence and hard work. What a shock to realize that those factors alone don't equal success. There are politics to consider, and prejudices. And always, always disappointment. It's as simple as this: Life isn't fair. The

moment you know this is the moment you become a woman.
I had just lost a child, and now this election. The night I
became a woman I wore a wonderful pink silk and wool
dress and coat. I had roses in my hair.

Arne was out on the floor. Soon he would have to make
a concession speech. I should be there with him.

"I'm going," I said.

"You can't allow her to go down there by herself, Harry,"
Jane said. "She'll do something stupid."

So Harry walked down with me. I wanted to cry. I felt
sober, but I was really so woozy that I can't remember a
thing Arne said to the crowd. The photographers snapped
photos of me looking so sad.

"What are your plans now that the election is over, Mrs.
Carlson?" a reporter asked me.

I answered, "We're going to adopt a baby."

10

Tucker

The call from Betty Collins (not her real name) came in the middle of Arne's mayoral campaign. I was home with Arne. We were frantic, eating on the run. Both of us had friends outside waiting to drive us to our various speeches for the night.

"Hello," I said quickly.

"Barbara?" came this nervous, angry voice. "This is Betty Collins, Amy's mother."

"Hi, Betty, I can't talk right now. I'm just on my way out."

"Barbara, I think you'd better sit down," she said.

Of course I didn't, I was in a hurry. "What is it?" I asked.

"Amy is pregnant," she said.

I sat down.

Amy Collins (also not her real name) was a girl my youngest brother dated. She and Bruce had met only a few months before. Obviously Bruce and Amy had gotten along famously.

I found out years later that Amy most likely became pregnant the weekend that Bruce took leave from the base to attend a Duffy Lumber party at Harry and Jane's. During the revelry, Bruce and Amy sneaked up to the guest room. A few minutes later, Harry walked in on them. They were stunned, Harry wasn't.

" 'Night, kids," he said, and shut the door, too drunk to care that his son was having sex with a young girl under his own roof.

After the Collinses discovered the pregnancy, they forbade their daughter to talk to Bruce, who had been transferred to Memphis, Tennessee. So I was the first Duffy to be notified about the pregnancy. I did the only thing I knew how to do. I went looking for Harry. I finally located him at Charlie's. The maître d' summoned him, and he must have stumbled over to the phone, because I waited forever before his voice came on the line.

"Harry, Amy's pregnant," I told him.

Long pause. Deep sigh.

"Barbara," he said, "will you handle this for me? I've had too much to drink. I really want you to handle this."

It struck me at this unfathomably inopportune moment that Harry seemed tired and old. I suppose it was the first time I ever saw Harry's human side or inability to cope. It was certainly the first thing he ever asked me to do for him. Once again, it occurred to me that Jane should be here in my place, taking charge. But she was in the hospital, as usual.

"Fine," I said.

I hung up and canceled my plans for the night. Arne had already left for his appointment. I drove to Amy's grandmother's apartment, where Betty was pacing the floor, to begin what I could sense would be a mammoth job of damage control. God, what a scene.

"How could you *do* this to me?" she kept saying. "How could you *do* this to me?"

And there Amy sat on the living room floor. She was a lovely girl with delicate features. Her pregnancy was just beginning to show. She didn't say anything. She just sobbed quietly, taking tiny breaths, so ashamed and so alone and frightened. My heart broke.

Betty told me that Amy would be pulled out of high school and would live with her grandmother until the baby arrived. The Collins family was so ashamed that they had decided to sell their house and move to a new town. I assured them that the Duffys would help them in any way we could and certainly make sure that Bruce lived up to his responsibilities. Betty talked on and on about the terrible position the family had been placed in because of the pregnancy, and whether Amy and Bruce should get married or if the child should be given up for adoption. Sitting next to Amy, who could not stop crying, I just listened. She must have thought her life was over. I put my arm around her and held her all evening.

A couple of days later Bruce called home from the base in Memphis. Our mother, who had just returned from the hospital, answered.

"Hi, Mom," he said. "How're things going?"

"Thanks for the bomb," Jane said.

"What the hell are you talking about?" he asked.

"Thanks for the baby."

"What baby?"

"Amy's pregnant."

Bruce was floored. But Jane's response wasn't driven so much by anger as by irritation.

"We'll get it taken care of," Jane said tersely. "Oh, and don't try to call Amy anymore."

"It's my problem, Mom," Bruce said. "I want to get married."

"Young marriages never work," Jane said.

"Bullshit." He hung up.

Poor Bruce never got the chance to do the right thing. Sometime the next spring, Harry called a meeting with Mr. Collins and Arne. Men to the rescue. They decided that Arne and I were going to adopt this child. It would be a replacement, if you will, for Kristin.

The adoption would be kept secret from Amy and Bruce. Hell, I'm surprised they told *me* about it. But believe it or not, Harry's logic made sense to me. Here was the chance to take care of our own, a chance to make sure that this baby stayed with its family, albeit under unusual circumstances.

Naturally I began to feel protective of Amy. She had been inside her grandmother's apartment away from her friends and siblings, still stinging from the wrath of her mother. Several afternoons a week, I picked her up in my car and took her for drives, let her help me with housework (even folding clothes was a welcome change of pace for the poor girl), and invited her to stay with Arne and me on weekends. She was forbidden to see Bruce, whom she missed terribly. Bruce wanted to be with her, as well, so one weekend in July, I allowed them one visit.

In August, Arne took a job as executive director of the Easter Seal Society, which at the time was embroiled in a political mess with the United Fund. But the infighting at Easter Seal was nothing compared to the byzantine intrigue surrounding the impending birth of our adoptive child. Amy's family refused to let her have the baby in Hennepin County, for fear that the neighbors would talk. So, they arranged for Amy to give birth a few miles away in Scott County. Arne and I met with Amy's doctor, who was not thrilled about the hush-hush adoption. He had been instructed to lie to Amy about the sex of the child, so she wouldn't find out that our adopted baby actually belonged to her.

One night around three A.M. our phone rang. It was Mr. Collins. "You have a baby boy," he said flatly. Despite the strangeness of the adoption, despite the pain the pregnancy had caused Bruce and Amy, I was ecstatic; I was going to give this child a home.

Arne and I got dressed and drove an hour to the hospital where Amy had delivered the baby. The sky was pink with sunrise by the time we parked in our appointed waiting spot, a block from the main entrance. I hid under the dashboard, and Arne watched until he saw Amy and her father exit the hospital and drive away. This was our cue. We would pick up the baby and, in order to maintain the secrecy of the adoption, take him to another hospital.

Arne drove up to the entrance and waited for five more minutes. Betty Collins appeared with a bundle in her arms and climbed into the backseat of our car with her grandchild. She didn't speak to Arne and me, only to that baby. It took twenty-five minutes to drive to our hospital in Minneapolis, and all the way there Betty talked to the child, trying to give him a lifetime of grandmotherly love. I'll bet she even gave him a name.

Sad whispers floated from the backseat. Whisper, whisper ". . . and we will always love you . . ." and more whispers. She sang and cooed and told him what a beautiful baby he was.

We reached our hospital, and it was time for her to leave him. "Here's your son," she said sadly and sweetly. She would never speak to her grandson again.

I have run across members of Amy's family over the years, but we did not stay in touch after the baby's birth. As far as I know, Amy has never been told who adopted her baby, and though we would tell Tucker years later that Bruce was his biological father, he has never pressed us on the identity of his mother or tried to find out on his own. He does know what she went through and that the pregnancy was very difficult for her family. I think he wants to protect her and not disrupt her life by confronting her now.

Arne and I decided to burden our new little charge with responsibility right away, so we named him Arne Carlson Jr. Because of his size and rowdy temperament, we nicknamed him Tucker, after Tucker Fredrickson, the New York Giants football player. Poor Arne Carlson Jr. Nobody in the hospital wanted to touch him. Because he was born in another hospital, because his mother was gone, because I had no legal claims on him (adoption in 1967 could be a willy-nilly affair), he was considered a tainted baby. He couldn't go into the nursery with the newborns until he was given a clean bill of health, so he was exiled to a room for big kids in the pediatrics ward.

He looked so lost, this seven-pound baby in this big kid's bed. I played the radio for him and fed him every three hours, but I felt like a baby-sitter. I tried to get him circumcised, but no one would do it. I wasn't his mother, they said. I couldn't make decisions like that.

Now, as if Tucker and I weren't feeling addled enough, add to this scenario a serious timing problem. Since young Amy and I had become friends during her pregnancy, it was going to be difficult to keep her in the dark. To make sure that she didn't make the quite obvious connection between her birth and our adoption, I had told Amy and everybody else that I was adopting a baby due in September. I thought that since Amy's baby was due in August, the time difference would put people off the track of the adoption. But now we hit a snag. It was August, and I had a baby.

Arne and I called my best friend Colleen, who was now married to a computer whiz and up-and-coming CEO named Dick Walter, and begged her to keep my baby for two weeks. This seemed easier than trying to convince Bruce and Amy and Jane and everybody else that the baby had arrived early. Besides, any child would be lucky to have Colleen as a mother, even for a little while. At the time, she had three children of her own and a menagerie of pets. If two parents can be perfect, Colleen and Dick are. Their family really did pray together and play together. Tucker ended up spending two weeks with Colleen, and during that time he and she developed a bond that would last his entire life. In the ensuing years of chaos that would be Tucker's childhood, the Walter house would become Tucker's place of rest. During Tucker's time at the Walters', I checked in with Colleen at least every hour if I couldn't be there.

Colleen began answering every phone call with "Hi, Barbara, he's fine."

"Hi," I would say. "Is his belly button falling off yet?"

At two weeks old, Tucker Carlson enjoyed a grand homecoming to our little duplex. I cannot describe for you the warmth I felt, having another baby in that house. He had striking hazel eyes and wonderful, curly brown hair. Soon after he came home, I found out I was pregnant again. I was delighted—I loved being pregnant. I loved eating all I wanted and wearing the maternity clothes in the second month. Another easy pregnancy. We named our new little girl Anne, and she looked just like her father. Blue eyes, blond hair, a beautiful soft, round face.

How I loved those babies.

If only I could have loved them enough.

11

Tornado Warning

I first stabbed Arne early in our marriage. Who knows what the argument was about—probably my drinking. No matter how our fights started, they always got around to the same issues—I was a drunk, and he was a cold sonofabitch. We were both right. One night I grabbed a knife from the kitchen and took off after him. When I caught him, I jabbed the blade repeatedly into his arm. Fortunately for him, I was not a good little housekeeper, and my knives were not sharp. No real damage was done.

The second stabbing occurred the evening of the bridal dinner held for his brother Lars and his fiancée, Mary. I was wearing a short black dress with pearls. It was a beautiful occasion. The food was wonderful, the flowers were lovely, the candles were glowing, the music was romantic. I had helped make all of the arrangements for Arne's parents, yet once again I felt all alone even though I was there with Arne. He ignored me all night. I reacted by being loud, obnoxious, and eventually picking a fight with the groom.

We got home, and Arne was furious. I had humiliated him in front of his family and ruined the dinner.

"I just want to be close to you," I wailed, drunk and sad and furious.

"You drink too much!" he hollered.

There on the dining room table was a ballpoint pen. I grabbed it and lunged for my husband, thrusting it squarely into his forearm.

He was shocked and started bleeding like hell.

It appeared the wound would not heal, so I immediately called a nurse we knew, the wife of our minister.

"Will he die of blood poisoning?" I asked. "Oh God, please let it happen."

She didn't quite know what to say.

Thoughts of divorce blew around in my head from the very beginning. The first time it occurred to me, I was pregnant with Kristin. Again, I don't remember what generated my anger. Maybe a violent row, maybe just another case of boozy ennui, but I drove to Anoka to get away from him. I sat in my mother's kitchen all through a stormy afternoon, crying, watching the rain dance on the pool, and listening to tornado warnings on the radio.

"How would I feel if the father of my baby got blown away by a tornado?" I thought to myself. And for some reason, the thought of Arne spinning helplessly atop a cyclone moved me to go back to him.

We would wait until 1977 to end our marriage. We should have done it earlier and saved ourselves and our children so much senseless brutality and cruelty.

Had it not been for Kristin's death, Arne and I might have sorted through our problems. But I could never forgive him for not being a husband to me when she died. So began a decade-long, deeply hurtful path of revenge on my part, which only pushed him further away. The only time I could share with him how much I needed to be held by him was when I was drinking, and my tearful, drunken pleading made him furious.

How I punished him for the love he withheld. I had always been sloppy when it came to . . . well, when it came to everything, and I made no effort to improve for Arne. This just drove him out of his mind. One evening when we were giving a dinner party in the living room, Arne went out to the kitchen, lifted up a garbage bag, and the bottom fell out, spilling grease and gunk all over the kitchen floor. I had emptied some kind of liquid into it without thinking, causing it to fall apart.

"Goddammit! You should have been in the Army!" he shouted, with tears starting to roll down his cheeks. *"They would've taught you!"*

I'm not sure why I recall that silly incident. Maybe because it was so telling. I remember laughing at him when he got so upset. I seldom saw the man cry, so those moments when I could bring a tear to his eye were precious.

He occasionally tried, God bless him. For Christmas one year he purchased a ring of tiny diamonds and emeralds for me.

"Oh, look!" I said. "Diamonds! No, diamond *chips!*" Nothing was good enough, nor grand enough, for Barbara Duffy Carlson.

The night I tried to have Arne arrested, I wore a pink peignoir, with no nightgown underneath. I had begun to gain weight, and it was *not* a beautiful sight. We had just returned from the University Club, where we had toasted the new year with forty of our closest friends, just as we did every year. Arne had spent the evening avoiding me, keeping himself in whatever room I wasn't. I'm pretty sure he kissed someone else when the clock struck twelve. I can remember pulling up my dress to adjust my girdle in front of the crowd. He was furious.

I was just as furious when we got home. While we got ready for bed, I asked him why he didn't love me (as always). He said something about my drinking (as always). Well I had had it. I became hysterical. Shrewish. I tackled the sonofabitch, pinned his arms to the carpet with my knees, and *Thwack! Thwack! Thwack!* I slapped his face like a wad of dough with both hands, over and over until both his cheeks were burning.

He shoved me off him and socked me in the eye with a punch that Tyson would be proud to call his own. As you can imagine, I was *pissed*. Arne was appalled at himself. He stumbled to his feet and helped me up and began apologizing, begging my forgiveness. I would have none of it.

"I'm going to call the police," I slurred. "I'll have your ass in a sling."

I dialed 911. Arne was weeping. My eye was swelling and turning an ugly blue. The police never showed up (fortunately for Arne's political career). So I called my attorney, Joel Mauer. It was now around four A.M.

"Joel?" I said, seething. "It's Barbara Carlson. Get over here now."

"I'm busy," he snapped. (I found out later that he and his wife were making love when I called.)

"The bastard just hit me, Joel," I told him. "I want a restraining order. I want him out of the house."

"I'll be there in a minute," he said, not at all pleased.

Joel arrived to find me screaming at Arne, who could say nothing except, "I'm sorry, I'm sorry."

"Barbara," said Joel, trying to play peacemaker. "He's trying to apologize. Listen to him a moment, will you?"

"I'm so sorry, Barbara," said Arne, shedding sincere tears and moving closer to me, as if my silence meant we could kiss and make up.

As fucking *if*.

When he got close enough, I kneed him in the groin with all the force of a hot Hell gale. He crumpled in pain.

I was satisfied, so Joel left, and Arne and I went to bed. I can't remember whether we slept together or not—most likely not. On New Year's Day, he was supposed to usher for a fancy political wedding, at which I decided to play the role of the battered wife.

So the next morning, I chose a yellow silk dress and jacket with rhinestones around the collar. To cover my black eye, I asked our live-in nanny to sew up a matching yellow silk eye patch trimmed with a colorful spray of sequins. For maximum effect, I grabbed a cane and covered it in yellow silk, and adorned it with a huge shiny silver bow. To make sure that no one missed me, I added a yellow bow to my hair. I entered the sanctuary, a giant sparkling banana dragging one leg behind me all the way down the aisle. People were speechless. When anyone asked what happened to my eye, I told them in a quivering voice that I had fallen down the stairs—*everyone* knows what it means when a wife says she fell down the stairs. And the Oscar went to Barbara Carlson. It was one of my finest performances.

Cards

I have come to realize that it was Harry whom Arne loved, not me. Harry supported Arne politically, supplied him with good social connections, and became a buddy. I really do believe that Arne put up with me so he could have the good father that he desperately wanted and never had growing up. For me, Harry, not my husband, was the significant man in my life. After Arne and I married, I continued to speak to Harry often, see him at least once a week, and drink with him. He loved me and told me I was wonderful and beautiful. My relationship with my father made up for what my marriage was lacking.

So, Harry's death, like the death of Kristin, was a crucial turning point in our marriage. Arne and I had lost the only person that was still keeping us together. Harry suffered his first heart attack in 1969 soon after Tucker and Anne were born. My parents had taken Arne and me to dinner at Michael's restaurant, where only four years earlier my father had sold Arne on the idea of taking me as his wife.

I wore a black dress and pearls. Arne, by the way, hated black. My father loved it.

In the middle of dinner, floating on a river of gin, I took the floor and announced, "I want a divorce."

Harry stood up to me. His chair flipped backward as he stumbled to his feet. "You are *not* getting a divorce," he bellowed. "You are *not* moving back home." He had had enough of my nonsense. He walked out of the room, into the hallway, and grabbed his chest. Jane rushed over to him and made him sit down. There was such pain on his face.

"He's okay," said Jane reassuringly, as much for his benefit as mine and Arne's. This tiny woman who had made a career of being taken care of for so many years put her arms around Harry's massive trunk, helped him out to the car, and drove him to the emergency room. Harry had suffered a mild heart attack. While I knew that I did not have the power to stop his heart, the guilt was overwhelming. Even today I can feel it. At the time, I salved the guilt with booze and simply drank my way through my father's final days.

We had seen those days approaching. My father had always been so together, so funny and clever when he drank. Blitzed nearly to the point of blackout, he could play bridge and drive a car. But lately he had become a messy, slow drunk. He wasn't fun, and it was painful to be around him.

Age and alcoholism turned him sad and a bit pathetic. My parents spent a month or so in Arizona, where he was supposed to recover. They returned to Anoka in time for the Easter holiday. On Easter eve, he suffered another heart attack. On April 6, 1969, he was pronounced dead on arrival at Mercy Hospital. He was only fifty-three.

The call came on Easter Sunday from my brother George, who had joined the Army after getting his degree from Harvard and had come home with Diana to Fort Snelling near Minneapolis. Arne answered the phone. He didn't say a word, just stood there with the receiver at his ear and tears welling up in his eyes. He looked at me sadly and offered me the receiver. Then he buried his face in his hands and began to sob.

"Dad just passed away," George told me. Although I collapsed inside, I didn't break down. I couldn't. Arne was breaking down enough for both of us.

"Why?" Arne cried. "Why do the good people die so young?"

We dropped Tucker off at a friend's house and took baby Anne with us to Anoka, to my parents' apartment. (They had sold the big house on the river a few years earlier.) Jane wasn't there, of course. She was in the hospital.

I remember walking in and noticing tracks in the carpet—from the gurney that had carried Harry's body out of the apartment that morning. I remember finding his smoking jacket on a chair in his room, wrapping myself in it, walking into his closet, and finally crying, letting go.

"Harry?" I whispered, hoping for his direction at this terrible time. "Who will be here to make decisions for me?"

Harry had made all the decisions in my life—where to go to school, where to work, whether to get married, to adopt Tucker. I remembered, as I sat wrapped in his jacket, what he said to me before I took off to New York that summer to be with Lou. Harry must have known I was lying about going there for work. "I don't think you should go," he had said. "You are going to fail, and here are the reasons why . . ."

He rattled off his reasons. He knew I wasn't listening.

"But I want you to know that I will always love you, and whatever difficulty you get into, I will always be here for you," he said at the end of our talk. That much I heard.

My father had died on the toilet, so I cleaned up after him. Then I found a deck of cards on the dining room table—they had naked women on them. I gathered them up and put them in my purse before anyone else found them. At the mortuary, an old buddy of Harry's named Phil came up to me. He had been playing gin rummy with Harry the afternoon before he died.

"Barbara," he said between sobs. "You didn't happen to find [sob] a deck of cards [sniffle], did you?"

"Don't sweat it, Phil," I said. "I saved them for you."

I placed a few cigarettes, a golf ball, and a bottle of good scotch in Harry's casket. I picked up Tucker and took him over to the casket for one last look at his grandfather.

"Say good-bye to Grandpa, Tucker," I told him. "You are our secret, Harry's and mine. Our precious, precious secret. Say good-bye."

At a year and a half, Tucker's command of the language wasn't terrific, but he managed a word or two, and looked around the room. What a strange place a mortuary must be a for a child, all those adults, red-eyed and vulnerable. I put him down and again remembered Harry's voice—something he said to me one night at Charlie's when I was a teenager.

"Barbara, there are things that you will do in your life that I don't need to know about. My belief is very simple. You raise children to the age of sixteen, you hope that you have instilled in those children a strong basis of morality and ethics, and after sixteen you just pray."

I began to cry softly to myself, and I felt my mother's hand on my shoulder. "You go ahead and cry, dear," she said with the faintest bitterness in her voice. "You can cry hardest, Barbara. You loved him the most."

12

Help

Not long ago, on my radio show, I admitted being guilty of child abuse. No, I didn't hit the kids. I didn't starve them or call them names. But child abuse is most often the sin of omission, not giving that child everything that he or she needs to grow—food, clothing, shelter, morality, love, and security. I loved them, but unconditional love was missing. When Kristin died, I didn't really grieve for her until years later. In the meantime, I simply anesthetized my irrational guilt and understandable pain with alcohol. Now I realize how that dormant grief kept me from completely loving another child. I suppose that somewhere inside I was afraid they would be able to hurt me as she did. I was afraid that if I got too close to Anne and Tucker, I would hurt them or they would hurt me. I can't imagine that my children ever felt secure.

Today, I'm trying to heal our relationships the best I can. I'm taking responsibility for my shortcomings and for repeating my own mother's curious methods of child-rearing, for being a mother in an altered state. By the time Tucker and Anne came along, I was chasing my liquor with Valium. In Tucker's earliest recollections of me, I'm on the sofa, ordering him to go downstairs to the refrigerator in the basement and fetch me a beer, or upstairs to the medicine cabinet in the guest bathroom, where I kept my pills. When he talks about it today, he will tell you about the pink tile in the guest bath, where he was constantly fumbling around on his little tippy-toes, searching for the right prescription bottle.

Anne and Tucker joined opposing forces when they were young. Tucker, my little hellion, did my bidding and kept up with my frenetic energy, while Anne stayed close to Arne. Just as I turned my back on Jane when she tried to show me affection, Anne turned her back on me. And like my mother, I couldn't show her affection when I was sober. She probably remembers me kissing her or trying to hold her when I smelled of liquor. What a terrible thought. I tried to kiss her, she put her head down. I held her, she stiffened her body. So, she gravitated toward her father, and who could blame her? She mimicked his actions and accepted his sentiments as her own. She was cute, smart, and didn't like me at all.

When Anne was nine years old, I dyed my hair blond. She came downstairs, caught sight of it, and panicked. She ran upstairs screaming.

"Tucker! Tucker!" she hollered. "She's a witch!" Anne says that this is her very first memory of me.

After Tucker came home, I quickly discovered that it was not easy to drink, fight with Arne, pop Valium, and watch the baby all at once. Having been raised by maids and baby-sitters, I naturally thought that live-in help was in order. My live-ins are legendary. Money was always tight, so we couldn't afford the finest. The first was Brenda (not her real name), who got the job simply because she was the friend of a friend's sister and I was desperate.

During her youth, Brenda had sliced off part of her ear in a motorcycle accident. So she often wore a prosthesis—a big fake ear that she glued on. It had an earring. One day I noticed a smell, the most rancid odor you can imagine, like spoiled meat or the rotting carcass of a squirrel in the chimney. (I don't know *why* the fake ear stunk, but it did.) As awkward as it was, I made her warn us when she wanted to wear the prosthesis, so the rest of us could evacuate the house. When she wasn't home, I enjoyed showing it to my friends. I held it up to the light, its delicate gold earring sparkled, but Jesus, did it stink.

After Brenda left, we decided that it would be a nice idea to hire live-ins in need of a home—foster teens, five in all, troubled youth that no one in the right state of mind would *ever* trust with their children. All of these foster children were sweet and very grateful to have a place to live. And ultimately they didn't hurt our kids. In fact, having them there forced our own kids to take some responsibility around the house. This is not to say hiring troubled foster kids as nannies was a great idea.

Our first foster nanny was a dwarf, and she had a deformed leg. Neither of these physical challenges made her a bad nanny, but she wasn't exactly equipped to wrangle Tucker, who could run so much faster than she could.

Eventually she learned how to trip him with her crutches, but she left after a few months when she simultaneously contracted VD and got pregnant. Next came Carol (also not her real name), a fifteen-year-old incest survivor who had already put two of her own children up for adoption. She had tattoos: a swastika on her ass, and a 69 on her arm. I made her wear Band-Aids over it wherever she went.

Mary, another foster girl, might have worked out fine if the rest of her family hadn't moved in. (By the time Mary came along, our family had moved into a big six-bedroom home on a curvy shaded lane called Lake of the Isles). Mary's sister came to live with us after she got pregnant. She was white, the father of her child was black—quite scandalous in the late 1960s—and she had nowhere else to turn.

Her brother came to live with us when he was around

fourteen. He wasn't retarded, but he had severe behavioral and speech problems, and a friend of his stayed with us for a while, too. Mary's father was a chronic inebriate—homeless, and spent most of his time in a downtown bar. On Christmas day, after all of the kids opened their presents, Arne drove Mary and her siblings down to the bar so they could wish their daddy a merry Christmas.

In order to afford my quality live-in help, I had to find a job. My knack for selling, which had served me well when I worked in the clothing business a few years earlier, led me to real estate soon after Anne was born. From then until our divorce, I was the family's chief breadwinner. This eventually enabled Arne to campaign full-time, and he resumed his political career in 1970, when he was elected to a seat in the state legislature. Even though I was drinking nonstop, mixing scotch and waters for my clients as I drove them from house to house, I was almost always the top-producing agent in my office.

Almost every day, on the way home from work, hung over from lunch, I bought Anne and Tucker toys, one after another. Tucker called them "guilt toys," which was very astute of him. One Saturday he took them all and stacked them in the middle of the basement playroom. Imagine all those toys—smiling dolls, fancy wooden Tinkertoy sets, playhouses, puppet stages, big red trucks, little yellow cars, G.I. Joes ready for action—hundreds of them piled and twisted, a merry, scary, mangled mountain of guilt.

Tommy

Tommy Weiser was a treasured friend, a valued real estate client, and the first gay man I tried to sleep with. He was built, smart, and gorgeous, with a country-club tan, strong tennis legs, blond hair, blue eyes, and green money. The fact that he preferred the company of men in bed did not stop me from developing a terrific crush on him.

Tommy's father, Joe Weiser, was a charmer, too. He made a fortune through two businesses, Minnesota Bearing, an industrial parts distribution company, and Dalton Gear Manufacturing. The ladies loved him, and he married a few of them. Along the way he produced four sons, two of whom are gay. As far as I know, this never bothered Joe Weiser—remarkable for a man of his generation. He was always very supportive of Tommy and generous with his wealth. Tommy grew up in Minneapolis, wintered in Arizona, and spent three years at Dartmouth College. In 1960 Tommy transferred to the University of Minnesota, where we met. We were both in our early twenties.

He was fabulous, a great friend to everyone, and we girls chased him like hormonal teenyboppers until we figured out that perhaps we weren't his type. (He began spending a suspicious amount of time with a local Catholic priest—that's what finally tipped us off.) Throughout our college days, Tommy visited me in the loony bins, offered me a shoulder when Lou turned his back on me, and made a nice, respectable escort when I was between married men.

Our friendship deepened over the years after I married Arne. Tommy was a great dancer, specializing in the fox-trot, which I loved. Arne didn't like going out so much and could never fox-trot. Tommy and Arne liked each other, and Tommy served as co-finance chairman on Arne's mayoral campaign. Tommy threw lavish parties and went on to become one of the nation's earliest leading fund-raisers for gay rights causes. In Minneapolis, he introduced many local gay and straight business people to each other and is largely responsible for laying the foundation of the gay and lesbian political power at work in Minnesota today.

Tommy also collected china, antiques, and—fortunately for me—homes. He was the cornerstone to my success in the real estate business. He would buy, decorate, and sell a new house about every nine months. I must have sold him nearly ten properties over the years, all of them expensive.

And I got smashed in every one of them. Sometimes other things got smashed. In a drunken fit one weekend (I was probably pissed at Arne, but I can't really remember what generated my rage), I reduced a few valuable antique dining chairs to kindling, and I never could pull out of the driveway without chipping away at his stone fence with my Ford LTD. Tommy never complained, and he had his handyman install rubber tires on either side of the gate so I wouldn't dent my car. Despite my shenanigans, his door was always open to me and to anyone else who needed a quick party. He entertained lavishly, and where Tommy went, so did a collection of bright young men.

There was a time that I was bent on saving my friend Tommy Weiser and luring him away from society's lavender margins and into the bright, happy realm of heterosexuality. The kids were growing up, Arne and I were growing apart, and—in the absence of Dexedrine and the presence of alcohol and Valium—I was simply growing. One magnificent spring day, he accompanied me to a benefit at St. Catherine's College. I wore a blue caftan with a floral print and white lace.

I was a vision, to be sure, but Tommy Weiser wasn't looking too closely at me. While I was preoccupied with the bar, he was preoccupied with the bartenders. Around midnight we made our exit with Tommy behind the wheel. We were laughing, singing along to the radio, and cruising along Summit Avenue. Suddenly, I grew extraordinarily quiet.

"Is anything wrong, Barbara?" he asked.

"Stop the car!" I screeched as tears poured from my eyes. Of course he must have thought I was going to be sick all over the leather seats of his new Alfa Romeo convertible. He pulled over to the side of the road.

I did not tumble out of the car as expected. I aimed my bloodshot blue eyes right into his crystal blue ones. He seemed confused.

"Kiss me," I ordered.

"Barbara," he said with saintly compassion and understanding—oh, his eyes were just beautiful—"You know I can't."

Hysterical. I became *hysterical,* sobbing and pounding the dashboard. I had offered this beautiful bastard every ounce of my 185-pound body, and he said *I can't!?!?!* Distraught, rejected, drunk as a Duffy could be, I put my head down in his lap, and I cried and cried and cried and cried. He sat there for the longest time, patting my hair, rubbing my great big blue floral back.

"Barbara, I love you more than anyone in the world," he said gently. "But I'm gay. You know I'll always love you, but I can't go to bed with you."

I sat up and put on my big sunglasses, which dimmed the moonlight, and cried all the way home to my children and my sad and loveless marriage.

This was not the only time I offered myself to a gay man. Homosexual number two was also fabulous. He was a bright, successful attorney in his thirties (we'll call him Jim). He was one of the first people I called the night Arne moved out of the house, just before our divorce. Actually, I didn't know at the time he was gay, though I should have known because he was so much fun to be around. He accompanied me to movies and art openings and dinner parties and generally helped initiate me back into single life. One night we went back to his house after a show at the Walker Art Center and ended up in bed together, as friends sometimes do and later regret.

We had a quick coupling in his king-size bed. When we finished, he rolled over to his own side. Here I was, alone again in a bed with a man. But in this case I felt more silly than lonely. We spent the night together and never discussed it again. Just a few months later he came out of the closet and has now been in a relationship for over fifteen years with a wonderful man. I love happy endings.

Good Housekeeping (continued)

Sometime in my early thirties, a friend of Tommy Weiser's, whom I'll call Sam, bought me my first dildo. Sam was dark-haired and spoke unabashedly of his exploits cruising the local baths and Loring Park, a quiet neighborhood a few steps from downtown Minneapolis. Sam always claimed that he could come seven to ten times a night. Not natural, I thought. This man must have been on something. One night Tommy and Sam and I were driving back from an art gallery that Tommy owned in Wayzata, and from the backseat I piped up;

"I've always wondered if I know how to give head properly," I said.

"Well, *don't* think I'm going to demonstrate for you," said Tommy. Sam, sitting behind the wheel, was more accommodating.

"I know what to do," said Sam. "We'll drive over to the dirty bookstore downtown, and I'll get a dildo so you can practice."

"Yippy skippy," said I.

We found the place on Hennepin Avenue, but it happened to be surrounded by about ten thousand men who were in town for a Shriners convention. They were all over downtown, spilling out on the streets in their stupid little red hats. I decreed that we would not let them spoil our good time, so I took over the wheel and circled the block while Sam got out and ducked into the bookstore. Tommy was mortified, just beside himself with worry that someone might see him and his friends patronizing a dirty bookstore in the middle of the night. He moved to the backseat and sat low behind my copy of *Good Housekeeping*. We passed by the bookstore twice. No Sam. Tommy was sweating by this point, bitching the entire time.

"Oh, relax, you big baby," I hollered.

On our third sweep, Sam was waiting for us on the curb, holding an oblong box. He climbed into the passenger seat and, as I aimed the car back down Hennepin Avenue, I opened the box.

I nearly veered onto the median.

There was the biggest, pinkest, most anatomically accurate dildo you have ever seen. It must have been a foot long.

"There is no way I can get that into my mouth," I protested, "let alone my throat!"

He held it up in the light of the glove compartment turned a little crank on the scrotum, and the head began to oscillate.

"It's alive!" Tommy screamed gleefully, tossing the *Good Housekeeping* onto the floor. He had come around.

"Come on, Barbara, you can do it," said Sam.

"Not until I clean it up," I said. "Imagine how *dirty* it is. We have to go home and boil it."

Back at Weiser's house, we left the dildo boiling merrily on the stove—blub, blub, bounce, bounce—and drank scotch at the kitchen table as we waited for all the little germs to die. One of Tommy's housemates came home (I have no idea who; Tommy always had a couple of hunks living with him, and I could never remember their names). Tommy's friend walked over to the stove, probably expecting pasta.

"My God," he said. "*What* are we having for dinner?"

13

$\mathcal{R}$ust

Except that I was a raging alcoholic and my marriage was awful, life was pretty good in the summer of 1971.

Arne and the kids and I spent the summer with friends on White Bear Lake and then moved into our dream home—a three-story Mediterranean-style house among the towering oaks and wide lawns of Fremont Avenue, with seven bedrooms, eight baths, and maid's quarters.

Because of a shift in school districts, intended to desegregate Minneapolis high schools, property values in the Fremont Avenue neighborhood had dropped. We picked up the property for about $65,000; today it's worth over $500,000. The home was Arne's reward for his victories in the highly scrutinized and often brutal battles in the legislature. It was my reward for years of diligent work in the real estate business.

Adhering to the decorating fads of the early 1970s, I colored the house in a navy-and-rust symphony of patterns. The spectacular dining room had a floor of Spanish tile and a soaring ornate ceiling with cove lighting and rugs and walls of orange and yellow and deep, deep magenta—remember, this was the 1970s.

Our days of taking in foster children to care for our own were over, thank God. On Fremont, we employed a fantastic young couple named Lynn and Norbert Smith to clean and help care for Anne and Tucker. She was a teacher, he was a law student, both exceptionally bright. Twenty years later, Arne would appoint Norbert a judge. With Lynn's help, I filled the house with booze and friends, who filed in and out for wedding receptions, cocktail parties, political fund-raisers, holiday gatherings humming with children, and sit-down dinners for eighty. I entertained the revelers with my famous rendition of "Mary Ann Barnes," and like my own childhood home, my dream house on Fremont Avenue vibrated with laughter and revelry.

Also like my childhood home, its solid, beautifully appointed walls contained the wreckage of two mismatched lives.

"Arne," people would say, "how do you do it all? You're married to that trying, crazy woman who drinks all the time. You do a wonderful job of managing the house and caring for those kids. You're a fantastic politician, and you give, give, give to your constituents."

Well, rumors circulated that while he was out giving, giving, giving to his constituents, he may have been giving more than his goodwill. Who knows if there was any truth to the rumors. But who could really blame him if there was? Our sex life was hardly lively, and hardly sexual for that matter. Not long before we moved to Fremont, I had my own affair with a lawyer in town. It had begun over the phone, but proved disappointing in the flesh. Now I was primed for action. Which brings us back to good old Lou.

Shoes (continued)

I hadn't seen or spoken to Lou in seven years. The last time I saw him was 1965, when I had told him I planned to marry Arne Carlson. I missed him. No matter how much time went by, I couldn't get over him. I was also nervous about contacting him—Would he still love me, would he even remember me? I employed my friend Judy Halleron, who lived and worked in Connecticut, to track him down. Ta-da! She contacted him, found out he was back in New York, still married, but he told her that he missed me, too. With the path cleared, I called him, and we planned to meet again in New York.

There was one problem. My last affair was so disastrous in the sack that I wondered if I would be able to make love to Lou—especially at my present weight. I was not exactly the svelte, pretty young thing who had lost her shoe in that horse-drawn carriage so many years ago. So I decided that I'd better have a run-through to see if I could still do it right. Who would the lucky man be? I flipped through my mind's carnal Rolodex and put my chubby little index finger on a married man with whom I had had an affair years ago before my marriage. We'll call him "Irving" since he still is married. I rang him at his office and asked him to dinner. We met the following evening, and my seduction went exactly as planned.

We drank and drank, and I told him that I had never gotten over him. We ended up in a ticky-tacky Minneapolis motel. We undressed hurriedly in the dark and hopped into the feathers. I felt something with my foot. I looked down, and Irving was wearing his shoes—loafers with black socks and garters halfway up his calf.

"What are you *doing?*" I asked.

"I can't take them off, Barbara," he said. "They're too tight, and I won't be able to get them back on without a shoe horn."

He explained that it would look suspicious to his wife if

he went home carrying his shoes. So we continued, loafers and all.

When we finished, Irving gave me a polite kiss good-bye, slipped on his trousers—it took a few minutes to get them over his shoes—and left. I spent the night at the motel, having told Arne that I'd be staying over at a friend's house. I drove to my friend's early the next morning and called Arne from there. I felt simultaneously a bit guilty about the lie and tickled silly with the confidence that now I was prepared to go to New York and see Lou.

Jewelry

My mother had her own room in our new home on Fremont. After Harry died, her drug addiction worsened, and there were frequent periods of time when she couldn't care for herself. Even though we knew that her various suicide attempts over the years had been nothing more than cries for attention, we were afraid that she might do some real damage with her arsenal of drugs if left alone.

She kept her riverfront apartment in Champlan, Minnesota, and Bruce, who was running Duffy Lumber by this time, checked in on her daily and administered her pills. Sometimes during severe bouts of depression, she stayed with Arne and me. She was at the Fremont house on the morning I was scheduled to fly out for my Lou rendezvous in New York.

Positively giddy with anticipation, I drove Anne and Tucker to school and returned home to finish packing. Jane was still in bed, so I went in to check on her. I found her out cold next to an empty bottle of Seconol. I didn't know where the hell she had gotten the pills, but I summoned the rescue squad, got in my car, and followed the ambulance to Hennepin County General Hospital. I was so accustomed to Jane's suicide attempts that all I felt was pissed. I was going to miss my flight.

County Hospital is a wonderful institution, but it is not one of the country-club treatment centers that Jane was used to. How delicious, I thought, that she will wake up with the drug addicts and young pregnant mothers, her throat and chest aching from the ravages of a stomach pump. After signing her in around 8:20 A.M., I realized that I could still make my flight if I hurried.

I called the house and got Lynn on the phone.

"Have my suitcases waiting on the lawn," I ordered.

I sped back to the house, scooped up the bags, and raced to the airport. I arrived at the gate sweaty and cranky and thoroughly winded just in time for the final boarding call.

Later that day Jane was revived.

"Somebody stole my jewelry," were her first words. She was right; I had taken it all, ostensibly because I was afraid it would disappear in the hospital. I really did it because I knew she would be horrified to find it missing.

I landed in New York without incident, and with three or four of the most adorable little bitty empty scotch bottles on my tray. I checked into my hotel and phoned Lou. He told me to meet him for drinks that evening. I wore a fabulous navy and white silk dress and, on my little finger, Jane's three-carat diamond ring, which I had slipped off her hand at the hospital.

I found him waiting for me in a banquette in the same Park Avenue bar where we had nuzzled a hundred times before. I don't know what he thought of me, but Jesus Christ, I thought, don't men age well? It hardly seemed fair.

"I have something to tell you," he said just as I sat down.

"What?" I asked. A number of possibilities occurred to me in that moment before his answer: He was leaving his wife to be with me. He wasn't leaving his wife and couldn't be with me. He was dying of cancer. I was too fat for him to fuck.

"I'm an alcoholic," he told me.

I looked at him blankly and answered, "Okay." There was no response, no more discussion of the subject, and he poured us both generous gin martinis. Obviously this diagnosis had not yet moved him to seek treatment. Nor would it for many, many years.

So we drank and later that night made wonderful love. Oh, I loved him. I still loved him for all the old reasons—his sense of humor, his intelligence, his body, his face. None of that had dissipated for me. He was that rare combination, someone I could talk to and laugh with, and the thought of being in bed with him, touching him, brought tears to my eyes. I loved him. I loved him.

I believe that he loved me. He told me that he did. Despite the weight I had put on since I last saw him, he was passionate making love to me. He didn't seem bothered by it in the least. But he also told me that he had a life that he couldn't walk away from and a commitment to his wife and three children. When I stepped off my cloud and faced that fact, my guts crumpled like tinfoil and I wanted to scream, but I did what I could. I resumed my affair with him. If that's all he could offer, I would take it.

When I got back home, we began speaking on the phone constantly. I would return to New York at regular six-month intervals for long weekends with him, always making some excuse to Arne—I was going to see friends or to visit relatives. I always paid a visit to Arne's father, whom I just couldn't stand, to give my trip some semblance of legitimacy.

And each time after I saw Lou, I would make that painful, drunken, tearful flight back to Minneapolis.

The Margarine Test

A year or so after the affair resumed, I returned from a visit to Lou in New York not only distraught, but plagued by guilt. I confided in a friend of ours, Charlie Leck. Charlie was a Congregationalist minister who had just separated from his wife and moved into one of our bedrooms for a few weeks.

"I've got to tell Arne I'm having an affair," I said.

"Don't do it," he advised, as I sat up late with him several nights in a row, weeping and debating whether to confess my transgressions.

Finally I made my decision.

"Why do you think I've been going to New York?" I asked Arne one evening at home. This was after a few mai tais at the Waikiki Room.

"To see plays?" he ventured, disinterested, from behind his newspaper.

"I'm having an affair with a man named Lou," I said angrily. "He's beautiful. He's smart. *He* went to *Yale.*"

"Oh really?" was all Arne would say.

This was a Saturday night. I felt better—absolved—though Arne's Cheshire cat grin all day Sunday didn't exactly put me at ease. On Monday morning as I was getting dressed for work, Arne walked into the bedroom humming something under his breath. It got louder and louder until I could make out the words "Boola, Boola . . ."

I realized that Arne was singing the Yale fight song.

I began to sweat. All day I walked around in a state of panic. Then on Monday night he really let me have it.

"I want you to call your friend and tell him that I'm suing him for alienation of affection," Arne said.

"Shit," I said, and not just because Arne had me by the balls. I had also missed my period. This I did not tell Arne. I cried in private. I considered running way. I thought about suicide. Fearing that Arne might find out, I would not go to my regular doctor for a pregnancy test. I was too embarrassed. I read in the newspaper about a confidential family counseling service across town and decided to go there. I called and got directions. In a fearful daze, I jotted them down and called and explained my horrible situation to Suzy Maurer, an old friend from high school.

"You have to go with me," I begged. "I'm scared to death to go alone."

On Wednesday Suzy picked me up at my house, I got in the passenger seat, put on my sunglasses, and handed her the piece of paper with the directions.

"Barbara, do you know where this is?" she asked, incredulously.

"Just go!" I said. I assumed that Suzy was afraid of driving into a bad neighborhood.

A few minutes later, I looked up and realized the clinic was *next door to the capital, within view of Arne's office window.*

We parked across the street from the little storefront where the clinic was located. As I ducked across the street, I bitched to Suzy.

"If this place is run by nuns," I said, "I'm not going in." I had enough guilt without *nuns.*

I knocked, and what can only be described as Quasimodo's mother answered the door—hunched over, crooked teeth. "Come in," she said.

We sat in the dingy waiting room, and from behind my

shades, I could make out the signs on the walls: "God Is Love," one said. "God Is Wonderful," said another.

"Shit!" I whispered to Suzy. "They're nuns!" I got up to leave. Suzy, a good Catholic, was not at all pleased with my attitude, and she ordered me to sit down and shut up.

I sat and stewed for about five minutes, arriving at the dreadful conclusion that I really didn't have much choice but to stay. Finally another nun appeared.

"Did you bring your specimen?" she asked.

"Yes," I said, and produced a Valium bottle full of pee.

"When did you fill this?" she asked.

"About 2:30 this morning," I said, tears filling my eyes. "I've been up all night."

"I think you should void again for us," she told me. Then she handed me a margarine container.

A margarine container. But by this time, I felt so defeated that I couldn't argue. Suzy just wanted to get this over with. She was so embarrassed to be with me, no doubt certain that she was doomed to eternal damnation by association.

So I went in the back, peed in the margarine container, surrendered it to the nun, and was ushered into another room to speak to still another nun. This one I recognized. She had taught me at Visitation. Now we could add mortification to the guilt. I tried to talk to her, but I was so horrified I could barely form sentences. Finally after what seemed like a month, Mrs. Quasimodo came in with the results.

"The test is positive," she said through her jagged smile. Oh my God.

"Are you sure?" I asked.

"My dear," she said, "our tests are ninety-nine percent accurate, and I have never *seen* a test as positive as yours."

What did that *mean?* I couldn't ask. I couldn't speak. I was in shock.

"Suzy," I said quietly, "write her a check."

We left and I went nuts, absolutely nuts. I got home and called Lou and gave him the good news first—that Arne was suing him for alienation of affection—and then the bad news.

"I'm having your baby," I said.

He remained calm. Too calm. He said nothing for a few moments, then decided the best thing to do in this impossible situation was to keep me from going crazy.

"You can come here and have the abortion," he offered.

"I can't have an abortion," I wailed. "I'm *Catholic!*"

I hung up the phone and rushed over to Tommy Weiser's house. Crying in my scotch, I told him what happened. He was absolutely terrified for me, beside himself with concern, and my only solace.

"Barbara," he said, "you have got to have an abortion. You don't have a choice. You must think of Anne and Tucker. This would tear your family apart."

Tommy called a doctor friend of his.

"Do you do abortions?" he asked over the phone.

"What the hell are you talking about?" the doctor asked—obviously this was the last question he would ever expect from a gay friend.

"I've got a friend who's pregnant, and she needs an abortion right away!" he said, agitated.

"How do you know she's pregnant?" the doctor asked.

Tommy rolled his eyes and yelled with exasperation into the phone, "She flunked her margarine test!"

In the background, the doctor could hear the violent sobs of a woman gone mad.

14

$\mathcal{B}$lue

Tommy had me wondering whether an abortion was the answer. That night I walked to the shore of Lake Harriet and sat alone in the dark. Frightened. God, how frightened I was. After a lifetime of trying to self-destruct, I figure I had finally done it.

I realized something very profound: Self-destruction isn't all it's cracked up to be.

For an hour or so, I listened to the tiny waves break on the rocks, looked at the stars, and I began to cry. But not because my life was a mess. The tears I shed were tears of resolution, accompanied by a strange kind of peace. I realized, sitting there, that I could *not* have an abortion. My soul told me. I heard a clear voice of conscience speaking calmly above my fear and confusion.

But how the hell was I going to explain this baby to Arne? The first problem was that we had not had sex in months. My solution, I decided, would be to seduce him soon. The second problem that came to mind was the fact that Lou had brown eyes. There was a very good chance that this child would, too. I had blue eyes, and Arne had blue eyes. I knew nothing about genetics, but I wondered if that might be difficult to explain if the baby came out brown-eyed. Then again, maybe two parents with blue eyes equal a baby with brown eyes. Maybe the baby could conceivably have brown eyes, since my mother had brown eyes. Who the hell knew?

Contact lenses. That was my next thought. I would have the baby, then color its eyes with blue contact lenses. Perfect! Yes, it was crazy, but such was my state of mind at the time. If there was a way around it, Barbara Carlson would find it. This, I now know, is the unrivaled arrogance of a drunk. No mountain too high. No ocean too deep.

I walked back home, crawled back into bed, and fell asleep. I decided to seduce Arne later, it had been a long day. Even though I had been too embarrassed and fearful to consult my own doctor for the pregnancy test, I realized now that I needed real help. The next day I called my obstetrician, Dr. Moehn.

"John," I said. "It's Barbara Carlson. I've just had a positive pregnancy test, and the baby's not Arne's. How soon can I see you?"

Short pause. "Would the next fifteen minutes be okay with you?" he said.

At his office, John ran a test. It was negative. The nuns were wrong. I bawled from relief. I thought about storming the clinic, giving those nuns a piece of my mind. But I never went back. Best not to push my luck.

The experience cemented my ideas on abortion. Having wrestled with the moral dilemma of an abortion for myself, I understand people in the pro-life movement, though I remain pro-choice. It's the fanaticism with which the pro-life movement operates that upsets me to no end. I hate the way they scream about dead babies and only add to the confusion and emotional intensity surrounding an issue that defies simple philosophy. There are millions of unwanted children in this world. If the pope and all the white men in Rome had to raise about three hundred or four hundred by themselves, maybe their ideas would change.

And what happened to Arne's idea about suing Lou for

alienation of affection? He just dropped it. I think we both knew that we'd be in court with each other soon enough.

The Obituary Bowl

By the time Harry died, Duffy Lumber's fortunes had begun to slide south. Bruce really had no more interest in running the family business than George and I did, but fate and Harry placed him there anyway. He sat at his father's old desk, dined at our father's old hangouts, and drank like our dad, too. Three martinis and two vodka stingers for lunch were nothing unusual for Bruce. He was only in his early twenties and the pressures of caring for this ailing elephant, Duffy Lumber, only exacerbated his drinking problem.

Duffy Lumber, once a million-dollar-a-year enterprise, now teetered near bankruptcy. Concerned about our mother's financial health, Bruce sold her interest to the lumberyard manager and to Uncle Pat, Harry's brother and partner in the company. So Jane sat comfortably on a trust the rest of her life. Finally, the company was sold to an outside concern, and by 1974 Duffy Lumber was no more.

I didn't care for my job being a political wife in the early 1970s any more than Bruce cared for running the lumber company. Since I loved politics, I had assumed that being a political wife would be ideal for me. I imagined sharing in the glory and the power and being there for my husband to share the disappointment. But once we were married, I realized that Arne was not the kind of man I wanted to share anything with. Or maybe, like Hillary Clinton, I'm just not the cookie-baking type. I was a kid who dropped her brother down a laundry chute because he was getting too much attention. I discovered that I did *not* enjoy watching my spouse stand center stage.

Not that I went unnoticed. Twice during black-tie parties I ordered several male guests to compare their nipples with mine. I wanted to take a peek so I could see whose were larger. I have teensy-weensy nipples in the middle of large aureoles, which I found absolutely fascinating under the influence. I would be standing in a group of men chatting politely, then suddenly, when the alcohol took hold, I would be challenging two or three of them to a nipple duel.

People seemed terribly amused by my behavior. I was a fun drunk. The press never witnessed these episodes. That could have hurt Arne. But among our friends, it only enhanced Arne's image as the careful, devoted public servant trying his damnedest while putting up with "Crazy Barbara."

As my drinking escalated—a feat that few thought possible—I tried pot once or twice. The first time I smoked it, I could not take my eyes off the crotch of a dear female friend of mine. I sat there stoned thinking that I had turned into a lesbian. But it wasn't much fun. Alcohol was my substance of choice. And for the hangovers: cherry Popsicles. I went through a lot of cherry Popsicles.

But for all my laughter and bravado and tits-baring contests, drinking had stopped being enjoyable. During these years, it wasn't unusual for me to suffer small nervous breakdowns during parties at the house, leaving eight-year-old Tucker to tend bar, and Arne to entertain the guests while I passed out upstairs.

Our dream home became a field on which to play an endless game of Arne vs. Barbara. I think that Arne not only didn't love me anymore, he didn't *like* me a hell of a lot either.

I spent a lot of time out of the house. Many evenings I stole away to drink with my friend Mary Baker and her mother.

Mary is my polar opposite. Thin with short, no-fuss hair, Mary is not what you'd call flexible. This is a woman who hasn't changed her shade of bright pink lipstick in several decades and still doesn't own a microwave. Can you *imagine* living without a microwave? Her father was the head of quality control for Pillsbury and taught her the importance of being meticulous. She plays mean tennis, eats right, and corrects people's grammar. We met during our college years when I was in the loony bin. She was with a mutual friend who came by to visit me on the afternoon the staff found me skunk drunk, wearing a mink stole, and with my head under the faucet of a utility sink. She liked me anyway.

Mary always wanted to marry a newspaper man, and she found one in John Baker. She was twenty-three, and he was legally separated from his first wife. After John's divorce, they married and moved to Japan, where he worked for a radio station. Mary taught English and recorded audiotapes of the *Encyclopedia Britannica*.

They divorced in 1973, after ten years of marriage, and since then Mary has lived in Minneapolis, working in management at a tennis club, caring for friends, and doing a great deal of volunteer work for her Lutheran Church and the American Civil Liberties Union.

I was crazy about her mother, Caroline. Caroline's family was one of the first to settle in Hollywood, so she grew up with the DeMilles and spent part of her youth in Florence and Kyoto, Japan. She was very bright and prim, but liked to drink as much as I did.

"Caroline," I would ask, "did you enjoy sex with your dearly departed husband?"

"Now, Mother, you *don't* have to answer that," Mary would say disapprovingly.

"No, I'd like to answer," Caroline would say. "Robert was very good."

Caroline would always answer. Many evenings we would sit in Caroline's living room for hours carrying on discussions about sex, religion, philosophy, and politics.

Caroline was also a little crazy at times. Mary and I helped her through her religious period when she was sending thousands of dollars to a radio evangelist, because she enjoyed the gospel music he played. But overall, Caroline's house was warm and old-fashioned and quiet, and the people there were loving and forgiving of shortcomings. It became my refuge.

In many respects, Mary became my baby-sitter, too. She insisted that I sleep over when I couldn't drive home and spent a lot of time at my own house, where she always took my side when Arne and I fought—even when I didn't deserve it.

She was there the morning Arne took a frying pan in the head.

She had spent the night at my home, and as we were putting away the breakfast dishes, Arne bundled up the kids in their winter coats.

"Do you want to go sliding with the kids and me, Barbara?" he asked me.

"Do *what?*"

"Sliding," he said. "Tobogganing."

"Of course not," I answered, surly as hell for no apparent reason.

He sort of lost it. "You never want to do *anything* with the family! You don't want to picnic. You don't want to go sliding. I'm getting really tired of this."

Suddenly an enormous cast-iron skillet, which happened to be connected to my hand, landed squarely in the middle of his forehead.

Konnnnng!

He was stunned. So was I. Why had I done such a thing? Imagine the unseemly pent-up rage I must have had. Mary went about drying the dishes, not knowing *what* to do. I was expecting blood to come gushing from Arne's head. But it didn't. In a moment he turned and left the kitchen without a word, collected the kids, and took them outside.

Mary stuck with me. We spent the morning inside, quietly playing Scrabble. Arne and I never spoke of the frying pan fiasco again. Maybe he was waiting for an apology that would never come. I suppose it should have, but I was also waiting for apologies that would never come. Our lives together simply went on.

When Caroline became ill, Mary moved in with her and stayed for fifteen months. She remained in her childhood home after Caroline died in 1981. Mary hasn't married again, though she is kept company by a terrible, horrid, hostile Siamese cat named Murray, who was named after Bill Murray. Murray has been known to bite her. Mary in turn hates my beloved Humphrey, who, just for the record, is perfection itself.

The great thing about watching your friends get older is seeing them develop their own eccentricities. Today, on Mary's dining room table, there sits a big antique covered dish, in which she saves newspaper obituaries—those of people she knew, as well as those that qualify as outrageous enough to be included. The practice began when she read about a man in Tokyo who committed suicide by leaping in front of an oncoming passenger train. His leg was severed, flew through an open window, and killed a commuter who was reading his newspaper. Mary recruits friends as obituary spotters in various cities. And she still wears the same lipstick. Silver City Pink. By Revlon.

15

Plastic Casket

Knees in the nuts. Skillets in the skull. It's a wonder Arne survived marriage to Barbara Carlson, and it's a wonder that I survived the endless stream of alcohol that coursed through my bloodstream. It was a close call. By 1975 I was dying.

In January, I visited Lou in New York. He was separated from his wife at this time and living in an apartment on the Upper East Side near Central Park. Flying back on the plane to Minneapolis, I was uncharacteristically numb and dry-eyed. I began searching for memories of my past few days with Lou, but they weren't there. In all my years of boozing, it was my only lost weekend. The blackout lasted more than a weekend, actually it was more like five days.

I had drowned under a wave of scotch and stingers. I had no concept of day or night. We were too gone to go out for dinner. I vaguely remember visiting friends and leaving early, knowing, as I tried to carry on a conversation, that I was making no sense. I remember cooking spaghetti at Lou's apartment. I remember being fat and having joyless sex. I vaguely remember another woman calling while I was there. But all I clearly recall was what I wore when I was with him—a wonderful double-breasted Irish tweed suit with loafers and a cashmere turtleneck.

Back home in Minneapolis, the drinking got worse. My friends were concerned. Arne and I had been talking about divorce for a while, and he had begun telling me that he didn't think I was fit to take custody of Anne and Tucker if it ever came to that. Often, in the middle of the night, I would hit the road drunk. That I didn't kill someone is a miracle in itself. Once, at four A.M., I found myself in my friends Colleen and Dick Walter's kitchen, feeding bananas to their new baby. How I got there and why I decided to wake their child and feed him, I don't know.

Like my mother, I began threatening suicide with nonchalant regularity. I had to have my stomach pumped one afternoon when I got tanked at a ladies' luncheon and swallowed a bottle of aspirin. This made Colleen Walter, my sweetest, most even-tempered friend, furious. She had watched me clamor for attention with this kind of stuff long enough. As punishment, she refused to take me to the high-rent hospitals I was used to. She drove me downtown to Hennepin County General Hospital, with its green walls and garishly bright lights and bums lying on the benches in the hallway. This was the same place I had taken my mother a couple of years earlier to have *her* stomach pumped. At least Colleen didn't take my jewelry.

But I survived that trip and continued my nocturnal rampages. Knowing that Colleen's patience with me was running out, I showed up at my friend Janella Slade's house and rang the bell until she came to the door in her bathrobe and let me in.

"Get out the Valium," I commanded, stumbling into the bathroom and grabbing a bottle out of the medicine cabinet. "I'm going to commit suicide."

"Okay, Barbara," she said, thinking very quickly on her feet for someone who had just been roused from sleep. "I'll plan the funeral. But it's going to be the tackiest funeral we've ever had in Minneapolis. It's going to be cheap wine, Jell-O salad, a plastic casket, and plastic flowers. And I'm not going to tell anyone that it's happening, so no one is going to show up."

Of course, I have always imagined my funeral to be a hot ticket, a black-tie affair. Janella's version was totally unacceptable. But in my inebriated state, the idea of artificial flowers and Jell-O salad at my final send-off was hilarious. I flung myself on the sofa laughing. She got the bottle of Valium away from me and made coffee.

Tommy Weiser didn't have to suffer my late-night antics because he had moved to Palm Springs by this time. At age thirty-nine, he decided that he didn't want to become a dottering old queen surrounded by antiques in a twenty-seven-room house. After my lost weekend in New York, concerned about my health and stability, I made a pilgrimage to see Tommy. His house was filled with camp, fun and boys. My first night there we heartily celebrated my arrival, and since the house was full, I slept in Tommy's king-size bed with my host. Another man, named Carl, lay between us.

I woke up in the middle of the night, and the bed was sopping wet. I was horrified, angry, and appalled that Carl had wet the bed. I climbed out of bed, stepped over the bodies in the floor, and found an empty sofa in the living room, where I finished out the night.

"Carl!" I screamed the next morning while Tommy was making coffee. "You sonofabitch, you *drunk*, you pissed on me! How dare you!"

Carl was slightly effeminate, mild-mannered, and very, very nice. Now he was also mortified. He began to cry. He couldn't apologize enough. I stayed angry and barely spoke to him the rest of the day.

Two evenings later I was having dinner at a restaurant with Tommy's stepmother and a friend of hers, when I reached down and felt my seat. My slacks were soaked. Carl hadn't wet the bed. I was becoming incontinent.

That night they took me to a hospital in Palm Springs. They assumed that my problem stemmed from minor kidney surgery that I had undergone a couple of years earlier. But I knew that wasn't it, not really. At age thirty-six, after nearly twenty-three years of booze, my body was sending a clear message: The party's over. Only it wasn't. My alcoholism carried on, dancing around the grave waiting for me, having a gay old time. And I simply wasn't strong enough to fight it. Not by myself anyway.

Minnesober

Intervention: the process by which a group of caring friends persuade an individual to seek treatment.

Interventions were and still are a big thing in the Twin Cities. This is recovery central. It has been ever since the Hazelden clinic opened 45 miles north of here in 1949. Hazelden was one of the first treatment centers in the United States to incorporate the philosophy of Alcoholics Anonymous into its program. It was cofounded by a Catholic priest who had lost his job because of his drinking and wanted a place where alcoholic clergy could seek help.

Kitty Dukakis, Senator Bob Packwood, Eric Clapton, and Liza Minnelli are all Hazelden alumni. Melody Beattie's book *Codependent No More* evolved from her treatment at Hazelden.

They don't call it "Minnesober" for nothing. It's where teenagers in recovery have a place to themselves—Sobriety High in Minneapolis—and Minnesota's fondness for sobriety was the subject of a hilarious *New York Times Magazine* article in 1995 by Neal Karlen, "Greetings from Minnesober."

It was, of course, an intervention, and eventually Alcoholics Anonymous, that saved my life. I believe my salvation began with a phone call between Colleen Walter and Janella Slade. Colleen I had known since childhood. I met Janella in 1959 at the University of Minnesota, where she was studying. She learned about compassion helping care for her father as his body wasted away from Parkinson's disease while his mind stayed alert.

She grew into an intellect, an athlete, and a woman of humor, with fabulous taste and a sense of high style. And she married well, to Jamie Slade, an heir to the fortune of railroad baron James J. Hill. Together they raised six children and survived Jamie's alcoholism together. In short, she spent her life caring for others. But she was never a pushover, and she still found the time to develop a terrific game of tennis. We worked together, selling real estate. And though I never lost my ability to persuade clients to buy houses, I couldn't have kept the details in order without her. With much rolling of her eyes, she helped me find certified checks that I had inadvertently thrown away, and she always seemed to be helping me find my glasses.

I told Colleen and Janella that I had become incontinent and that I was afraid. They spoke privately on the phone and decided that it was high time for an intervention. Since interventions are supposed to be a surprise for the subject, Colleen and Janella had to act quickly. They called friends in New York and Washington, D.C., they called Tommy out in Palm Springs, and they made them all promise not to take me in if I got ticked off and boarded a plane to get away.

Along with another friend, Kay Johnson, they recruited about twenty-five people who cared about me and scheduled meetings for the group at the Johnson Institute, an organization here in Minneapolis that, among other services, trains people in presenting their "data" to the person in trouble. "Data" are examples of the person's self-destructive behavior. I had data out the ass.

But at each meeting at the Johnson Institute, fewer and fewer friends of mine showed up. Some of my friends were heavy drinkers themselves and weren't ready to face their own problems. Several others said they simply didn't want to risk losing my friendship. My brothers refused to take part in the process, I'm not sure why. So did my boss at First Minneapolis Realty, who said that he didn't have any data, because I was still the top-producing agent in the office.

Arne didn't want to be a part of it either. "She's hopeless," he said.

Colleen and Janella decided that was for the best, knowing that I tended to listen to Arne's advice and then do the opposite. If he had shown up at my intervention, I probably would have responded with a lost month.

Even though the intervention was supposed to catch me off guard, I had listened to Janella and Colleen and Kay voice their concerns long enough to know that it was just a matter of time before they tried something. A year or so earlier I had made a pact with my good friend and drinking buddy, Elaine Miller, who was the only person who could match me double scotch for double scotch and who kept her pot stuffed under the skirt of a Virgin Mary statue on her piano. We agreed to sabotage each other's intervention, should any of our friends ever try it.

When Elaine Miller was tipped off and alerted me, Janella suggested they postpone the intervention, but Colleen Walter insisted on launching an offensive strike right away. Because of the short notice and so many people dropping out, three friends out of the original twenty-five—Kay, Janella, and Colleen—had to face big bad Barbara all by themselves.

Early one rainy, blustery winter morning—I was wearing a red Lanz nightgown with a white floral print—my doorbell rang.

"They're here," said something in my gut.

I poked my head out of my bedroom window on the second floor. I looked down at such a sad and hilarious sight. There were Kay, Janella, and Colleen in trench coats, guerrillas in the mist, three little concerned Davids up against one spoiled, raging Goliath.

"I know you're here to confront me!" I bellowed from my perch, my face raw without makeup, my eyes puffy, my hair pillow-matted and spiked. I was the hangover personified. "And you *can't come in!*"

"Goddammit!" said Janella, shouting from below and squinting through glasses spotted by rain. She was pumped with adrenaline and would take none of my nonsense. "You get down here and open that door!"

Knowing they wouldn't go away and thinking I could outsmart them, I let them in. But boy was I pissed. They took their seats in the living room, and I plopped down on the sofa with my arms crossed.

"Okay," I said. "Go ahead."

"We are very concerned about your behavior and drinking," Janella began. "You're destroying your marriage, your children, your health, and your job . . ."

"If you're concerned about my drinking, I'll stop drinking," I said. "I've never *tried* to stop drinking. I appreciate your concern. Now, would you leave?" Arguments followed. They knew I couldn't stop. I ranted and yelled and stomped my feet, but they wouldn't let up.

Then Colleen spoke to me softly. "You know, Barbara, we go way back," she said. "You know that I love you, but this has become too painful for me to watch. If you will not do this, if you will not go in and get help, I can't see you anymore."

That hurt. The anger rushed out of me, and sadness set in, but I would not go gently.

For a couple of hours, what seemed like all day, I listened as each of them fired off their rounds of data, their ammunition against me.

Colleen replayed my greatest hits. She recalled the nocturnal rampages (Joan Crawford had nothing on me), the time I woke up her baby to feed him in the middle of the night, my attention-getting suicide attempt at the luncheon. All my ugly, humiliating behavior. Of course, I hardly remembered any of it. Janella reminded me of the evening I backed out of her driveway and crunched a tricycle under the wheels of my Ford.

"My God, Barabara," she said. "What if one of the kids had been on it?"

And on and on and on.

"I've got to go to the bathroom," I announced. I jumped up and disappeared into the far reaches of the house and called Elaine Miller.

"They're trying to take me to rehab," I whispered panicked into the receiver. "Get over here *now!*"

I returned to the living room and listened to more data. Pretty soon the doorbell rang again. Elaine, who lived a couple of blocks away, must have run all the way to my house.

Janella tried to bar the door, but I managed to shove her aside and let Elaine in. Her hair was wet, and she was out of breath. She ordered the women to leave me alone. They wanted to tell her she was a goddamn drunk herself and how dare she ruin the intervention. But they didn't. They allowed her to stay and listen to the data, hoping it could change her mind. She sat silently for a while, then slowly became convinced that I did need help. It must have made quite an impact on her, since she eventually went through recovery and now works with substance abusers.

Next I called Arne at his office to tell him what they were trying to do.

"Happy birthday early," was all he said.

"Sonofabitch!" I yelled, then hung up.

Now I knew I was defeated. One of the women gave me more data—something about me flashing my tits at a dinner party. That I remembered. But I thought it was funny when I recalled it on my own. Hearing about it from someone else, it just sounded pathetic and embarrassing.

"When you flashed your boobs, Barbara," said Janella, "no one was laughing *with* you."

I finally agreed to go look at treatment centers. But *look*—that was all.

I took my time getting dressed, put on the same tweed suit and cashmere sweater that I had worn during my lost weekend with Lou.

"Goddammit, *what* did I do with my glasses?" I hollered. I tore through my purse and drawers searching for them. I couldn't find them, and I wanted to cry. Finally I gave up. I sucked back the tears, stood up straight with what little dignity I had left, and marched downstairs. Colleen Walter was on the phone, alerting one of the treatment centers that we'd be there later that afternoon to tour the place.

"Ask if they have recreational facilities," I said. I opened the front door. My head ached, and as I walked through the icy rain toward the car, my girdle began to chafe.

16

One for the Road

I sat glum in the backseat as my three friends and I drove about an hour to a treatment center outside Minneapolis. I can't remember exactly where it was or its name, but it was a tacky old building in the middle of a muddy cornfield. They were expecting us, and we were met at the door by a young man who was nearing the end of his own treatment and had been assigned the role of tour guide. He told us that the place was built as a mudbath facility during the Victorian era.

We walked through a couple of spartan, vacant rooms with single beds and rickety nightstands. This place was a disaster, especially to an old girl who had seen some of the finer hospitals in her day. Worst of all, it smelled like hell. The man took us through the depressing dining area and into another room where a few zombies with cigarettes were lounging on sofas.

"This is our recreation area," the man said.

"Where are the bridge tables?" I asked.

His answer: "Bridge? What's that? We got some pool tables, and sometimes we get to go home."

"Ladies," I said, "this is *not* a viable alternative."

As we pulled out of the muddy driveway, I announced, "I want to go look at Hazelden. The best people go to Hazelden."

"There's a little problem, Barbara," Janella told me. "Hazelden wants $500 up front, and I'm not willing to pay it. Do you have it?"

"No," I said, defeated again. But for some reason, the fact that I didn't have the money for Hazelden infuriated me. By God, nobody was going to keep Barbara Carlson out of a decent treatment center, whether I thought I needed treatment or not. So the first step toward getting into a good center was getting insurance to pay for it. That meant undergoing an evaluation by a therapist. We went down the checklist to see if I was indeed an alcoholic.

"If booze is available, do you keep drinking as long as possible?" the therapist asked me.

Check.

"Do you drink at home to get started before going to a party?"

Check.

"Have you ever told loved ones that if they can't handle your drinking, that it's *their* problem?"

Check.

"Do you ever become less sociable and more isolated after drinking?"

Check again and again, on down the list. I passed with flying colors. A bed opened up at St. Mary's, where both my mother and I had been sent for repairs in the past, but I would have to wait thirty days to get in.

I felt so smart and fancy getting into one of the Twin City's better treatment centers, especially after seeing how the other half lived in that stinky converted mudbath. But I still wasn't convinced that I needed help. Maybe I could dry out on my own, after all. I decreed that I would not drink for the next thirty days. I would show *them*. And I quit, cold turkey. I also threw out my remaining Valium. For an entire month, I surprised everyone by not taking one drink or popping one pill.

It wasn't difficult to quit, really. A lot of drunks can stop drinking for a few days, weeks, even months. It's called going on the wagon. My eyes cleared a little. I was amazed that I felt so good in the morning without the hangover. But I was living—*living*—for that glass of scotch waiting for me at the end of the thirty days. All right, I would drink a little less from now on, moderate my intake. I could do that.

This, of course, was bullshit—self-deluding, arrogant bullshit. For an alcoholic, going on the wagon is like pruning your disease; it makes it stronger. If you want to stop its growth and prevent it from strangling you with its snakey vines, you have to dig deep and find its roots.

But I didn't know any of that at the time. I finally agreed to go into treatment because I feared losing custody of my children in case of a divorce, and on the off chance that I could save my marriage. And there was something about that little crushed tricycle.

"My God, Barbara, what if one of the kids had been on it. . . ."

One evening in late March during a harsh Minneapolis blizzard, the phone call came from St. Mary's. They could take me the next day. Part of me felt relief. The other part hoped the snowstorm would keep me housebound so I couldn't go. I hung up the phone and called Elaine Miller, who had tried her best to keep me out of treatment.

"I'm going in tomorrow," I told her. "I want to have one last drink."

She came trudging over to the house through the terrible wind and snow and sat with me in the kitchen. The only liquor I could find was a bottle of vodka in the freezer. I poured two small glasses of it and sipped it slowly to make it last. It was a sad occasion. I didn't even like vodka. A big tumbler of scotch tinkled in my head, but there wasn't any in the house. So I finished the vodka and sat at the table a

133

little frustrated and very depressed, watching the snow whip through the air outside.

Severely Deluded

I checked into St. Mary's recovery program on March 29, 1975.

Arne drove me to the hospital and left me with my counselor, as instructed. Oh, I was angry. Angry at myself for failing at marriage. Angry at my friends for putting me here. Angry at Arne for bringing me here.

"How much do you drink?" the counselor asked me during my evaluation.

We conservatively determined that my daily alcohol intake was at least four drinks. I would have ten drinks if I wanted to get drunk.

"My drinking is not a problem to me," I said defensively, "but it is to my friends." I told her that I would do my time at St. Mary's, but I planned to spend it playing bridge.

I looked down at the notes she was taking and made out the words "severely deluded."

Day One. I woke up with a splitting headache. I demanded that my doctor give me aspirin and spent the day in my room.

Day Two. The headache had spread to the back of my neck and was making me sick to my stomach. I insisted on skipping lunch, and they told me this meant I had to forgo other activities. No visitors. "Fine," I said. "All I want to do is stay in bed."

Day Three. Orientation to group therapy. I made it clear to the counselor and the half-dozen patients there that I was above all this. "I'm only here because I'm thinking about a divorce, and then there will be a custody fight. I have to stop drinking, but I *don't* think I'm an alcoholic."

Another patient told me I seemed hostile. "No, I'm *not!*" was my response.

I spent the next few days in group, sitting nervously in my chair, tapping my feet, swinging my legs, tearing my empty paper coffee cup to shreds, and basically resisting any and all efforts to get me to participate. God, I hated it. I hated the counselor's psychobabble and the group's whining and all the goody-goody concern they had for each other. There was a prostitute in her twenties in the group who was trying to get her life together. "You know, Barbara," she said to me. "You and I are very much alike."

"No," I hissed back. "The difference between you and me, sweetheart, is that I fucked with my mind. *You* fucked with your body."

The staff got so tired of my arrogance that they humbled me by moving me into a double room, which I shared with a 300-pound welfare mother.

I was cranky. I missed the alcohol. I longed for that out-of-control feeling it gave me. Here I was without my means of escape, and these people meant to take that exit from me for good. I missed the Valium and its sense of calm. I was simply fighting back, protecting what was mine. More than that, I was fighting for what I thought was myself.

The counselors and veteran A.A. disciples talked of experiencing one's feelings, confronting and overcoming the fears and frustrations that I had anesthetized all those years. I had a pretty good idea what those numbed frustrations were— Kristin's death for one thing, my marriage, for another. I had spent a decade nearly killing myself in order *not* to think about those things. Did they really think that I was going to deal with them now, here in a hospital with strangers?

135

I put another patient on the defensive by asking him, "How come you wear your wedding ring if you're divorced?" He did not take kindly to the inquisition. He looked pissed.

"How does that make you feel?" the therapist asked him.

"It makes me feel angry at Barbara," he said.

"Barbara?" the counselor said, urging me to respond.

"I have no reaction to that," I said sarcastically. "I guess I'm out of touch with my feelings."

The counselor noted on my records that I was "phony, deluded, and out of touch with feelings. Is dumping her anger towards outsiders on group members."

The group ordered me to be quiet until I was ready to take about myself. I spoke up a few days later to tell them I still wasn't sure that I was an alcoholic. I had been studying my pamphlets, and knew the first of A.A.'s 12 steps is admitting that you're powerless over alcohol and that your life has become unmanageable.

"I can't imagine taking the first step because I'm *not* powerless over alcohol," I said, "and my life is *not* unmanageable." I was a sexual being, I had a husband and a lover. I had two beautiful children. I ran a magnificent home. I worked and made lots of money. *How* could I be powerless? So, I had a slight drinking problem. How could I know if alcohol was controlling me if I had never tried to stop? In my mind, to admit I was without power would make me a soulless marionette.

"So why do you stay here?" someone asked.

"I would leave," I said with all the arrogance I could muster, "but the insurance wouldn't cover my stay so far."

Before long, they transferred me to another group. I decided to try to get along, to get through this as pleasantly as possible, and then get out. Funny how much you learn when you decide to listen. I began to realize that I wasn't so different from the hooker who woke up in a strange bed, not remembering how she got there or who left the $50 on the nightstand. I wasn't far from the welfare mother whose booze left her so foggy she couldn't remember her children's birthdays.

I heard myself in their stories. Rich or poor, we all drank for the same reasons. We were all insecure. We feared that without the booze we'd be devoid of personality. We drank to forget our responsibilities. We drank to forget, period. I had a deep and important connection to these people, these alcoholics. Maybe I was powerless, powerless to stop at one drink, or two, or three. Alcohol *was* pulling the strings. But how could anyone expect me to dismiss it from my life? Without it, I would crumble into a pile of splinters.

Each Tuesday was family day, which was hardly as sunny and sweet as it sounds. First of all—*what* family? Arne came only occasionally, my kids were too young to come very often, and my mother was a worse drunk than I was. Colleen and Janella and Kay understudied for my family. I sat in a chair ("the fishbowl," as it was called) surrounded by my friends ("concerned persons," as they were called) and listened again to their data and how it had affected them.

If it was meant to shame me into listening, it was beginning to work, but I still had bad days and made sure everybody else came along for the ride.

One of the St. Mary's staff members told the group that she was feeling closer to me.

"Well, I don't like *her!*" I told the group. "I couldn't care less what she thinks." I blamed such behavior on the bunions that were developing on my feet—I always got bunions during times of high stress—which I soaked every night in hot water, alone in my bathroom.

And then there were good days. The group became less and less threatening. There was nothing that I could tell this group of my fellow drunks that they couldn't understand.

They had all been there. I was able to share my most painful memories, like the joint birthday party I threw for Anne and Tucker when they were little. Their birthdays are close together, so I always gave one big party for the two of them. On this particular day, my home was filled with mommies and children.

The mommies were drinking gin and tonics, many gin and tonics, and at the end of the party I passed out. The kids had talked about it several times over the years, how scared little Tucker was when he couldn't wake me up, how it embarrassed Anne for the other parents to take care of her and tell her it would all be okay.

One of my dearest friends was in a serious accident on her way home after the birthday party. Two of her children were severely injured in the accident, and her husband told her he would never—*never*—forgive her for hurting his kids in such a stupid, careless, selfish act as driving drunk with them in the car.

The thought that alcohol was such an important part of my existence that I had to serve it with babies and children around is one of the most appalling memories of my entire drinking history. I am still ashamed.

My life, I slowly realized, *was* unmanageable. I discussed my vulnerable points in the group. I talked of my marriage, how shameful it was to have failed. There was my weight, too. How did I get here? I asked myself that over and over and over. The sad montage played out in my head—flying to New York long ago to be with Lou, then marrying Arne Carlson for all the wrong reasons; Arne and I riding in separate cars to Anoka the night Kristin died; drinking to forget my grief; drinking more to numb the guilt I felt for not giving my other children the love and support they needed; running away from home in the middle of the night; resuming my affair with Lou, the man I could never have; hitting

Arne in my rages; and humiliating myself in order to embarrass him in public.

On April 22, just over three weeks into treatment, I sat in the fishbowl, gazed upon by my faithful concerned persons, Colleen and Dick Walter, Janella, Kay Johnson, and Arne. My counselor told me for the umpteenth time that it was my time to "let go"—a way station on the way to A.A.'s 12 steps. Someone read to me, once again, the A.A. instructions:

"To 'let go' does not mean to stop caring, it means I can't do it for someone else.

"To 'let go' is not to judge, but to allow another person to be a human being.

"To 'let go' is not to regret the past, but to grow and live for the future.

"To 'let go' is to fear less, and love more."

Loving someone else was an alien idea to me. My life— with my children, my husband, my mother and father—had been spent not loving, but trying to get them to love me. I couldn't listen anymore.

"I can't do it," I said, and began to cry. "I don't want to . . ." I looked around the room for help. My eyes were flooded, and I could not see any of their faces clearly. It seemed that others were crying too. I could feel their energy, their pleading, their support.

"You don't have to like it, Barbara," my counselor said softly, weeping with me. "You just have to do it." And so I let go.

How can I describe the feeling to you? Peace. No more pain. God had taken the pain away, wiped away those years of keeping the balls in the air while I bottomed out internally. Now I had dropped the balls, the appearance of having it all together. The relief was bliss. It was the most important step in my life. I needed to be held by my husband. I wanted him to tell me that it was going to be okay, that I was wonderful for having broken through my defiance. I walked toward him, and he held out his arms. He touched my shoulders, but left his arms extended. He wouldn't let me come close. There were three feet, a gulf, between us. Once again we were unable to meet one another's needs.

All he could do was pat me on the back.

17

Grief

Before long, I became one of those patients that I used to hate. I confronted—some would say bullied—the new group members if they weren't participating or if they were engaging in the same destructive defiance in which I had specialized. I could get hurt and sad and pissed. I had moods for all occasions, and they were all wonderful, even when they were gut-wrenching. They came and went, good and bad, and I knew that if I could weather the storms, bright euphoria would follow. I could rattle off data on the other group members and hug them within an inch of their alcohol- and drug-withered lives. I was very good at recovery.

"Is definitely in touch with her own feelings and is working well with other group members in regards to her alcoholism," the counselor noted on my chart two days after my breakthrough. "Patient continues working on first step." My reviews were stellar.

In my grief therapy group, many patients came to work through a recent loss—a spouse, a mother, or a child. But as was the case for so many alcoholics, we discovered that other deaths in our lives sat dormant, ungrieved, for many years. Instead of grieving, I had submerged my feelings in booze and drugs. But the grief did not go away. It quietly fed on me and might have ultimately destroyed its host. The group was frightening at times; the membership included murderers who had killed under a chemical influence and had come to grieve and make some kind of peace with their victims. Some had killed with a knife, some with a car. Mothers were there grieving for children they had aborted.

Kristin's death felt like an open wound stinging deep inside me. Not that the death of a child shouldn't hurt forever, but my disease had convinced me that I killed her by not loving her enough. My disease told me that if I drank enough, I could make that guilt go away. My disease also told me I had killed my father by giving him a heart attack. All those feelings were, of course, irrational, but I felt them, and I felt them deeply and painfully.

At St. Mary's, I could finally grieve for my child and my father—feel the grief and work through it. With the help of a wonderful minister, I was able to talk about Kristin and remember the night of her death. For the first time I recalled picking her up moments after she had died. That memory had been buried, it had been just too painful to deal with until now.

The only recollection I had of that moment was that her body felt warm. Now I could see her face. I could see her little hands clinched, the blood on the side of her rosebud mouth. Through Gestalt therapy, I was able to hold Kristin, talk to her, tell her how much I loved her, and, finally, to say good-bye. Can you imagine the feeling? I had a second chance to see that precious little bundle again and relive the feelings of motherhood.

Working through my feelings for Kristin, I realized that I had never let go of my father after his death six years earlier. But grieving for him was much different than grieving for my child. As I tried to speak to him and let out my feelings, I was sobbing so hard that I thought I would stop breathing.

Here I was, sober for the first time in my adult life, trying to have a conversation with my father without a drink in my hand. How strange it seemed, how surreal, how impossible. I have wondered in the years since if I could have had a sober, genuine relationship with Harry Duffy, my first true love. What would we have liked about one another? Could we have been friends? Would I have laughed uproariously at his jokes? Would I still want every man in my life to be just like Harry? But it's impossible for me to deal with the What Might Have Beens. I learned at St. Mary's that I loved him, and I accepted that he was dead. Now, I could move on.

On April 26, I got a call from a friend telling me that Colleen Walter, who had cared for me when Kristin died, whose home had provided a place of warmth and discipline for Tucker, had lost her seventeen-month-old Jimmy, the youngest of her five children. Colleen thought Jimmy was with the baby-sitter and backed her truck out of the driveway. The baby-sitter and a couple of the other kids came running up to the car, panicked. Colleen put on the brakes and knew immediately what had happened. She got out and ran to him and picked him up in her arms. He was already blue. "Why now?" she prayed. "Why is he dying *now*? Why can't it be *me* dying?"

The baby-sitter tried to resuscitate little Jimmy mouth-to-mouth. The paramedics showed up, and Colleen rode in the ambulance with her baby. She watched the line on the monitor go flat before they reached the hospital. My God, how my heart broke for Colleen. It seemed just impossible that this woman who loved everything, and whom everyone loved, could possibly have to endure this. Tall, freckled, full of fun, with a husband who adored her, she seemed too *good,* too *lucky* for this kind of tragedy. There was not an animal that she could not care for, nor a life that she could not make brighter. Children loved her. I've never known

143

another human who is more loved than Colleen. That's what made this so devastating.

I requested a pass right away to go see Colleen and her husband, Dick. "What can I possibly do?" I thought. "What I can say?" I got to their home and spoke to the Walters' four other children, none of whom were out of grade school yet. I remember talking to their daughter, Tiff, trying to console her, watching the little tear that dangled from her lower lash.

Colleen and Dick, shaken by unfathomable grief, were surviving on the strength they had gained in participating in my recovery at St. Mary's. They had learned about powerlessness, unconditional love, and letting go. Oh, how they missed that baby. But there was a strength and a support and a love and a forgiveness that this family had for one another that was beautiful. Inspiring.

And I was there. *Right there.* I could feel. I was not anesthetizing the pain with booze. Again, this time with compassion, I recalled the deaths of Kristin and my father and prayed that I would never allow myself to anesthetize those feelings again.

The funeral took place on a Sunday, and on the following Tuesday, Colleen and Dick Walter returned to my family group at St. Mary's. They put their own pain aside to finish their commitment to me, a friend. To me it was the most extraordinary gift of selflessness that I have ever witnessed.

Their commitment and love and friendship strengthened my commitment to sobriety. Now it was time to begin again. "God," I prayed, "don't let it be too little. Don't let it be too late."

After five weeks of intensive recovery therapy, I was discharged from St. Mary's on Mary 6, 1975.

The first few months of sobriety can only be described as euphoric. I can remember that fall, looking at the trees and thinking that I'd never seen the orange and gold in the leaves. The blue sky was magnificent, intense. When pressures mounted, or the old appetite for alcohol came back, I called old friends and new friends from A.A. who could talk me through it. The phone became my lifeline.

I called Colleen to tell her I planned to have another drink, and she drove over and sat with me on the porch all afternoon trying to calm me down.

"Barbara," she said, taking my hand. "You are grieving for alcohol the way that I am grieving the loss of my baby."

"Oh, Colleen, that's not true," I said. "It can't be the same. There is nothing more painful in the world than losing a baby."

"You've lost your best friend," she said quietly. "You have lost the thing that you went to in your hours of pain and happiness and loneliness. Every feeling that you had involved alcohol. Of *course* you miss it."

And it all fell into place. The clichés were true. Giving up alcohol *is* like giving up a best friend, more than a friend, really. For an alcoholic, to give up alcohol is to give up God, for booze has filled the hole in the soul where God should be. The loneliness afterward is devastating. Prayer to one's "higher power," as A.A. calls it, is the only hope. First I had to define that higher power for myself. My higher power was not the same God I had learned from the nuns in Catholic school. At last I realized that God was tangible and caring. God was manifested inside me. God was my survival instinct that made me stay in recovery. God was my compassion— the thing that gave me the selfless strength to be there for the Walters when they lost Jimmy.

Not that it was easy. I still wanted the alcohol. It had gone everywhere with me since I was thirteen years old. I had accommodated my bottle as if it were a difficult loved one that could spin my bed and inflict terrible hangovers. But it was worth it. It was all worth it for my faithful friend, whom I sorely missed.

Barbed Wire Fence

Instead of drinking, I threw myself into therapy. There was not a group I did not join. There was not a book I did not read. My sobriety library included self-help books like *Alive and Aware: Improving Communication in Relationships* ("We distinguish four specific relationship states. We call the first one *togetherness . . .*"); Barry Stevens's *Don't Push the River* ("Simplify. Who are you trying to impress?"); and *Peoplemaking: Because You Want to Be a Better Parent* by Virginia Satir (*Chapter Two*—"What's *Your* Family Like?").

God knows, I had spent enough time getting sick. Now I could certainly give myself time to get well. How did I have time to sell real estate? I did—I had to—but I moonlighted, persuading my friends who still drank to go into recovery. Honestly, I was out there bossing any person whom I'd known longer than thirty minutes to go into treatment. It became my crusade.

Arne and I both felt ambivalent about saving the marriage. Arne met Joanne, the woman who would become his second wife, before our marriage was over; but even with someone else in the picture, it was still hard. You still think, "Do I want to give up my family? Do I want to give up my house and everything we've built together?" We existed in a strange Never-Never Land, dreaming that we could save the marriage. But the more involved in treatment I became, the more I knew that I needed to count. I needed to be a partner in this marriage. The more I thought about it, the more I

Four generations. *Left to right:* Mamie Simons Duffy (my grandmother); me, one year old; Harry (my father); and Henry Simons, Sr. (my great-grandfather).

Me, three, at our fancy new house in Anoka. The baby fat would *not* go away.

Me, five, and George, three. I introduced him to my parents' collection of "blue" party records and taught him the facts of life.

Me, six, at home in Anoka with Harry, and George, four. This is the last time I wore pigtails.

Me, ten, with George, eight, and our father having lunch at the grand old Nicollet Hotel.

My high school senior photo—the last time I was a virgin in white.

My high school graduation photo, taken by the pool at my house. I'm sitting in the bottom row, far left. Almost all of us went on to find husbands. A few would find divorce attorneys after that.

My mother as a bride in 1937,
and me as a bride in 1965.
We're wearing the same
strand of pearls.

Standing before the
Minneapolis skyline as
Lady Liberty in 1981.
Look! I had a neck!

Down to my "fucking
weight" in 1981, standing in
front of City Hall. Then
again, maybe I look better
heavy.

1982 City Council
campaign photo. *Left to
right:* Annie, Tucker, Jane,
and me.

Holding court with staff members and my City Council constituents at an early morning "Breakfast with Barbara."

The forty-four-year-old bride and Pete, sixty, my second husband, with the minister, in 1983. I wish I could remember her name.

My new family in 1983. *Left to right:* daughter-in-law Jerri; Pete's son, Kent; their daughter, Cici; Pete's son, Scott (with the beard); Jerri and Kent's son, Scott; Pete; me; Annie; Tucker; and my mother, Jane.

The governor and me. Arne always makes an appearance on my radio show during election years. He's always nice and seems very nervous.

Assaulting an innocent bystander with my KSTP microphone at the state fair.

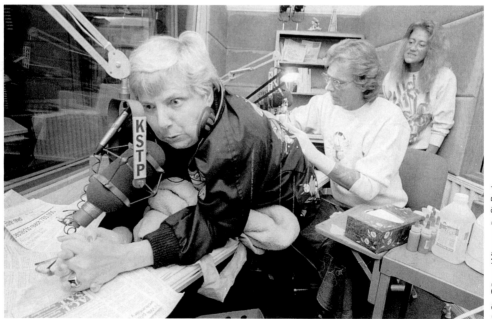

Having my posterior tattooed on the air. Sometimes it hurts to fly in the face of convention.

realized that Arne and I were worlds apart, and we weren't growing any closer.

"I don't know why you want to stay in this marriage," he told me one morning. "I have never loved you."

I convinced myself that he had said this in confusion. But I was the one who was confused. Getting sober was making my life so much better, I refused to think that my marriage was hopeless. I forced Arne to attend couples groups at the St. Mary's after-care program run by an outrageous Irishman named Bill Kelly and a quiet, demure woman named Marian Mann, who had founded St. Mary's recovery program with her husband, Dr. George Mann. Bill was a recovered alcoholic, a big, large, wonderful fellow with bushy eyebrows and a booming voice, and people adored him. I trusted him as much as I trusted my father. If he had told me to keep my legs together for the next ten years, I would have listened to him. I didn't make a move without asking him first.

In group therapy, as desperately as I tried to reach Arne, he kept his distance across the ocean of animosity we had put between us. He would never admit that he shared responsibility in the faltering of our marriage. As I screamed and begged and reached and cried, he sat back with his arms crossed.

"See how crazy she is?" he said to the group, in a calm, condescending, well-modulated tone.

"You see? He doesn't love me!" I screamed. "He does not care about me!"

But Bill did not suffer self-pity. "I wouldn't sleep with you either," he answered. "You are a barbed wire fence."

On a Saturday morning, after I had cried and ranted at Arne during a session that included Anne and Tucker, we stopped at McDonald's to pick up lunch. He was seething and I was weeping as we pulled into the parking lot. The kids filed out of the back seat, but I stayed in the car, too tear-streaked to go inside. Arne climbed out of the driver's side and stood there a moment. He bent down and looked in my eyes, his face purple with rage.

"I hope you rot in hell in loneliness," he said, then turned and walked into the restaurant.

18

$\mathcal{P}$issed

During recovery I decided to take a course called Pharmhouse, which was offered by the Junior League and designed to help women understand alcohol and drug addiction. It was very popular, and pretty soon all the women in it were throwing their husbands helter-skelter into St. Mary's, Hazelden, and any other treatment center with a spare bed.

After completing the course, we participated in a support group run by Dick Cargill, a large hairy man who instructed us in the vintage 1970s ways to get good and pissed off. All the proper little Junior Leaguers assigned great big cushions to play our husbands, and we just beat the shit out of them with big red foam-rubber clubs. You had all these Junior Leaguers screaming and crying, *"I'm pissed!"* wielding these bats, and you would think, "My God, the world's coming to an end."

I had never had trouble venting my anger, but that was unusual among the Junior League set. The free-thinking, get-in-touch-with-yourself decade of the 1970s was very tumultuous for these women. We had watched the Vietnam protests on the news, Watergate had instilled in us a cynicism about the male power structure, we had seen one revolution after another in fashion and art, and we came to realize, sometime during our late thirties, that there had to be more to life than keeping plates warm for our successful, philandering husbands. There had to be more to life than drinking, entertaining, and being good hostesses—those generations-old values we had picked up from our mothers.

We had done enough easy volunteer work and decorated enough homes. Unfortunately, the self-help movement also fostered a culture of blame. So many women of my generation blamed their husbands for their unhappiness, and as a result, great waves of divorce papers flooded the country. These women got in touch with their frustration and anger in the 1970s, and they got rid of the sonofabitch they had married, but they were also lonely and scared. Now they had to raise children on their own, and enter a workplace where former housewives were unemployable. Even if they were lucky enough to find a job, they were grossly underpaid.

I was one of the lucky few, having been the main bread-winner in my household. I watched my friends file unprepared into the real world, dressed for battle in their Pappagallo shoes and Ann Taylor suits, away from their big homes and housekeepers. They found themselves banging their heads against some very low glass ceilings and kicking down office doors. Let me tell you, young women of the 1990s, no one was particularly happy about opening those doors for you. We weren't thinking of you. We were getting through it the best we could.

Downdrafts

In May of 1975, about a month after I left St. Mary's, I decided to test my new sober strength by visiting Lou. Maybe I could convert him to sobriety. Maybe we could then live happily ever after together. And maybe I was still the same desperate, deluded broad I'd always been.

This time, the excuse for traveling to New York was the wedding of my old friend Mary Prichard. Mary was the daughter of a Minneapolis grain baron, and the groom's parents were part of the wealthy set of Short Hills, New Jersey. It was to be a grand affair, and I couldn't wait to go. But mostly, I couldn't wait to see Lou. I boarded the plane clutching my little A.A. 12-step book to my bosom. We took off, and I was gripped by panic. I had never flown sober before, so I had never realized that I was *afraid* of flying. Imagine my surprise.

I tried to calm myself by reading my little book. The flight attendant noticed my reading material, sat down next to me, and told me that she was in the program also. It was very comforting to be part of this wide-reaching and caring support group. I shared with her my fear of flying, and she tried to comfort me. But then she started talking about something called downdrafts, which sounded very dangerous, so she ultimately wasn't much help. I was relieved when she had to get up and serve the snack.

That night, before I went to the bridal dinner, I stopped by Lou's apartment. I looked quite smashing in my long flowing blue dress cut to my navel (my breasts were still perky) and matching floor-length coat. I had hit a high mark of 185 pounds before recovery, and once I stopped drinking, my weight had dropped about 50 pounds, which seemed a miracle in and of itself.

I felt proud and beautiful, and I couldn't wait for him to lay eyes on me. Lou wasn't quite so smashing. He looked pale and gaunt and, in fact, he was not very happy to see me. But I didn't care. I was here on a crusade. I had been saved, and the man I loved was going to join me. No more martinis, but instead a life of happiness—a life to be experienced in the glow of sobriety—was waiting for us.

"Lou, I want you to get help," I told him. "We have spent

too many years drinking together. You told me that you were an alcoholic years ago. There is help. It's called St. Mary's. I know I can help you get well."

I began to cry, but Lou didn't reach out to comfort me and tell me that it would be okay. He just sat there, staring at me coldly, with a glass of straight vodka in his hand.

"I'm happy for you, Barbara," he said. "I'm happy that you got help for yourself, but this is my affair. I am not ready to stop drinking. It is a very important part of my life. I appreciate your concern."

He got up and poured himself another drink.

I kept hearing his soulless words: *I appreciate your concern.*

I stayed a few minutes longer and then left for the bridal dinner. It was a black-tie affair, complete with a band and glorious food and all my old friends, but all I wanted to do was see Lou. After the first course, I excused myself and went back to his apartment. I knew that if I was just smart enough, pretty enough, wise enough, loving enough, hysterical enough, tender enough, and angry enough, I would be able to get through to him.

I tried going for the soft sell when I got back to his place. I offered myself to him, and we tried to make love, but he was too drunk to maintain an erection. Years of booze had left him impotent.

I spent a sleepless night next to him. The next morning I threw my gown in a paper bag, put on my high heels and pearls, borrowed one of Lou's raincoats, kissed him good-bye, and hailed a cab on Park Avenue alone. I liked the idea of riding naked under a man's trenchcoat in a cab, and I plan to do it again someday.

I think the sky was overcast, or at least that's how I remember it. I had been in love with Lou for nearly fifteen years, and now, in my newfound clarity, I knew it was never going to work out. I went back to the apartment where I was staying and cried most of the afternoon. I barely made it to the wedding. I remember that the bride was unhappy because her mother was driving her nuts.

I left the wedding early that afternoon, to go back to Lou, to keep trying to persuade him to get help. After two more days of pleading, it was time for me to leave. I was exhausted, and he was comatose. I remember the same old sad feeling when I got on the plane pointed toward Minneapolis. I had always been so happy in New York with Lou, dreaming that this time it would last, that we could be together. Drunken dreams are still dreams. Now that pocket of hope and joy in my life had been emptied. I fell asleep on the plane thinking about downdrafts.

Orangutans (continued)

Not long into my postrecovery crusades to get the entire world into alcohol and drug rehabilitation, I realized that the sinners who needed saving the most were the Duffy's themselves, starting with my mother.

After Harry died, Bruce had slowly taken over Jane's care and feeding; my relationship with her had deteriorated almost beyond repair since I had checked her into the hospital, borrowed her jewelry, and left for New York. When I returned this time, I discovered that, far from being treated for her addiction to pills, she had accumulated even more prescriptions. I called her psychiatrist to plead for his help in getting my mother into treatment.

"It's not going to work," he said. "You know how manipulative your mother is."

Next, I spoke to her brother, also a physician, and some

of her friends. Not one of them thought that health and sobriety were possible for dear little addicted Jane.

Her doctors and friends weren't totally to blame, though. Her children had ignored her sick, crazy behavior for far too long, simply because it seemed absolutely normal to us. We had grown up with her suicide attempts. We thought all children visited their mothers in the psychiatric ward every couple of months. Once, when she slept at my home on Fremont after a party, I went in to awaken her the next morning, and she was gone. She hadn't received the attention she thought she deserved during the party, so she had called a cab in the wee hours of the morning and checked herself into the hospital with some made-up ailment.

By this time, Bruce had married a wonderful woman named Mary. Since they lived close to Jane, they stopped by several times a day to administer her pills and often saw her home after parties when she had had too much to drink.

On Christmas Eve, 1974, just two days before Mary would give birth to Shannon, their first child, Bruce and Mary were helping Jane home when she got pissed and tried to shove Mary down a flight of fifteen concrete steps at Jane's apartment complex. Bruce was livid. He grabbed Jane by the scruff of her neck and tossed her into the apartment and slammed the door. Before that the police had arrested Jane in a restaurant when she was eating with George's children, who were in town for a visit. On the way there, she had sideswiped a parked patrol car without noticing, and she was charged with a hit and run.

The years of abuse on Jane's body had left her with tremors. Her lower lip quivered almost constantly. Her hands shook. X-rays revealed lesions on her brain. Her perfect little figure had become slightly puffy, and her face was bloated. She was a mess and looked like hell. Without the help of her doctors, the intervention consisted of Bruce, Arne, Anne,

Tucker, and me. George declined his invitation, citing no data. I thought to remind him of the cop car incident, but if his denial was so great, we would do it without him. Being a veteran of psychiatric hospitals, Jane was surprisingly amenable to the idea. Just before Christmas of 1975, eight months after I had checked out sober, I checked my mother into St. Mary's Hospital.

She was not, however, prepared for the journey in store for her. She was teeny, frail, and angry and said she couldn't read the literature.

"Well, Jane," her nurse said, "I'll read it to you."

As soon as she realized no one was going to let her off easy, pamper her for a few weeks, then send her back to her life with a new batch of prescriptions, Jane became hostile. Susie Brixius, who always thought Jane epitomized some glamorous ideal of a woman, was there as a concerned person. I believe she always loved my mother much more than I was ever able to. I don't remember Jane's having a breakthrough, which is a normal step for most recovery candidates. With Jane, it was a slow, laborious exercise of tiny steps. She could not absorb the information we gave her. She would get angry, lower her eyes, and puff out her bottom lip in a pout, Sometimes when I looked at Jane, I thought a demon had taken possession of her. Many demons, really. They lived deeply in her soul—the cheating husband, a brush with death, unrealized grief for her own father and her own dead child, countless substance addictions—and they fought hard to keep their hold on her.

"Is this worth it?" I wondered over and over.

It was. I now realize, when I think back on her horrific, defeated behavior during her first few weeks in therapy, Jane was actually fighting like hell. My mother rang in 1976 sober. She made friends in her A.A. group. She would cook them dinner in her apartment. She was driving and entertaining and being a wonderful grandmother to Anne and Tucker. She gave them lessons in painting and sculpting, which she had resumed with a vengeance. And as Arne and I slouched toward divorce, she became a constant for Anne and Tucker.

Her recovery was one of the few miracles I've been lucky enough to witness. She got her old, petite figure back and dressed immaculately. The tremors ceased. Even the brain lesions cleared up. It was just astounding.

My relationship with Jane, which has always been competitive, still wasn't perfect. But it was five million times better. I liked her. We laughed together, and I came to see her as Suzie Brixius had always seen her. I had spent thirty-six years battling her, hating that she could only tell me that she loved me when she was drunk, hating the way she and my father would fight, and hating the way she slurred her words. I judged her harshly. She was my mother, and I had not understood her alcoholism and drug addiction. So now, this wonderful woman who emerged from treatment was truly a gift. I like to say that St. Mary's gave me back my life, and it gave me a mother.

St. Mary's also gave me a brother. Bruce's drinking had worsened after Duffy Lumber fell on hard times. It consumed his life. I had tried to convince him to seek help, but he wouldn't listen even as he was helping our mother through recovery. Throughout his early adulthood, he strove to emulate his father. He had affairs and told his wife that other women had nothing to do with their marriage; it was just a need that Duffy men had. Mary accepted that. He drank, smoked, and swore. He was loud. He was the spitting image of his father. The trouble was that my brother was the spitting image of his old, dying father, and Bruce was still in his twenties.

It all changed for Bruce one morning in December when he woke up and realized that he had driven home from a restaurant in a blackout. His baby daughter, Shannon, had been in the car with him. Imagining what might have happened, he panicked and ran into her room and saw she was sleeping soundly. But knowing that he could have killed her, Bruce began to think that the best way to end this kind of behavior was to end his life. He seriously considered suicide, the old Duffy standby.

The next day he took a more positive step. He attended one of Jane's group sessions at St. Mary's as a concerned person. Bruce had always maintained a kind of nervous calm about himself. He seemed quiet and friendly, but there was a raging temper brewing underneath the facade. On this day, he seemed edgy, like he was about to erupt. Another man in my mother's group said something—I can't recall what—that upset Bruce. He blew up in group and left the room.

As he passed the reception desk, he stopped to ask, "What can I do to get in?"

Bruce went home and told Mary that he had checked himself into recovery. Well, she was absolutely dumbfounded.

"It's not your problem," she argued. "It's other people's problem." Mary, who was so compassionate and stable, had tried to hide his problem from herself. This, ladies and gentlemen, is what they mean by codependency.

"No," he said. "I'm as sick as my mother."

Mary backed down immediately and agreed to see him through his recovery.

About three weeks into his treatment at St. Mary's, I showed up as his concerned person. I began spouting data at him. This was nearly as difficult for me to say as it was for him to hear.

"Anne and Tucker don't respect you, Bruce," I lectured. "They *fear* you. There's a big difference." And then I began to talk about our father. I talked about how strange it was for Harry to turn me into his surrogate wife, just as strange as turning his little boys into adult men before they hit puberty, leaving them home alone to cook their own dinner, allowing them to drink and tend bar at parties. Bruce was shaking.

Then, suddenly, he straightened up, and a real calm—a sense of peace that I had never seen in him before—washed over his face. It really was as if someone had taken a planet off his shoulders. His tears fell freely. Bruce had admitted to himself he was powerless over his alcoholism, over his anger, over his sense of failure. For a son of Harry Duffy, this was the bravest thing he could have done.

"My father was a sonofabitch," he said crying in pain and smiling in freedom. "I loved him, and I still love him dearly, but there were a lot of things he did that I never thought of until now. Did I miss playing catch with my father? I didn't think so. But maybe I did." With that, Bruce took the first painful baby step out of the fatal family cycle and on the way to life.

19

Don't Go in the Closet

"Goddammit, what did I do with my glasses?" and "If only . . ."

These are probably the ten words uttered most often throughout the course of this broad's life. As I struggled against all logic to save my marriage after recovery, "If only" became my mantra. If only I was more attractive, Arne would come around. So I lost weight and became more diligent about treating my allergies, which had plagued me since childhood and caused unsightly skin rashes. I looked healthy now and felt sexy for the first time in years. If only he could learn to touch and express physically whatever warm feelings he still had for me, then he could love me again. So I signed us up for the Sexual Attitude Reassessment Seminar at the University of Minnesota. For an entire weekend he patiently watched the films with me and listened to the therapists. Apparently it meant nothing to him.

We decided to stick it out through his 1976 election to the legislature. Even though the divorce rate in America was skyrocketing, politicians had to play by different rules. This was not a consideration lost on a man whose campaign literature at the time billed him as "one of the best-known political figures in Minnesota."

In 1976, Arne's campaign newsletter sung his praises and featured a picture of Arne and me, sitting in our living room with the kids. When I look at that photo, I see a composite of so many truths and lies. Nine-year-old Tucker is poised and confident in his little sweater. I'm smiling, or at least baring my teeth. Anne, eight, stares down the camera, intense and somber, a child of the damned. Arne is gazing down at me from his perch on the arm of the sofa, grinning like a schoolboy in love. He was quite an actor.

Arne and I were in therapy together and separately. By this time we were seeking help primarily to keep our split as amicable as possible, for us and for the kids.

"In all my years of practice," my therapist said to me, "I have told very few people that they must leave. But you must get out of this marriage, or you will die. This is the most hostile symbiotic relationship that I have ever witnessed."

We conducted separate lives in that house on Fremont. I can remember going downstairs because a few friends had come by one evening. Arne hadn't told me that we were expecting company.

"Barbara, go back upstairs," he said. "This is my party."

I still had a hard time accepting the option of divorce, which I saw as an admission of failure. I really believe that it was easier on Arne than on me. Men simply have an easier time cutting emotional ties. Is that sexist? I don't know, and I don't care. There's a part of me that would still like to go back and try again with Arne. I still get lost in thoughts imagining if only I'd been different, better, neater, thinner, if only I'd gone sledding or on picnics and hadn't nailed him in the head with a frying pan. It might have worked if only I hadn't been such a hostile bitch, if only I had not been that barbed wire fence, as Bill Kelly had called me at St. Mary's. If only . . . If only . . . If only . . .

My divorce was the most difficult thing I have ever gone through in my life, including the deaths of my child and my father. It still says to me that there was something wrong with me. Why else could he not be intimate with me? why else wouldn't he love me? Why else would he pull away from me in bed at night?

One afternoon when I was alone in the house, folding clothes in the library, my body began to sway back and forth. I began to wail and could feel myself slipping outside my head, going mad, teetering on the verge of a nervous breakdown. I remembered hearing the story of a woman I knew, whose children had found her cowering in a locked closet when they came home from school.

"Don't go in the closet," I kept thinking over and over, under my howls and pain. I found myself on the floor still rocking back and forth, back and forth. I became incontinent—wet my pants—and went numb on the right side of my body. I thought I was suffering a stroke. I remember crawling to the kitchen and thinking Arne would be home at four P.M. I had no idea what time it was, but I knew I had to stay alive until four. I hugged myself, rocking, rocking, rocking. I pulled myself, dragging my legs behind me, my pants soiled, across the kitchen, into the living room. By now there were tears. I curled up in a fetal position on the floor next to the couch and stayed there waiting for salvation. Arne finally came home and found me lying there.

"I need help," I whispered. "Hold me."

All he saw was this woman he despised, curled up crying like a baby, and he wanted no part of it.

He shook his head no. "I cannot hold you," he said. "You have killed every feeling that I have ever had for you." After a while I was able to pull myself together enough to go find Tucker. Tucker held me until I fell asleep. He did it without flinching. He instinctively knew that this was what had to be done, and he rose to the task. He was just a scared little boy, forced to be the man of the house.

The End

Arne won the election that November. We had a large party with campaign workers and friends to celebrate the occasion. I didn't turn in until almost three A.M. Arne was already in our bed. I crawled in and faced him. He put his right hand on my cheek and held it there for about five minutes. We lay there looking into each other's eyes, not a word spoken. I believe he was thanking me for coming this far with him, and maybe for the children. I will never know what was going through his head, but I do know that it was our most intimate moment in twelve years of marriage. I also knew that we were done.

The Walters' Thanksgiving parties had become a tradition with Arne and the kids and me, but this year, Anne and Tucker and I went without Arne. I had asked him to stay at home because wherever we went together tension and very often an all-out brawl followed. I returned that night with a doggie bag of turkey and dressing for him. He slept on the couch that night, and the next evening he left. He stayed out all night.

Of course, Arne had stayed away at night before, but at least he always offered an excuse—working late, a business trip. This was the first time he had not come home without calling. When he walked in on Saturday morning, I lost it.

What followed was our last battle in that home. It ended with Arne retreating from the house with his suitcases packed. Instead of dead, bloody soldiers left on the Fremont battlefield, there were two sobbing children.

"Daddy, don't leave," Anne cried. Tucker tried to hold back his tears. Arne knelt down and looked them both in their little red eyes.

"This has nothing to do with you," he said, as he began to cry, too. "It has to do with your mother and me, and I have to go." He hugged them both and walked out the door. I stood in the kitchen, knowing the war was over, knowing that all of us had lost.

I celebrated my first single Christmas Eve in a smart red silk pantsuit that once belonged to my mother. I greeted friends at my home, laughed and entertained. But this year, at the Carlsons' annual Christmas party, the host was missing. At least I missed him. During the party I went upstairs and phoned Arne. I began to cry. "You've got to come back," I pleaded. "I can *not* do this alone. I'm sorry, I'll do anything you want."

He let me cry for a minute or two, then said, "I can't, Barbara."

I threw the phone down and rejoined the festivities.

Soon after he left the house with his suitcases, Arne hired a lawyer and filed for divorce. Once he made his decision to leave, he was out of there, and he didn't spend a lot of time with the children. This really upset me, but as I was told by a minister, a lot of men are unable to separate the anger they have for their spouse from their children. He was angry, he had Joanne, and he didn't seem to want any part of his old, broken family. He stopped by occasionally and took Anne and Tucker out for a bite to eat, but there were no definite visitation times. Thank God my mother was well. She became Anne and Tucker's mother, father, and grandmother. She was their world. She was living at the Calhoun Beach Club, where both she and Arne had apartments.

Screams

Most of 1977 remains a blur of pain generated by the divorce and excitement about my new life. Anticipating a property fight, Arne's attorney advised him to put the house in foreclosure.

We finally sold the house, and I moved out at the end of June to a small rented duplex. My friends helped me move. On our last day in the house, the trash man was to appear to pick up the mountains of crap and trash bags that we had produced cleaning this enormous house. At nine A.M. he hadn't arrived yet. My phone was scheduled to be disconnected at 9:30, so I got a little anxious about the trash. I dialed the gentleman at home.

"Hello?" said a quiet female voice.

"Well, where *is* he?" I growled.

"He's gone," she answered.

"What do you mean, he's gone? He's supposed to be *here!*"

"I'm sorry, he died," she said.

It turned out the poor man had been killed the night before—electrocuted. I felt just awful. I went to sleep on the last night in our house and woke up around two A.M. to find that my cat had given birth to two wretched, screaming black kittens in my bed. It was not a promising beginning to my new life.

I wasn't the only open who wasn't having fun. I could see that the divorce was wearing on the kids. Anne missed her daddy. I could only imagine how I would have felt if Jane and Harry had split up, and I had been packed off to live with my mother. I would've killed myself. Anne held it together, but I worried for her. Tucker was afraid to leave the neighborhood where he had developed a network of friends over the last few years. Fortunately, the first house we found was close by.

Our next stop was divorce court. Arne wanted half of everything, even though I would take custody of the kids and despite the fact that I had been the principle breadwinner in the family. I was making a substantial income selling real estate at the time, while Arne was making only about $12,000 a year working in the legislature. Some men just walk away from a marriage and start over. Not Arne. He had never given me a honeymoon. I didn't have an engagement ring.

I wasn't bitter about it, but ... Well, I suppose I was a little bitter about it.

As we entered the court to hack out a settlement, I heard that invitations to Arne's wedding to Joanne had begun landing in people's mailboxes. I couldn't believe it. I knew that he had been seeing Joanne before we separated. But couldn't that bastard have waited until *after* the divorce was final? Oh, I was angry.

The trial dragged on for three days. Details of our vapid sex life came up, so did tales of my drinking and Arne's coldness. Friends came to watch, and every day my camp went to eat lunch at Charlie's. Tommy Weiser came all the way from Palm Springs for the show. He said, "I've never known a divorce that I enjoyed as much as this one." Another day at lunch, one friend told us all about a nightmare she had had in which Arne pushed her over a railing down through the atrium of the courthouse. It was getting a little tense.

Friday came, and we still hadn't settled. Arne's wedding was supposed to take place a week from Saturday. If I played my cards right, I could drag this proceeding out long enough to wreck their wedding plans. Wouldn't that be fun? Then I spent some time over the weekend with Bill Kelly, the man from St. Mary's who had held my hand through couples therapy with Arne. Bill was scheduled to testify on Monday.

"Barbara," he said. "You know I'll testify for you. And you know I'll do anything that you want me to do. But I have to tell you, because I care about you, that you have to let go. It's just like in recovery, when you admitted you were powerless over alcohol. You came to the realization that you could not control it, and therefore you had to get it out of your life. You're powerless over Arne. You *can't* control him. You can't make him love you. You're powerless over the decisions he's made, and you have always been powerless. He's going to do what he wants, no matter how you feel. All this is doing is hurting you and the children. Go and get on with your life. You have a fabulous life ahead of you. I think you're wrong in continuing the trial."

I gritted my teeth and called my attorney.

"Give him whatever he wants," I said.

"What . . ."

"Give him whatever he wants." I hung up the phone.

I received $20,000 out of the sale of the house. We divided the furniture, the silver, everything.

A couple of days after the divorce became final, Arne wed Joanne in a ceremony in Duluth. He did not invite Anne and Tucker, which destroyed them. Their cousins were invited, their friends attended, but Arne for some reason did not want his own children there. Maybe it was some misguided sense of protocol. Maybe he was angry at me and taking it out on them. Charlie Leck, the minister who had lived with us for a while during his own divorce, came over for dinner the night of Arne's wedding. Anne and Tucker were visibly upset. I tried to explain to them that they shouldn't take it personally, that their father was doing what he thought was best. But inside I was just furious. I wanted to kill him.

"Let's raise a toast to the happiness of your father and Joanne," Charlie said. We extended our glasses and held back our screams.

20

Shitska Goddess

When he was fifteen years old, a young man named Chuck Mark and some other brave Jewish teenagers would stand outside the church of anti-Semitic Minneapolis evangelists. They politely handed out leaflets on behalf of the Minneapolis Jewish Council, an organization that fought against and exposed hate groups. When anyone cared to listen, they would also discuss their literature, trying to counteract the hate spewing from the pulpits.

That same year, 1946, Minneapolis was called the United States' "capital of anti-Semitism" by journalist Carey McWilliams. Jews were excluded from the Minneapolis Athletic Club, the Minneapolis Automobile Association, the Kiwanis, the Rotary, the Lions, and from living in several neighborhoods and suburbs around the city.

Unlike most Jewish men of his generation, who couldn't find jobs in the major industries in town, Chuck Mark found a job as a stockbroker at John Kinnard and Co., which was owned by the father of Sally Kinnard, my old drinking buddy. By the time Chuck entered my life, he had left brokerage, moved into insurance, and had divorced his wife of twenty years. He had three adult children of his own, all of them fairly religious—at least more religious than their father. But I'm sure those early experiences, calmly fighting anti-Semitism with brains instead of brawn, shaped his personality. He was gentle, smart, caring, and underneath he was seething with passion and righteous indignation.

I met him the night Arne moved out in 1976. He was invited along by some friends who came over to play bridge and try to cheer me up. Chuck seemed cute and smart, and sort of quiet on the surface.

He called the next day. The last thing I wanted was another man in my life, but I agreed to go out to dinner. I kept my distance, but began seeing him occasionally. I think that he probably saved my life that Christmas. He escorted me to Christmas and New Year's parties and took my mind off the divorce I would face after the first of the year. It was a time of tremendous highs and lows for me. Sometimes I enjoyed a sense of freedom and relief because Arne's feelings and judgments no longer had to be factored into my life. At other times I missed Arne terribly and gave in to purely sentimental feelings.

I was down to what I call my "fucking weight," about 135 pounds. So I decided that amid all the pain of losing Arne, I could at least try to enjoy single life. Chuck and I began dating, and we continued to do so on and off for about seven years, never exclusively, but often intensely. He was short and balding—no one's idea of an Adonis—but he was passionate. I think of such passion when I think of our affair. I think of having orgasms, which were so few and far between with Arne. It was heaven. Chuck is the main reason I say my best lovers have been Jewish.

Chuck and his children became my second family. They all enjoyed my fractured Yiddish—I turned *shiksa* into "shitska," and continued to say it that way after I knew better, simply for their amusement. When his daughter Laurie married a rabbi, I gave her a bridal dinner. Though when I went with Chuck to visit her in Vancouver, I had to agree not to go to services at her husband's synagogue. I mean, how would they introduce me? "Here's the shitska that good old

Dad's sleeping with"? I gladly stayed at the house and cooked.

And oh, How Chuck and I fought. I can remember driving to a party once and deciding on the way that I simply didn't want to go. I showed Chuck what a petulant horror I could be. Chuck insisted that we go at least for a little while. We had said that we would be there, he reasoned, and we were on our way. I fought back. He yelled at me. I yelled back. Neither of us gave an inch. We got to the party, and he got out of the car with the keys, knowing that nothing else would keep me from driving away and leaving him stranded. I sat alone in the car for a few minutes, fuming. Then I decided that he had won the battle. I went in and stayed for hours. We had a great time at the party and great sex when we got home.

Running

Here it was, 1978. Carter was in office and I simply could *not* listen to that disco drivel on the radio. Olivia Newton-John and John Travolta were singing "You're the One that I Want," and every *other* song was by a bunch of castrati wannabes who called themselves the Bee-Gees. On June 21, I celebrated my fortieth birthday with a black-tie affair backed up by a full orchestra (playing my favorite standards from the forties and fifties) and with about four hundred guests.

I decided that I should invite Arne and Joanne. It was appropriate that he be there. After all, he had been a large part of my journey up to this point. He and Joanne accepted. It had been a very important day for Arne, since he had just been endorsed by the state Republican party to run for state auditor. This was his first try at a major political office. After he received the nomination, he left the convention early, went home, and put on a tuxedo for my party. I'm sure it was difficult for Joanne and Arne to come in as a couple and see so many of Arne's old friends, but it was a magnificent thing that he did. That night a new, supportive, professional relationship between Arne and me began.

I was not happy about turning forty. I was bored with real estate. I got no excitement from getting listings anymore. I had lost my husband and my good friend liquor, so depression became my hobby. I had crying jags and thoughts of suicide again. I couldn't sleep, and a shooting pain in my right temple visited me like a goddamn candy striper every hour on the hour. One evening, not long after my birthday, I called a friend and A.A. sponsor, Bob Harvey, and asked him to have a glass of cognac with me (which shows how deluded one can get).

"You can drink if you want to, Barbara," he said, "but I want no part of it."

I dropped the idea and poured out the cognac since I didn't want to drink alone, but Bob spent the entire night with me on the telephone. It scared the hell out of me when I realized what I had almost done. I needed help.

I hadn't had a drink since I left St. Mary's in 1975, but my commitment to A.A. had waned. I suppose I just got bored with it, and I was arrogant enough to believe that I could do it on my own. I had failed to fully work through all 12 steps that are necessary to stay sober. My friends were concerned about my depression, concerned that my life was becoming unmanageable again.

On July 20, 1978, not one month after my big splashy birthday blowout, I checked into St. Mary's asking for help again.

I talked to the therapists about anger. I was one angry woman. Angry about the divorce. Angry that I hated my job. Angry about turning forty. If Harry had been here, he would have told me what to do. But he wasn't. And I was still angry at him for dying. During clay-sculpting therapy at the hospital, I took my index finger and violently jabbed the wad of clay full of holes. This was duly noted on my therapist's report.

After less than a week, I decided to leave. The staff suggested that I stay, but I was restless. I felt like getting back to my kids. I agreed to continue an outpatient program and attend a grief group to help me continue working through the deaths of my father and Kristin, as well as the death of my marriage to Arne. I also agreed to take a more active role in A.A.

My self-involvement and Arne's second marriage had left Anne and Tucker at loose ends. Anne still remembers getting physically ill and throwing up whenever she saw Arne touch Joanne. Tucker had always played the role of peacekeeper in our home, not a healthy occupation for a prepubescent boy, but an occupation nonetheless, and he felt lost without it. At home he had begun to act out and rebel.

After I came home from the hospital, Tucker began misbehaving so badly that the nanny, a beautiful young woman in her twenties named Bobbie, told me she would have to quit. Then one evening Anne and Tucker engaged in a screaming fight, and something in me snapped.

"I can't handle you kids anymore!" I yelled. The next thing I knew I was on the phone to Arne.

"Goddammit!" I told him. "This was *not* part of the deal. I did not agree to raise these children alone."

Arne was surprisingly kind. He tried to calm me down. He tried to tell me that he understood how I was feeling. Arne offered to let Tucker live with him, and I accepted.

"He's a big asshole!" screamed Tucker. But I insisted that he go and tried to convince him that he would be better off. Anne said she didn't want to be separated from her big brother. The divorce had brought them closer, and they learned to count on each other more. Anne insisted on going to live with Tucker at Arne's, at least for the summer. Arne agreed.

So I gave up my children. Anne and Tucker ended up staying past the summer, living full-time with Arne throughout the better part of their adolescent years. Maintaining two kids couldn't have been a picnic for poor Joanne, who was only twenty-six at the time. Based on what Anne and Tucker have told me, it wasn't a picnic for them, either. Joanne had been raised in a large family and was big on assigning chores and establishing rules. Tucker continued to rebel. He refused to make his bed. He would mow only half the yard. Joanne kept the candy and cookies locked in a cabinet, so Tucker stole the key and had it copied.

While the relationship between Joanne and the kids became strained, I eventually overcame the fact that she was Arne's new wife and got along with her. She liked me, too, I think. She and Arne generously helped me move several times when I was bouncing from house to house during my postdivorce era. I will be eternally grateful to Joanne for trying so hard to be a stable, traditional kind of mother to my kids. That was more than I had ever done for them. I kept in touch with her after she and Arne divorced, and after Tucker's high school graduation, I called to thank her.

"I'm sorry you weren't there to see it," I said. "You were largely responsible for getting him there."

I must admit that giving my children up wasn't difficult at the time. Living with the decision during the ensuing years has been hell. I have a lot of regrets about raising my children. It was, quite frankly, easier to love them when I was drinking. But when it came to the sober day-to-day reality of changing diapers and potty training and walking them to and from nursery school, I wasn't there. I went back over old photographs taken when the children were young. The only pictures I could find of our family together were campaign photographs, taken for Arne's literature. The rest had the children with the baby-sitter. I love my children more than anything, but I have often asked myself if that was enough. Would I have laid down my life for them? I don't know. I think my own sense of survival and my own needs transcended their care. These are the betrayals and shortcomings that I have tried to make up for during their adult lives, but coming face to face with those regrets at the time . . . Jesus, was I lost.

That fall Arne won his election to state auditor. He was elected on a platform that called for increased protection of whistle-blowers, informants who came to his office with discoveries of government waste and fraud. He also vowed to make the auditor's office a resource center to help local government handle new programs, committing himself more deeply to the GOP's liberal wing. Tracking him through that risky election, I felt the same pride and love I had for him when I first saw him speak at a rally during our courting days. And even in my morass of confusion and guilt about ending our marriage and its effect on our children, my leftover feelings for him were beginning to hurt less. Maybe I would live through this divorce, after all.

Home Alone

While I was sitting on my duff trying to decide what the hell to do with my life, Charlie Leck came to my rescue. He offered to pay my rent for a while. Charlie had lived with me off and on when we were single. He was there the night my divorce became final. We were platonic friends, but women loved him. I introduced him to his current wife—one of my more successful shots at matchmaking. She had a lot of family money, and Charlie became something of a gentleman farmer. Fortunately for me, he was happy to spread the wealth.

I moved to East 18th Street, not the best neighborhood, but the apartment I had was adorable. It was a third-floor walk-up with a gorgeous view, two little bedrooms, exposed brick, a fireplace, and enough space to hold my beautiful mahogany dining room table with eight chairs, as well as my grand piano. I hired a carpenter to build floor-to-ceiling bookcases. Over the next couple of years, I filled them with my expanding library. I read a novel a day. Friends took me out to dinner. Basically, I had no expenses.

Unfortunately, there was also no maid, no husband, and no children to pick up after me. Tab cans filled the car. Cigarettes burned in a dozen ashtrays at once. The bed was covered with clothes, about four outfits deep, which I slept on and dry-cleaned when I found I had nothing to wear. I suppose I went a little mad, though the severe depression I suffered when the kids left slowly let up. I had stumbled into some kind of weird bliss here at home alone.

I didn't mind not working. Sitting at home all day reading wasn't boring. Boring was writing up purchase agreements, boring was seducing clients into buying houses they couldn't afford. But what else was I qualified for? Every morning I stood in the shower, praying, "God, what do you want me to do?" as though a bolt of lightning were going to come down and say, "*This*, my dearest Barbara, is what I want you to do."

That never happened. Every New Year's Day my friend

Kay Johnson, one of the trio who had driven me into treatment, threw a party at her place and invited a friend, the psychic veterinarian. I don't know how she was with animals, but she was a very good psychic.

"What is new in my life?" I asked her each year.

And each year, three years in a row, she answered, "There is no new man, there is no new job, and there is no new money."

Oh God. *What* do you want me to do?

21

Cocks

The psychic was wrong about one thing. There were plenty of men. I hadn't seen Lou in a couple of years, and I knew that I couldn't be with him as long as he was drinking. That could ruin me. But Chuck Mark was always around, and I hopped in the feathers with several others in the five years between Arne and my second husband, Pete. I did not bed all of the men I dated, but I did go out nearly every night. And why not? I was thin, and the last thing I needed was a deep commitment. I had tried that in the only way I knew how—and failed miserably. I still wanted it. I still wanted to be married in sobriety. But I had to dig deep inside and figure out a way to maintain a commitment and be happy, too.

My mother was always eager to meet the men in my life, and not because she was crazy about me. She liked to flirt with them. When I visited her apartment with a date, she would get all dressed up to be as sexy and cute as possible and sit there as coy as she could be. Once she even came to the door in her peignoir. Jane never wore a bra. Without any cosmetic surgery, she still maintained amazingly perky breasts.

Henry Stevens (not his real name) was one of my favorite interim lovers. He was always up for the symphony or balls, and he loved TV. Sometimes he had three shows going at once, and he could follow all of them. He was smart, thoughtful, and sweet. When we weren't together, he would call me to wake me at 6:30 A.M. because I hated to sleep late. In fact, he called several women early each morning—wakeup calls for women all over Minneapolis.

He was also my first toupee wearer. I liked his looks, but I would have preferred him without the brown roadkill sitting on his head. My God, it felt like a badger.

"Take it off," I pleaded the first time we tried to make love.

He refused.

Then I started laughing. I couldn't follow through. Something about that toupee was so funny. "I cannot make love to someone who's wearing a rug," I complained. "Take it off!"

He always promised me that he would take it off some day, but I think he was very self-conscious about the top of his bald head. His noggin was evidently scarred pretty badly because he had tried hair transplants and all sorts of things. I tried to be understanding, but every time we got in the sack, I had to giggle. Sometimes we got past it, sometimes we didn't and just watched the three TV's.

But there was one hurdle the affair simply could not clear: geography. Driving home eastbound from his house at 5:00 or 5:30 in the morning, I had to face the rising sun, which practically burned my eyes out and gave me a headache for the rest of the day. I complained a lot, he got tired of hearing it, and he eventually stopped inviting me over.

I was fond of all the men I went out with, but my only real crush was reserved for dear old Harold, a short, dark, and handsome rancher. He was into fruit and cows, and he was probably the best-looking of all the men I've known. We had been introduced by a mutual friend, but it was not a match made in Heaven. Harold was a little straight and told people behind my back that he didn't think putting up with me was good for his heart condition (even in my sobriety, I could be quite an adventure). The fact that he didn't absolutely adore me, of course, made him that much more appealing. I was dying to see his ranch, mostly because he wouldn't take me there.

"Why won't you show it to me?" I asked.

"You know nothing about cattle ranching," said the condescending sonofabitch. "You're not interested, and that is my private retreat."

He kept saying no. So one weekend when I hadn't heard from him, I decided to drive up to the ranch and surprise him. I couldn't think of an appropriate gift at first; then I remembered that Colleen Walter has the most beautiful, multicolored rooster. She raised chickens in her backyard in a fancy section of Minnetonka. All Colleen's neighbors had Afghan hounds and toy poodles and probably didn't approve of the chickens, but Colleen is very much her own woman. Anyway, the Walters had no use for this rooster since it had only one leg, but I thought Harold might appreciate it. Surely this would win him over.

On a Sunday morning, Colleen happily handed the rooster over to me. I plopped the little hummer in a box and took off for Brooton, Minnesota, in my big Ford sedan. The ranch looked healthy and rustic. I just loved it. However, as I pulled into the driveway, there seemed to be no one home. Suddenly a car drove up, and out popped Harold. There was *another woman* in the front seat. I was horrified and aghast. There I stood with egg on my face and a squawking, squirming, one-legged rooster in my arms. All I could think to say to Harold was, "All my lovers have been Jewish, and I don't want to give you up."

Then I started sobbing. I tried to be nice and polite to Harold and his girlfriend, recalling that my mother taught me never to throw a scene in front of another woman. "I happened to be driving up this way," I tried to explain with

179

tears rolling down my cheeks, "and I thought you might like this rooster." God, I was pathetic. He told me that he really didn't need a rooster, but that he appreciated the gesture. After a minute or two of very awkward conversation, I took my one-legged rooster and drove away, weeping all the way back home. That was the end of Harold, and I don't know what in hell ever happened to that rooster.

New Year

New Year's Day, 1981. I sat down with the psychic veterinarian, expecting the same prediction again: "There is no man, there is no new job, and there is no new money." But this time she studied the cards a bit longer than she had in years past. Then she looked up at me.

"Something is going to happen in February," she said. She was as surprised as I was. She thought for a moment longer and spoke up again. "And something really wonderful is going to happen in November. There's going to be a total lifestyle change in November."

In February I read that Parker Trostel, the alderman of the seventh ward, in which I live, had decided not to seek reelection. The idea that this would change my life popped into my head. The first person I called was my ex-husband.

"Arne," I said, "this seat is available, and I'm not happy sitting here doing nothing. Do you think I should run for seventh-ward alderman?"

I knew that politics was Arne's life, his vocation, and avocation. If anyone would know whether I could handle the job, he would. Plus, I had no desire to put any crimp or difficulty into his professional life. But I wondered, even as

I dialed the phone, if I was regressing by seeking the advice of a man whom I had allowed to exercise such control over my feelings during our marriage. No. I respected his opinion—something that I could never have admitted in all our years together. He offered me his support and assistance.

"I think you'd be dynamite," he said. "I think you should go ahead and do it."

I began to contact the delegates from the seventh ward and received good feedback from them, but I still had my doubts. On a long sheet of paper, I listed all of my positive and negative factors that would come into play during an election.

The positives: I had been involved in politics for a number of years. I had been active on the city and state levels. I was just as bright as the people I knew on the council. I had a knack for public speaking. I had sold real estate all over the seventh ward, so I knew a lot of people.

The negatives: I was divorced. I was not a college graduate. And I had only recently moved back to the seventh ward.

The positives list was longer that the negatives, so I decided to go for it. We had a rip-roaring convention, and I ended up on top of the three candidates seeking the Independent Republican nomination. Arne was there and worked the delegates hard, and I became the endorsed candidate.

Now for a brief lesson in Minnesota politics. There's the Democratic Farmer-Labor (DFL) party and the Independent Republican (IR) party. The DFL was formed back in 1944 when the far-left Farmer-Labor and the more moderate Democratic parties merged. By 1946, the radical Communist faction had been weeded out of the party by a young politico named Hubert Humphrey. A year later, a student from St. Paul's Macalester College helped organize an anti-Communist takeover within the DFL's youth faction. His name was Walter Mondale.

Minnesota Republicans became the Independent Republican party in 1975 in an effort to shake off the stigma of the Watergate scandal by tweaking their name. I had joined the Republican party when I was young because of my ties to Arne. I stayed with it because it's always been fairly progressive.

I held some views that others would consider very conservative. I still believe, for example, that prayer in public schools is a good thing. If it has to be instigated by calling it a "moment of silence," I say fine. It's good for kids to spend a little time looking at their souls, at their hearts, to take a good look at what they plan to do with their day and try to contemplate the world outside their personal needs. And I'm very conservative fiscally. I hated the way the liberal DFL members of the Minneapolis city council tossed around municipal funds. I decided that if elected, my role would be to prevent spending.

Still, I'm more liberal than many Republicans on social issues. For example I'm very vocally pro-choice, although I would never be able to have an abortion myself. But the party was changing when I entered politics as an alderman, and my professional honeymoon with it would be short-lived.

22

Who's Afraid of Barbara Carlson?

I had some fabulous ideas for the campaign, but there was one problem: money. So in March, just before I won the IR endorsement, I decided to try selling a house. I still had my touch: I sold the house and pocketed a $15,000 commission. I found a dynamite campaign committee which included attorneys, bankers, and conservatives. It also included Fred Krohn, a Minneapolis political brain who had worked for Arne in the past. Also on the committee were Fred's lover at the time, Tom Hoch, a recent law school graduate, and my friend Kay Johnson, who had helped get me into recovery. We managed to tap into wide-ranging voter blocs, from Junior Leaguers to the gay community.

We had a wonderful time and littered the seventh ward with lawn signs in the colors of Tab cans—shocking pink, yellow, and white—with the words "Who's Barbara Carlson?" I had wanted to print "Who's afraid of Barbara Carlson?" but they wouldn't let me.

Midway through the campaign, we switched to signs bearing the words "This Is Barbara Carlson," with all of my positive traits listed underneath. In November, in accordance with the psychic's timetable, I won the election.

Arne wasn't faring as well. His second marriage was unraveling. While the relationship between Joanne and the kids had always been strained, Anne was brokenhearted about losing another mother. Joanne had been a far more attentive mother than I had ever been, and Anne, who was experiencing all the turmoil of adolescence, had come to appreciate and like her. About six months after I had won the election, Anne learned that Arne and Joanne were ending their marriage. She called me, and I drove out to pick her up and take her for a drive. I tried to comfort her as best I could, but I knew what she was thinking. "Anne," I said, "you have to know two things: One, everything is going to be okay, and two, this does not mean that your father and I are getting back together."

Meanwhile, my relationship with Chuck Mark was reaching its end. I had always known that Chuck and I were not for the ages. For one thing, all we did was talk, talk, talk about the relationship. Talking, sleeping, playing bridge— that was our life together. He was in love, he was out of love, I was in love, I was out of love. We spent so much time on self-examination. I've never thought the whys of life mattered so much, it's the life itself that counts, and I've always been in favor of just getting on with it. Chuck didn't see it that way.

When the city council election began to take up all my time, he found another woman to take up his. Of course, when I found out that I was losing him to someone else, Chuck became the love of my life for a few intense months. Like a madwoman, I professed my undying love for him, begged him to come back and ask me to marry him. I even offered to convert to Judaism.

Thank God Chuck was more sane than I was. He knew I didn't mean it. Deep down, actually not that deep down, *I* knew I didn't mean it. I just didn't want to lose anything. We had to go our separate ways, and I don't think that the realization was actually very painful for either of us. We had played a lot of bridge. We had had a lot of sex. We had had a great deal of fun. I missed him, and as I entered the city council, I was beginning to come to grips with the fact that I might spend the rest of my life alone.

In January of 1982, I became an alderman, representing the seventh of thirteen wards in Minneapolis. For the next eight years I would earn a salary that ranged from $30,000 to $50,000 protecting the interests of the poor in Elliot Park, which had one of the lowest average household incomes in Minneapolis, and the wealthy in a neighborhood called Kenwood, where the railroad barons built their mansions in the early 1900s. Kenwood rests near bucolic Lake of the Isles and is flanked by two tourist attractions: the Walker Art Center and the Victorian mansion featured in *The Mary Tyler Moore Show*.

Kenwood was rich in both civic and personal history. For a short while in the 1940s, Sinclair Lewis resided on a tree-lined Kenwood lane named Mount Curve, and Robert Penn Warren lived there in the 1950s. On Lake of the Isles, my paternal great-grandfather, Henry Simons, had built one of the more notable mansions in the 1920s.

My first battle on the council was to play peacekeeper among a bunch of Kenwood busybodies who were pissed that another Kenwood homeowner was converting his old mansion's carriage house into rental property. As far back as 1948, an association had been formed to fight high-rise development in the area and keep the population in the area from booming. I told them that they had to work it out, especially since the carriage house had been stalled in mid-construction and was getting to be an eyesore. The neighbors were troubled because they thought the owner had been housing tenants in his main house in the past. So I made him promise not to do that, and everybody seemed to settle down. The carriage house was completed in a month or two and looked beautiful.

I would fight a lot of battles on behalf of the Kenwood rich. They were not to my mind the most sympathetic constituents, but they were taking a bath on property taxes. I remember a widow whose disproportionate taxes were about to cost her the home where she had raised a family and outlived a husband. I was one of five IR members on the council, versus eight DFLers, so we conservatives stuck together. I helped fellow IR Sally Howard get the subsidies she needed to develop a shopping center in an area where our two wards overlapped. But for the first few months I sat quietly and listened and learned.

Bubbles

I briefly took a lover in January of 1983, a man named Ken who was recently separated from his wife and lived in my district. It was, I admit, an affair of convenience. He was perfectly sweet, but the real drawing card was his bathtub. I love taking baths—*love* taking baths—but I didn't have a tub at home. Ken had a great tub, and sometimes I stole away to his house in the afternoon to fill it with bubbles and relax for a while, even if Ken wasn't there to share it with me.

One afternoon, as I sat soaking alone in the house, I heard his adolescent son come home from school with some of his friends.

Shit, I thought, now what? I sat there, praying no one would barge into the bathroom and hoping that they would go play somewhere else. They didn't leave. I could hear them in the kitchen, watching TV and laughing. The poor kid—

he was thirteen, which is hell enough, plus his parents were getting divorced, and now he was about to find a strange naked woman in the bathroom.

The floor plan of the house prevented me from leaving unnoticed, so I finally stepped out of the tub, got dressed, walked down the hall, and introduced myself. "Hi, I'm Barbara Carlson," I said. The kid stared at me blankly. I couldn't think of anything else to say, except "I'm your seventh-ward alderman." I shook his hand like a typical politician and left.

I was sitting in my office at City Hall one day in January when my old friend Wyman Spano called and said, "Barbara, I have a man who I want you to have dinner with. His name is Pete Anderson." Wyman was also a lobbyist of great credibility and a Democrat who had supported me. I trusted him.

"How much money does he have and how old is he?" I asked, joking. Sort of.

"I'm not talking marriage, Barbara, you impossible bitch," said Wyman. "I'm talking dinner. He's a constituent of yours, he's a client of mine, he's interested in energy conservation, and *you* should be interested in conservation."

I procrastinated for a while, but Wyman kept pushing. Then I thought, what the hell? This thing with Ken wasn't going anywhere, despite my fondness for his bathtub. "All right," I told him, "but I won't go out with him alone. You have to come with us." We met for dinner at a low-key Italian restaurant called Pronto's.

Pete was a businessman sixteen years my senior. He had been wildly successful in the insurance business and was now in the process of manufacturing and marketing a gadget with which homeowners could monitor their energy consumption and save on their bills.

He was tall, cute, funny, and charming. But he was too old for me. Too many wrinkles, I thought. Pete drove me home that night, and I decided to pass him along to Alice Rainville, who was president of the city council and a little closer to his age. Pete was single, straight, and relatively sane. I thought I was doing Alice a real favor. The next day I told her about him, and she agreed. "Fabulous!" she said.

Well, Alice never had a chance.

Later that afternoon, I got a call from Pete. I had left my perfume in his car, a little bottle of L'Air du Temps. I told him that I would come pick it up, so he gave me his address. It turned out that he lived in a certain converted carriage house that I was already very familiar with. I was dying to see what he had done to it on the inside.

I drove over to his house in the snow wearing a black sweater, pants, and green rubber boots.

Workers were still finishing up the interior as Pete gave me a tour of the place. The house was bare except for a dining room table (I assume there was a bed, but I didn't get to the bedroom). We ended up sitting at the table over coffee and talking for hours. He was divorced, like myself; a child of an alcoholic, like myself; and a recovering alcoholic, like myself. I took a long, close look at his face, and somehow the wrinkles disappeared. He was both dashing and shy, handsome and cute—Droopy the dog and Cary Grant rolled into one.

That night I went to a bridge party, and throughout the game my thoughts kept returning to old Pete.

A couple of days later I called and invited him to a party in St. Paul. On the appointed evening the following week he fetched me, and I was fetching myself in my natty little paisley cocktail dress (I was maintaining my weight at 130 to 135 and had a small waist, so I could get away with paisley). My friends seemed to enjoy him, and I soon discovered that Pete was a toucher. Some people hate that, but I love touchers. After the party we went to dinner, where there was more touching. I was infatuated with him, but I still wasn't sure how he felt about me.

On our way home from the restaurant, I delivered what may be my very best line ever uttered in my long and arduous romantic history. May every woman who reads this memorize it and use it well.

"I have something to confess," I told him as we sped along the freeway toward the lights of downtown Minneapolis. "I'm in my celibate period."

"Your *what?*" he asked.

"I really want to know if I can have a deep, meaningful relationship without sex," I said. "I know how men are, Pete. I know what you're probably thinking about right now, and I was wondering if you would be willing to just hold me?"

"Sure, honey," he said. "Would you like to come to my house for coffee?"

"Well, I guess," I said. Yippy skippy, I thought.

My celibate period didn't last through the night. There was much kissing and holding and cuddling—foreplay and lots of it. We made wonderful love, and when I walked into his bathroom before going to sleep, I was elated.

I'd never seen such a beautiful tub.

23

Hair

Within two or three days, enjoying unlimited access to that wonderful tub, I had all but moved in among the rubble of Pete's under-construction carriage house.

Pete Anderson was born in 1922 in Minneapolis and never knew his father very well. Pete's dad spent his money on booze, disappearing on binges for days and weeks at a time, leaving Pete's mother to care for him and his sister on welfare. As Pete grew up, his life took on the same shape as that of many men born to the World War II generation. In 1942, twenty years old and ready to escape his unhappy upbringing, he was drafted and shipped off to Texas Air Force bases in Big Spring and Odessa, where he waited out his duty. The dropping of atomic bombs in Japan ended the war before he had a chance to go overseas.

Back in Minneapolis, Pete attended school on the G.I. Bill and married a beautiful, statuesque Scandinavian blond named Dorothy, with whom he had two sons. They moved to Edina, an affluent suburb, where Pete made a killing in the insurance business and slowly began killing himself with alcohol. By the time I met him, Pete was picking up the pieces of a broken life. His marriage to Dorothy had ended in 1971, and he then began a rocky relationship with a woman named Marilyn, whom he had known all the way back in kindergarten. After Dorothy died of cancer, Pete became estranged from his adult sons. He hit rock bottom and, while he was living in an apartment near downtown Minneapolis, he got piss-drunk one day and decided to end it all. He went to the roof, a dozen or so stories high, took a flying leap, landed on a ledge three feet below, and passed out. I'm certainly glad he didn't do himself in, because I'm very fond of him.

Finally he got sober with the help of Alcoholics Anonymous, and began lecturing at A.A. groups. He even volunteered to organize A.A. groups for a prison. He ended the relationship with Marilyn and planned to set up the carriage house as a swinging bachelor pad just before he met me.

We had a lot in common, and he shared with me his distress over his frayed relationship with his kids. One Sunday night soon after we met, I insisted on inviting his sons, Scott and Kent, over for dinner at his house. Kent and his wife, Jerri, had a new baby, Cici, but since there was no furniture, we didn't know where to put her. We found some dry cabinet space underneath the sink and made a little bed there. Jerri and Kent, children of the sixties, showed me their wedding pictures. He had a big handlebar mustache in the pictures and long hair, and Jerri wore a big floppy Janis Joplin hat with her wedding dress. I laughed at that and endlessly grilled Pete's other son, Scott, about why he had never married. Pete and the kids talked and laughed. I could feel their healing begin.

Others weren't so happy for us—namely my campaign committee. They were getting nervous about my car being parked outside Pete's carriage house every night.

"My God, this is sophisticated Kenwood," I said. "No one can be upset about a woman cohabitating with a man."

They disagreed. They were frantic. So, one evening I set

about proposing to this wonderful, dear man, who, by the way, seemed to adore me. Since I had never proposed before, I took my time complimenting him on his good looks, the dearness of his spirit, and the wonderful delight I had in sharing time and space with someone who was also in recovery. Finally after about two hours, I informed him that I had something serious on my mind. Not being able to get straight to the point, I elaborated on the concerns of my campaign committee. He got a funny, bright look in his eye. He knew what I had on my mind. I popped the question.

"Will you marry me, Pete?"

He smiled and said that this was not something that he had anticipated doing quite this early in a relationship, but yes, he would.

We set the date for June 2, 1983, a few weeks before my forty-fifth birthday. His best man was a gay barber, who for years had suffered such unrequited love for Pete that he couldn't bear to touch Pete's hair. But he was over that by now. We were married in a beautiful setting in Charlie and Ann Leck's garden, which rolled down to a lake. Ann and Charlie worked for weeks getting ready for the event, commissioning topiaries made of flowers. Charlie hired a trumpeter to hail the beginning of the ceremony. Charlie gave me away and spoke before the service, mentioning that he was doing this in place of my father, Harry Duffy.

"I didn't know Barbara's father," he told the congregation. "I'm sure I would've liked him."

My two children and Pete's two sons were all in the wedding. I wore a gray chiffon dress with flowers in my hair. We honeymooned at Miniki Lodge in Canada, where I had vacationed as a child with my parents and Daddy Doc.

Dupont and Fart Blossom

Pete informed me early in our relationship that he was nearly impotent. This problem had been with him for many, many years, and he didn't know if it was a psychological or physical ailment. I didn't really mind the absence of sex with him. I was happy sitting with him, and talking and cuddling in his big porcelain tub. But before we were married he did undergo a penile implant, which would enable him to produce an erection with a small manual pump in his scrotum. The operation left his balls swollen to the size of a horse's. They were huge, purple, and ugly. More than being horny, I was fascinated by the little device, so of course I wanted to play with it right away.

"You've got to wait six weeks, Barbara," he said patiently.

So, I waited for the swelling to go down, and he said I could try it as soon as he was out of pain. Up I pumped it, and it worked beautifully. Then I squeezed the apparatus to make it go back down. Nothing. I tried it again. Again, nothing. So here was Pete, stuck with this erection. He couldn't leave the house. I called a friend from A.A., Gay Parker, because I thought she might have some advice.

"Well, you probably weren't supposed to pump it up this early," she told me. "What does the doctor say?"

"We can't call the doctor," I said, "because we're not supposed to be playing with it yet."

This is when I nicknamed Pete's penis "Dupont," after a one-way street in Minneapolis. Finally he did get to the doctor, who took care of the situation. Today it works fine, I'm happy to report.

As I write this, Pete and I have just celebrated our thirteenth anniversary. It's so hard to imagine that we have been married now longer than Arne and I were. Considering some

193

of the difficulties on our road from then to now, it's difficult to understand how marriage to Pete Anderson turned out so beautifully. When I look at my marriage to Pete, I look at tranquillity, laughter, and gentleness. My first marriage was trauma, angry crying, and a general gnashing of teeth. I did not feel counted, did not feel loved, and I filled those voids with liquor and unbearable longing. *Peaceful*—that is how, by and large, I can describe my marriage to Pete Anderson. I hope I bring him some peace of mind, as well. I don't think I do, but maybe, sometimes.

He suffers gladly my messy, messy ways and loves my cooking, even though I leave the kitchen in shambles. He follows behind me, shutting cabinet doors and wiping up flour. So many men have wanted to change me, and there have been so many men I have wanted to change. Pete and I accept each other rather than try to own each other. And, fortunately, he doesn't seem to mind that I fart indiscriminately. He thinks it's cute. "Fart Blossom" is his pet name for me. Now, that's love. That's caring.

Secrets

When he was very young, Tucker was informed that he had been adopted, but he never seemed to have any curiosity about who his biological parents were, so the subject didn't come up very much. In the years since the adoption, my mother had been told where Tucker came from, but my brother Bruce still thought that Tucker was his nephew. Still, he and Tucker had always had a special connection. They looked alike, for one thing. Tucker had the dark hair of his biological mother, but his clear, expressive blue eyes came directly from Bruce.

When he was a kid, Tucker hated how the other kids called him "Tucker the fucker" in the schoolyard. He briefly considered renaming himself Bruce, after his favorite uncle, and I considered telling him that Bruce was his biological father. Arne and I thought it was important that Tucker be told that he actually had Duffy blood in him, but we decided that we would tell Tucker about his origins when he turned sixteen, when he could better understand the hows and whys of the situation.

I had an elaborate ceremony planned. The entire family would be there. A therapist would be present to talk Tucker through his inevitable shock. There would be tears and music and, finally, love and laughter. Well, that's not how it happened. Just before Tucker's sixteenth birthday, Tucker went out to dinner with Arne. For reasons still mysterious to me, Arne decided to divulge the family secret without telling me first. Tucker came home and very nonchalantly told me how cool he thought it was that Bruce was his father.

Well, I went crazy. Tucker seemed fine with it, but my God, I thought that Bruce had no idea, and he had a wife and two children to whom he would have to explain this. I thought that Bruce would just go nuts. He had quite a temper. I called his house. His wife, Mary, answered and told me that he wasn't home.

"Well, Mary," I said, "you'd better sit down, because I have something to tell you."

I gave her the news, and she was surprisingly, impressively calm. Bruce had already told her that he had fathered a child that had been put up for adoption, and that it was quite likely that the child would surface some day. Mary told me that she would tell Bruce, and that they would tell their children, Sean and Shannon. As it turned out, Bruce wasn't all that surprised when Mary gave him the news. In fact, Bruce had suspected as much over the years. He liked Tucker, but also accepted that Arne and I were his parents now. His feelings for Tucker wouldn't change, and neither would Tucker's for Bruce.

I still thought that a family meeting was in order. Even though Tucker didn't seem upset by the news, I knew that he would look back on this as a pivotal moment in his life. He had just found out that his uncle was his father. This is not the kind of thing one simply takes in stride. So, we all gathered at the carriage house—Bruce, Mary, Tucker, Pete, and I. I took the floor and made my carefully rehearsed and dramatic speech.

"Tucker," I said, "I want you to know that you have always been loved by this family. Part of this family is not here, and that's your grandfather, Harry. Harry said many, many years ago that we always must take care of our own, and you are our own. I know your father has told you who your biological father is, but I want you to know the whole story."

We did not tell Tucker anything about his mother other than her first name. I wanted to protect Amy's privacy, but I told Tucker that if someday he decided that he wanted to contact her, I would help him do so. During our meeting I told him about Amy's mother calling to tell me that Amy was pregnant with Bruce's baby. I described for him how scared Amy was the day I met her, how I cared for her during the pregnancy, and about the night he was born, when Arne and I drove to the hospital to pick him up. I talked about his biological grandmother singing to him as she held him in the backseat and then handing him over to me, knowing that she would never have a chance to get to know this grandchild of hers.

Tucker sat and listened, neither upset nor terribly touched.

196

But I could see something in his eyes—happiness. He was happy. I couldn't figure out why. When I was done with my story, I asked him if he had any questions, if there was anything he wanted to talk about. He said no. Then he announced, "I'm going to go see Nana."

That was it. Tucker loved Jane so much, he was elated to find out that she was his biological grandmother. Anne had always teased her brother about being adopted and teased him about not belonging in the family. It never seemed to bother him, but it must have, at least a little bit. Now he knew that he belonged to Jane every bit as much as Anne did. Tucker left the house and boarded his motor scooter and rode to his grandmother's apartment. Once again, Jane was his anchor, his constant. I don't think I've ever felt more grateful toward my mother than at that moment. I realized that night just how much she meant to my children. Tucker needed her. And she would be there when he knocked on her door.

24

Born Again

My Kenwood constituents proved to be a high-maintenance lot. During my engagement, a group of residents sought a permanent injunction against the building of a 5,000-square-foot recreational center that would be connected to a high school gym in my ward. The construction of the project and its attendant parking lot would mean the uprooting of a clump of trees and the rerouting of Franklin Avenue. One of the plaintiffs in the lawsuit complained to a newspaper reporter that the project would "impair very seriously the aesthetics of the house I live in."

It was always a difficult line to walk, between developers, who could bring money into the seventh ward, and the residents, who deserved to have their environment protected, especially considering their outrageous property taxes. For some, those taxes pushed the $35,000-a-year mark. But I supported the recreational center, partly because the neighborhood didn't have anything like it. Finally, the park board got its way, but agreed to cut down nine trees instead of eleven.

During the 1984 election year, the IR Senate District 59 convention took place in April. There, delegates to the state national Republican convention would be nominated. A few weeks before it took place, I received a phone call at home.

"Are you a born-again Christian?" the caller asked. I had seen this coming ever since Reagan took office in 1980. These

Republican assholes were calling people—people who had been loyal to the party for years—trying to determine if they were fit delegates for the Republican party. They were basing that determination solely on religious beliefs. This infuriated me.

"Madam," I said, "I was never *un*born." Then I taught her a few words she probably wasn't familiar with and hung up.

During the convention, many old-guard party members like Parker Trostel, who had held my council seat before I was elected, and Sally Howard, a terrific, reasonable Republican voice on the council with me, were defeated by the far right-wingers who billed themselves as "pro-family." These delegates would go on to the state and national conventions with one thing on their minds: abortion.

"How can I carry the banner for a party that does not treat all human beings with respect?" I asked Pete.

He didn't have an easy answer right away, and neither did I. I had been part of the Republican party for years. I felt loyal to it and betrayed by it all at the same time. I couldn't sleep. Then Pete made it easy: "You have to do what is right," he said.

The next day I announced that I was leaving the party to become an independent. It made headlines, and I got to say my piece. As I made this announcement I discovered that I liked the media and the media liked me.

When I stepped up to my second term in January of 1984, DFL members outnumbered—and outvoted—us conservatives 10 to 3. Hindered by that imbalance, the media became a great place for our dissenting voices to be heard, rather than squelched as they often were amid the morass of politics and favor-mongering of City Hall.

I became the appointed spokesperson for the fiscally conservative IR leg of the council. When we feared we would be outvoted on a piece of legislation, I took our grievances to the public and tried to persuade constituents to push their DFL representatives over to our side. By 1985, I had become a local personality, famous for my omnipresent string of pearls and flannel Lanz nightgowns printed with flowers and teddy bears and such, in which I greeted guests at home.

I made good copy, and my adorable little Llaso Apso, Humphrey, was always up for a photo op. He became known as Humphrey of Kenwood. The local newspaper called me "a woman who courts the media, who has an openness that puts people at ease, who often decides issues on gut feelings rather than research, and who works hard bringing people together for compromise on issues." Some of this was good, some was bad, but all of it was true.

Seagulls and Waves

I think I was a good member of the city council. I was not great at handling the pressure, and, whereas in the past I would have picked up a Valium or glass of scotch, I now began picking up anything edible. In the three years since Pete had accepted my marriage proposal, I had regained 40 pounds that I lost after getting sober. This did not please either of us. I was also smoking three packs of cigarettes a day. There were burn marks everywhere, in my clothes, my furniture, and my office. My beleaguered staff burned out too because of my disorganization and general grumpiness and found it impossible to keep me happy.

Apparently my behavior was becoming even more erratic than I realized. A few friends, including Fred Krohn and Tom Hoch, the two men who had worked on my campaign, decided to organize a *behavioral* intervention. As I said before, Minneapolitans love interventions. One day my friend Kay Johnson invited me over to her place, where I was greeted by about twenty friends. They told me in concerned voices that I was becoming too frantic. They worried that I was going to drop dead of a heart attack or at least alienate all my friends who were becoming exhausted by my behavior. But I would have none of it. I had been through treatment, and I was not Liz Taylor. Or so I thought at the time.

My friend Mary Lufkin was concerned about my weight and thought that a weekend at a nice, peaceful fat farm would do me some good. I had met Mary years before through Frank and Suzie Brixius. Frank wanted to introduce Mary to me, just to see for himself who talked the most. Somebody put a tape recorder in front of us, and off we went. It was a draw, and Mary and I have been talking to each other ever since.

I don't know how Mary ever got heavy, because although I adore her, she's a terrible cook. I don't know how she eats it. Anyway, I agreed to go to the fat farm with her, and we drove to one out west of St. Paul. They made me hike. I hated it. But I stayed the weekend, did my best to touch my toes, center myself, and thought the entire time about work.

As Mary was driving us back on Sunday afternoon, I started feeling chest pains.

"Mary," I said quite calmly. "Have you ever been with someone when they had a heart attack?"

"Yes," she answered.

"Well, I think I'm having a heart attack."

"We're going to a hospital," she said, putting the pedal to the floor and sounding a little panicky.

"No, we're not," I said. I sort of enjoyed the drama, even though I could no longer feel my left arm.

But she insisted, and on the way home we ended up in an emergency room in a small country hospital.

"My friend is having chest pains," Mary explained to the woman at the desk. "We've been exercising a lot, and I'm concerned."

"I'm okay, goddammit!" I grumped. I wasn't convincing. My face was beet red, and I was out of breath.

Mary called Pete. She told him where we were and that she was arranging for an ambulance to take me to Minneapolis. Meanwhile, I was off in a small private room where a nurse was hooking me up to monitors and sticking little plastic gadgets all over my chest and back.

Once all the monitors were on, of course I had to pee. "I have to go to the toilet," I said. "Get these things off me."

"We have a commode right here," said the doctor.

"What do you mean, a commode?"

She showed me a fancy bedpan on the floor.

"I'm not going to sit down on that thing."

"Yes, you will, or I'll get a catheter," he said. I could see that I did not amuse these people.

So with all these wires dangling from my person, I squatted neatly on the little commode, within eyeshot of Mary and the doctor and whoever else might walk in at any moment. I couldn't do it. I simply couldn't pee.

"Close your eyes and think of the beach," the doctor said. "Think of the waves washing in and the seagulls . . ."

"Are you drinking?" I asked. But it worked. After a few minutes of seagulls and waves, I was able to relieve myself.

The monitors didn't reveal anything terrible, but the doctor insisted that I board the ambulance and get more tests in Minneapolis. There I received an angiogram and was eventually diagnosed with pleurisy, an inflammation of the lining of the lungs.

The same chest pains flared up again a few months later in my office at city hall. I took another ride in an ambulance and woke up in the hospital feeling fine. Pete was beside me, and the phone was ringing.

It was someone from the morning show on WCCO, a local radio station. They thought it would be funny to patch me in for a conversation with Dr. Bob Vantassel, who was head of the coronary unit at the same hospital I was staying in. Dr. Vantassel had no idea who the hell I was and really didn't care, but since it was heart month in Minnesota, he said that he would tell me what to do. They briefed him, told him who I was, that I was in the hospital for an angiogram, and that I was a three-pack-a-day smoker. He wasn't terribly excited about being on the air.

"Lady, I don't know who you are," he said to me and the Twin Cities. "But I know that if you're a forty-seven-year-old smoker and in the hospital for an angiogram, that you're going to die soon. You must stop smoking. Good-bye."

So I stopped smoking. I quit cold turkey on a soothing, uplifting habit that had carried me through a difficult adolescence, a volatile twelve-year marriage, alcohol recovery, and the city council wars. Gone was my last crutch.

No, the *second* to last crutch. The only thing left was food, and I should have known it wasn't going to be pretty.

Cookies and Condoms

Besides eating more, I took up needlepoint—anything to keep my hands off cigarettes—and clicked away at it during council meetings when I wasn't popping jellybeans into my mouth. Two months after I quit smoking, a friend gave me a giant pacifier, which dangled from my neck on a string of fake pearls. I recommend a pacifier to anybody who wants to stop smoking. It helped a lot, and sucking on it at opportune moments during council meetings was a nice, quiet way to say "Fuck you" when the Democrats acted childishly. God, was I cranky. The *Star Tribune* duly reported the pacifier and my quitting smoking on what must have been a slow news day.

"My disposition is hideous and vile," I told the reporter. "I am mean, nasty, cynical, and abrasive." No one would argue.

The papers loved covering me. They'd never had a Minneapolis politician willing to talk about her affairs, her alcoholism, or her failed marriage. My attention-getting stunts didn't make my free-spending opponents on the council happy. I was adamantly opposed to the city giving tax dollars to support a state arts high school, which Lola Perpich, the wife of Governor Rudy Perpich, was supporting.

When it looked like the council was going to side with Lola, I surreptitiously placed a teeny tape recorder under my seat in the council meeting chamber, where we all sat at a long U-shaped table and debated issues. At each council member's seat was a small light, which he or she flicked on if they wished to take the floor. A few minutes into the debate, I punched "play" on the recorder and Gwen Verdon began belting out "Whatever Lola Wants, Lola Gets" from *Damn Yankees.*

Everybody went crazy. The orange lights went on boom, boom, boom, one after another. It looked like the Minneapolis city council was playing *Family Feud.* I loved it. The arts school did not get its money from the city of Minneapolis, so I felt I had made my point.

As I think of it, critters also played a big part in my political career. When a cock-eyed proposal to license small animals came up, I disrupted the vote by showing up with a bunny for everybody. Another time a friend called and asked if I would show public support for farmers in the Twin Cities area who were going through a terrible time because of foreclosures.

"Okey-dokey," I said. "What do you want me to do?"

"Well," she said, "we have this nice Holstein that we want you to walk down the street."

Within a few days I was parading down Marquette Avenue with a cow on a leash. My insatiable thirst for theatricality forced me to hang my pearls and pacifier around its neck. The damned cow wasn't terribly fond of me. As we made our way down Marquette, she stepped on me and shit on my high heel.

But my favorite stunt of all unfolded in December of 1986. I sent out invitations for a "coffee, cookies, croissants, and condoms press conference" at my house. I planned a small speech and set out trays of holiday goodies in my living room and kitchen, with little condom packages mixed in with the sweets. I made a speech encouraging more safe-sex education for our children and announced that my own children and unmarried friends were all getting rubbers for Christmas. You would've thought I'd shot the Pope.

No less than the archbishop of the Twin Cities came out fighting, calling my little party "a new low in bad judgment and bad taste." We duked it out on page 3B of the *Star Tribune*. "In Bethlehem, the angels sang," he proclaimed. "[Sunday] night in Minneapolis the angels had to cry."

I retorted that "[The archbishop] can deal with mangers in Bethlehem and the baby Jesus. Meanwhile, our country is dealing with real babies."

"I'm gong to have to continue to live in a world that knows pain and suffering," he said, "the barbarous taste of a condom gift-giver and a world which totters on the edge of self-destruction."

I took the high road. "I prayed for the archbishop this morning," I said. "And I will continue to do so."

But by April of 1988, the middle of my third term on the council (the first two terms ran two years, then the city switched to four-year terms in 1986), I was growing weary of the city council political battles, but far from ready to give up politics. We were coming up on an election year, so I started flirting with the idea of running for mayor.

My fiscal conservatism and social liberalism gave me a large, diverse constituency of homeowners, gays, and yuppie liberal Republicans. The incumbent, Don Fraser, wouldn't be easy to beat, but I also knew I would have one hell of a good time running a mayoral campaign. "It'd be just a hoot," one of my fellow council members predicted to a reporter when I first began considering the bid. "It'd be just wonderful as far as a show goes." This was not meant as a compliment.

A 1988 survey seeking voter's opinions about the possible mayoral candidates revealed that 84 percent of the respondents had heard of me, which indicated that I had excellent name recognition. But, according to the *Star Tribune,* I was criticized for being "loud and brassy, too stubborn, too outspoken, too candid on her personal life, using 'too many four-letter words' and for being 'a bit of a loose cannon.'" The novelty of Barbara Carlson was beginning to yellow with age, and this loose cannon was about to get looser.

25

Don't Worry, Be Happy

In the summer of 1988, Bush was in office, the United States of America seemed to be sitting still, and a singer named Bobby McFerrin was telling us, "Don't Worry, Be Happy." My favorite birthday gift that year was handed down on June 20 by the Supreme Court. It was something I could share with women across the country—a unanimous decision to uphold a 1984 New York City law that prohibited men-only "business-oriented private clubs" from excluding women from their memberships. But that was small consolation to someone turning fifty and weighing in at nearly 200 pounds. After suffering through one of those diet programs that required me to drink a shitty powdered drink every day, I had shed 75 pounds, only to gain most of it back immediately. Don't worry. Be happy. I wanted to strangle Bobby McFerrin.

Arne Carlson was among the 280 members of the Minneapolis elite who gathered in July to celebrate my fiftieth birthday with a charity roast for Project Self-Sufficiency, an organization that helps single mothers get off welfare. Police chief Tony Bouza said roasting me was "too easy . . . I much prefer a challenge." He had a point. The roasters took the podium with tales of my drinking, bad housekeeping, and the needlepoint and pacifier I took to council meetings. Even Arne, who was state auditor at the time and a likely candidate for governor, took the podium. Like I said, we had a friendly professional relationship by this point, so it seemed natural that he show up. His jabs were gentle, God bless him.

"Going to a Barbara Carlson party wasn't like going to a party and having a couple of cocktails and hors d'oeuvres and then going home," he said. "It was a *commitment.*"

I promised the mayor that night that I wouldn't run against him in 1989—"at this weight." We laughed a lot and raised $5,000 for Project Self-Sufficiency, but I didn't have a good time, really. Two council members showed up to speak, but the rest of my colleagues didn't come to the event, which hurt. I went home and salved my wounded heart with several hefty pieces of strawberry cheesecake.

Take Off Pounds Safely

I dream of crème brûlée. *Crème brûlée,* with its calories and cream, its eggs and butter and brown sugar and God knows what all.

I want jellybeans, jars and jars of the cheap kind that come in big bags, two-for-a-dollar, not Ronald Reagan's tiny gourmet kind. No. I want the big, fat jellybeans. I want to lick the outsides off and suck the insides dry. I want to be covered in whipped cream and lick it off myself. I want a bathtub overflowing with crème caramel. I want to soak in it for hours. I cannot imagine anything more wonderful than licking every glob off my fingers and toes. I want a man to cover his penis with chocolate mousse and let me go for hours.

And I want to be thin. Thin, the way Harry Duffy said I should be.

Do you know what it's like to be fat? Let me explain. It's not like alcoholism or drug addiction, which can be hidden from, and perhaps even forgiven by, the world. *Fat* is a very public failure. *Fat* is okay to laugh at. *Fat* means I can't see my own snatch, the very thing that makes me a woman. I occasionally look at it with a mirror, and it's like I'm looking at someone else's.

I tried it all—Optifast, Weight Watchers, something called TOPS (Take Off Pounds Safely), and self-help groups, which I betrayed by sucking down homemade caramels on the way to meetings. I played Richard Simmon's stupid little card game, Deal-a-Meal. I know that Richard has helped people, I've seen them late at night giving infomercial testimonials. But if I ever meet him, I'll choke the little bastard. Hopping around the way he does, I just hate him.

Actually, I hate Barbara Carlson. I hate her for being fat, for not being able to control it, for falling for the slick ads of a weight-loss industry that sells billions of dollars worth of hope instead of help. The bulk of the over-the-counter diet programs dish out at best temporary immediate gratification. At worst, they force the body to feed off its own tissue with their plans. And all for nothing. Most participants in these weight-loss programs gain the weight back immediately, like an alcoholic who gets stinking drunk after six weeks on the wagon. Regaining the weight leads to depression, anxiety, and frustration. Chronic fluctuations in weight may lead to heart failure. I hope to meet Kathleen Sullivan in a dark alley someday.

Why don't these diets work in the long run? Genetics? Mental illness? So many theories, but I know why Barbara Duffy Carlson Anderson got fat: I love food, and life is hard.

By the end of the summer of 1988, I topped the scales at 234 pounds, and I began to routinely pass out at night from overeating. I was bottoming out, and so was my marriage. I had been fitted for a wedding dress soon after Pete and I decided to get married in the spring of 1983. By the time I got to the altar, I had gone up two full dress sizes, from a 10 to a 14. I had done the same thing when I married Arne. I suppose I did it to make myself less desirable to punish him somehow. A therapist told me I was just like a black widow spider. "Come, come," I said to my men. "Come into my web of love and desire." And then, *Gulp!* I had them and ate myself to gluttony. The more they complained or voiced their concern, the more I ate, and the more they pulled away. Which was fine with me.

I don't think that my weight problems were connected to my alcoholism, which made them even more difficult to explain. I do know now that I was using weight to keep men at a distance. I told Pete that if he left me I would immediately go back to my fucking weight. I would make myself attractive to other men. Try to imagine how much that hurt him; I can't. Because I felt so unattractive, we had not made love in nearly five years. He told me to get help. I said no.

Finally my cruelty and defiance got the best of him.

"Shape up or ship out," he told me one night in July. "I can't stay here like this. I have to take care of me, too."

"Take a flying leap," I told him.

He went upstairs and started packing. I started crying. I would not fuck up another marriage. I would not kill myself with food. I asked him to forgive me and to help me. He held me and said he would.

Next stop: recovery. Back to the loony bin, back for repairs.

Bulimics Vomit

I had watched my friend Bill Kelly, the wonderful man who helped me through my recovery and divorce, relapse and ultimately drink himself to death after I married Pete. In the end, he looked like the victim of a concentration camp. His gums had receded, his eyes were sunken, and his stomach was terribly distended. He had been very fat—he'd probably weighed 350 pounds at one time—but he wasted away to nothing after he resumed drinking. I did not want my addictions to kill me the way Bill's had taken him.

We found a recovery center up in Oconomowoc, outside Milwaukee, called Rogers Memorial Institute. There they treated everything from eating disorders to sex addictions with a 12-step program, which I was already familiar with. I really wanted to sit in on the sex addicts' groups, and listen to them admit they were powerless over fucking.

I'm not making fun; sex addiction is far more glamorous than being powerless over cheap jellybeans.

I called and elbowed my way to the top of Rogers' two-month waiting list by convincing the woman on the phone that I was an emergency case. God, I was dreading it, but within a few days I was in a car pointed toward Wisconsin. On the way, I began screaming at Pete that I didn't want to go in, that I had changed my mind. He wouldn't hear of turning back, but he did allow me a stop at the Chocolate Factory in Oconomowoc. I ate a lovely turtle sundae made with four scoops of vanilla ice cream.

A few minutes later, I was checking in. Rogers Memorial Hospital is headquartered in a stately four-story red brick building that is surrounded by outbuildings shaded by more than seven acres of trees and rolling lawn. A bunch of doctors and psychiatrists sat with me and collected my life history on standardized forms. Right then they told me I was bulimic.

"Bulimics vomit!" I snapped at them. "I hardly *ever* vomit." Jesus, I thought, I know more about my illness than these jerks.

They explained to me that patients who binge then punish themselves with starvation diets are driven by the same impulses as those who binge then purge by running an index finger down their throat.

I wasn't so sure I liked it here. It wasn't air-conditioned, and this was August. It was no place for all the soft Lanz flannel nightgowns I had packed. I really started hating the place when they told me I would have to sign up for showers.

"I am *not* signing up for showers," I protested. A few of the other patients condescendingly offered to switch places with me. "I just won't *take one*," I said. In spite of all my protests and disappointment I was soon signed in. Pete left. I soaked my head in cold water and went to bed.

26

Strokes

I began group therapy the following day. I was resistant at first—just as I had been at St. Mary's thirteen years before. My head pounded from caffeine deprivation, and the hospital food was just god-awful.

"The food *sucks!*" I told my counselor, named Theresa. "You're making the food so boring, it won't ever be an issue again."

Within a few days, Theresa was so fed up with my intimidation techniques that she forced me to carry around a brown teddy bear. She thought that if I seemed less fearsome, the other patients in my group would be more likely to reach out to me.

It so happened that at the time I was fighting to get into Rogers, a reporter named Kay Miller from the *Star Tribune's Sunday Magazine* was doing a story on me. She had heard through friends of mine that I was struggling with my weight and emotional malfunction. I had heard that she was fair and sympathetic. However, I must not have fully engaged my powers of judgment when I invited her to visit me at Rogers.

Kay arrived on the appointed day and witnessed a group therapy session. She listened as I talked about my father, who, I told the group, had riddled me with Dexedrine so I could be the size he wanted and look good in the furs and jewelry he purchased. "Nothing was ever *quite good enough!*"

I cried. I buried my head in my hands and boo-hooed to beat the band. I had lots of people to blame for the predicament I was in, and I was just warming up.

During the second week at the hospital, I suggested that Pete join me for therapy.

"It's his fault I'm here," I told Theresa. I invited Kay to come along and record my session with Pete. He wasn't thrilled to have a reporter along. He had every right to complain; my life was also his life. But I was pissed at him, irrationally blaming him for my weight problems. I refused to take responsibility for them and used him as a scapegoat. Plus, I *liked* having reporters around. The insecure, needy part of me thinks they make a wonderful accessory signifying importance.

"She's not only coming to our therapy session, Pete, I've given her access to my counselors and psychiatric records," I told him.

"Fine," he said, resigned to save his energy for bigger battles. We embarked on a two-hour therapy session, moderated by my therapist and with Kay watching from the sidelines.

"What kind of strokes do you get for your ego from having reporters constantly tagging along?" Theresa asked me.

"I do get positive reinforcement for being open," I answered. The bullshit meter was threatening to malfunction from overload, and I knew it. So of course I didn't stop. I threw my teddy bear to the floor.

"I've been in so much *pain!*" I wailed. "That's all I can think about, how much pain I'm in!"

My rant left in its wake a moment of silence, which was rudely interrupted by the counselor, who said, "Give me a *break,* Barb. Have you ever considered being an actress?"

This gave Pete license to let me have what I deserved.

"It's a sad situation that you're so goddamned *fat,*" Pete told me. "But *that's* not the problem."

"That didn't sound like sadness to me," Theresa reprimanded. "That sounded like *madness.*"

Pete denied his anger, said that weight wasn't a big deal for him. Nobody believed that, not even Pete, and we told him so. Finally he relented.

"I don't like the fat," he said, sounding a little whipped. Then he reminded me of all the times I had said that I would lose the weight if he left me. God, it sounded horrible, having that repeated back to me. "The message I get is that I'm not worth losing the weight for, or else it's all my fault that you're fat."

Theresa tried to explain to me how I had replaced sadness and shame with rage. I had raged at my father, at Arne, at my colleagues on the city council, and at Pete. She said that I employed rage to humiliate people and push them away. She said I used my rage to generate hate or, at the very least, animosity in the people who loved me so they would be afraid to get too close to me. She explained that I used food to anesthetize the loneliness.

I was quiet for a while. I couldn't argue. I just sat and marveled at the depths of sadness and shame that would make me want to hurt people so badly.

"How are you feeling?" Theresa asked.

"Terrible," I said quietly. "I'm feeling fat and ashamed and mad."

Pete leaned over and kissed me. "We ought to be able to hang in there," he said. We were both crying. So was the reporter.

She Begged for Help

The trip to Rogers was successful in repairing my relationship with Pete, but there's no happy ending. There would
be no clarity, no blue sky, no green leaves, none of the spoils
I enjoyed after getting off alcohol. I would not conquer my
eating disorders at Rogers. I truly wish I could be enlight-
ening on this point, but I don't know why I couldn't overcome the weight thing. I still haven't. Some people say we
all have to have one vice, and maybe food has to be mine.
I certainly have clung stubbornly to it. I did lose 15 pounds
at Rogers, and as the August heat let up, I was able to wear
my Lanz nightgowns to therapy.

On October 2, the *Star Tribune's Sunday Magazine* appeared with my face resting on folded hands on the cover.
My glasses were positioned on top of my head and my baby
grand piano sat open in the background of my living room,
amid yards of the blurry floral chintz that draped my
windows.

"FIGHTING FAT WITH BARBARA CARLSON," blared
the headline. And under that: "Her increasing weight was
ruining her marriage and her life. She begged for help." I
would *need* help after everyone read the article. It was all
there. Our nonexistent sex life. My alcoholic father. Our
money worries. My tears. My headaches. My binging and
passing out. It was accompanied by an inside photo of me
smiling uncomfortably on my bed, sharing a big bowl of
popcorn with Humphrey.

Compassionate, well-written, but overall *not* good p.r. for
my political career. Soon enough, I would discover that Minneapolis had finally heard more about me than they ever
wanted to know, and my constituents would doubt whether
this crazy bitch who screamed, ranted, and binged, and with-

held sex from her long-suffering, penile-implanted husband, then *talked* about it to reporters, was really the person they wanted protecting their interests on the city council.

I remember on the Sunday it appeared I was playing touch football in a charity game at the University of Minnesota. I was out there rolling around with a bunch of former Minnesota Vikings and Dave Dahl, a gorgeous local weatherman from KSTP. I don't know why I was invited. One of the local anchors, Cindy Hilger, came up to me and congratulated me on the article, called it very moving. Others were embarrassed for me and didn't talk to me at all.

Soon after, a two-year-old lawsuit filed against the city—and naming me specifically—resurfaced. The plaintiff alleged that I had put his strip bar out of business as a result of a city renovation plan. He requested my psychiatric records, apparently hoping to prove that I was crazy and as a result acted irresponsibly toward him. I refused to hand over my records.

I was learning the importance of keeping my mouth shut. It was a little too late.

Details, Details

A couple of years ago, I visited a mortuary where the body of a young man named Brian Coyle rested.

I had been on the city council for six years with Brian, but I had not said good-bye to him when he was dying of AIDS. The mortuary was filled with little memories of his life, pictures of Brian and his friends and colleagues. There was even a picture of me. Standing alone over his open casket, I looked at his face, once so passionate and smiling and photogenic, now gaunt and lifeless in his coffin. I wondered if I would ever be able to grieve for him. I wondered if I even wanted to grieve for him.

Brian was a DFLer who had been the only openly gay city council member when I was on it, and we had butted heads numerous times over fiscal issues. We were particularly at odds as the only two council members who diligently courted the allegiance of the Minneapolis gay community. At a gay pride rally in Loring Park a few years earlier, I took the podium and said that the people in the audience should demand legal domestic partnerships. The crowd went wild, and Brian was livid. He had planned to make that his issue, and I had beaten him to the punch. Finally he was so fed up with me that he planned to do what he could to unseat me in the upcoming 1989 election. He was dispatching a search party to find a seventh-ward DFL candidate who could take me on.

So, during 1988 in the dead of winter, an article appeared in the *Twin Cities Reader*. It was both sourced and set up by Brian Coyle. Alongside this devastating attack ran an almost life-size, candid shot of my face, obviously taken during a shouting match at a press conference. I was wild-eyed in the photo, teeth bared as if I were a savage animal about to rip into the neck of my prey. If there was any doubt left in the public's mind that I was a certifiable raving lunatic, this would certainly help people make up their minds.

The story focused on my waning support among constituents and a blunder I had made when I allowed a twenty-one-story residential development to slip through a zoning ordinance loophole.

"I am *not* a detail person," I argued in print, thereby destroying any future I might have had as a defense attorney.

Brian Coyle was also quoted, accusing me of skipping meetings and blaming me for other zoning snafus. I must admit, I had given him ample ammunition with which to attack me. With my political career in shambles, thoughts of my mayoral bid seemed silly at this point, so I scrapped those plans and was now seriously wondering whether it was time to gracefully bow out of politics instead of running in the upcoming election and losing. I was tired of the front lines of city hall, sitting around with a dozen people who basically didn't like me very much, who called me ineffectual, and said I didn't know what I was talking about. They wanted to wear me down, and they did.

I knew that I had done my best. Should I have known about the zoning ordinances that would become such a rallying cry against me during the campaign? Yes, I should have known. Even the *Star Tribune* ran an editorial urging me to retire.

What would I do next? I still had very mixed feelings about the council. Despite the political brawls on the council, my position could still be so gratifying when it came to serving the people in my ward. Also, while Pete and I weren't totally dependent on my salary, we really didn't want to lose it.

So I stood rocking in indecision, the black dog of depression nipping at my ass. The depression took on a life of its own. I had problems, but they weren't bad enough to keep me from getting out of bed in the morning; yet there were times when I just couldn't rally to get up and get dressed. I asked my doctor if he could help, and he prescribed a miracle. It was called Prozac, that marvelous little nonaddictive antidepressant that was becoming so popular at that time.

The scientific community generally refers to Prozac by its generic name, fluoxetine. I call it "fan-fucking-tastic." It keeps serotonin, a neurotransmitter, from being too rapidly reabsorbed by cells, and somehow that gives you a lift. Fluoxetine has fewer side effects than other antidepressants—

which can cause constipation and weight gain and anxiety—though loss of sex drive can be a big problem with Prozac as well. Any interest in sex I had vanished, but if I never have another orgasm again, I wouldn't mind. Pete doesn't mind so much, either, as long as the Prozac helps control mood swings. It's not as if we had such a sterling sex life to begin with.

Prozac worked wonders and alleviated some of my anxiety; I stopped focusing on the future so much. In January of 1989 I was able to take the plunge. I formally announced that I would not seek a fourth term.

A sense of nostalgia descended on Minneapolis. The papers carried stories reminiscing about my cow on Marquette Avenue, my Lanz nightgown in council meetings, my pacifier and pearls. Tom Hoch, who had helped orchestrate my campaigns and public appearances over the years, was quoted in a local gay paper called *Equal Time* saying, "I think Barbara will be missed. As much as we need gay and lesbian leaders, we need straight people to stand up for us. Barbara is very open and very much 'I am what I am.' I don't know of any other politician who is as open and as creative. Everyone will miss her antics, which made us howl for weeks."

27

"Bizarre Behavior"

At the end of February I visited Colleen and Dick Walter at their home in Florida for two weeks. I petted the dogs, walked on the beach, basked in the sun, and just went nuts. I was so afraid of going back home and being a lame duck for the rest of my term and not having a job after the end of the year.

Before I left for Florida, Tom Hoch had called me to ask for my blessing and support. He had decided to run for my seventh-ward council seat. He had learned much of what he knew about Minneapolis politics working with me. We liked the same people. We didn't like the same people. I adored him.

Some background on Tom: When he was sixteen years old—before he figured out that he was gay—he began dating a woman three years his senior. He never worried about birth control, thinking he was too young to get a woman pregnant. So of course, the woman got pregnant. Neither of them ever told their parents about the situation. She was already out of high school and was able to move out of her parents' house and lay low for nine months. Tom simply kept his mouth shut. He told no one. On the day she went into labor, Tom was scheduled to work at his job as a cook in a restaurant. He hadn't been working there long and feared that if he called in sick, he would lose his job. So he asked his identical twin brother to work his shift and pretend to be him. I swear this is true—you just can't make these stories up.

Tom's twin did such a bad job that Tom almost lost his job anyway. The birth of his daughter went off just fine, but try, if you will, to imagine the scenes that ensued. Tom told his parents and then went with his girlfriend, babe in arms, to tell *her* parents that they had a grandchild. Eventually the baby girl was put up for adoption, and years later, when she was a teenager, she and Tom reestablished contact. They have a wonderful relationship now.

Even if Tom had been a bastard, I would have had to love him for that story alone. But he wasn't, and no one could have asked for a better political successor. He respected me. He had helped me. He had put up with me. He had learned from me. In spite of all this, while I was in Florida I began to wonder whether the seventh ward would elect an openly gay man to the council. Obviously my need for job security had addled me or the sun had baked my brain. The seventh ward had the largest gay population in Minneapolis. Tom was an attorney, young, good-looking, and talented. In short, he was the perfect candidate for my constituents. But I told myself that he just wouldn't be able to muster the votes. This was such complete arrogance on my part. What I was really telling myself was, "That seat's *mine!* I've done a good job, and I'm not going to let anybody take it away."

So I came back and told Tom I was going to reclaim my council seat. I tried to explain myself, but he was hurt that I didn't think he could win and disappointed that I had returned and pushed him out of the race. But he was big about it. He scrapped his own campaign and agreed to work on mine.

On March 29, 1989, the *Star Tribune* announced on page 1B that "Carlson now says she's in the council race."

So much for reminiscing about my charming, nutty antics. My opponent would be DFLer Pat Scott, the chairwoman of the Minneapolis school board, and she was gearing up for a nasty fight. She had already taken me to task in public for my "bizarre behavior" and said that my decision to reenter the race was "just another example of Barbara's indecisiveness." It was going to be a tough eight months.

A tax revolt brewing among Kenwood residents promised to be a key issue in the campaign, as would the questions of development around Lake Calhoun. The adventure began.

Brian Coyle jumped wholeheartedly into Pat Scott's campaign. He had plenty of time. You're going to find this hard to believe, but he was running for reelection in the sixth ward against a homeless man who was apparently not even living in Minneapolis, since he had given up his bed at the shelter before election day.

I didn't have it so easy.

I had a good committee and great campaign material, but my efforts at getting my face back out in front of the people were being sabotaged. We papered the seventh ward with magnificent lawn signs bearing a Warholesque photo of me. They were very classy and very expensive at around $14 a piece. Right away they began disappearing. The ones that weren't stolen were defaced with a mustache. So, we kept printing more and more posters. Because of the printing and other careless spending on my part, my campaign would ultimately cost $74,811. It would be the most expensive campaign ever waged by a council candidate in Minneapolis up to that point, running over budget by more than $25,000. We were never able to make good on the entire debt and finally settled with various vendors for about 56 cents on the dollar.

Waterloo

During the campaign, city officials announced that they were considering an "anticruising ordinance" in Loring Park, a hip, gentrified gay mecca in my ward between Kenwood and downtown. Male prostitutes staked their claim on certain side streets, which led to drug dealing and heavy car traffic that kept residents up during the wee hours. The ordinance would prohibit cruising between ten P.M. and two A.M. If the ordinance was passed, any driver who was seen cruising the same place three times in a row on the same night could be fined $200.

I not only supported the ordinance, I helped police write it. My God, there were cars honking their horns at three A.M. This wasn't fair to the people who lived there and paid taxes. But the radical fringe of the gay community accused me of courting antigay voters. This was ridiculous since I marched in every gay pride parade and both my campaign managers were gay. But getting behind such a volatile ordinance during the campaign, one that would undoubtedly alienate some loyal voters, was nothing short of self-destructive on my part.

One night in October, several carloads of protesters stormed my house on Uptown Avenue South to vent their rage about what Tim Campbell, the editor of a local gay newspaper, called the "homophobic situation." Several Barbara Carlson drag queens showed up in black dresses and pearls, wearing masks fashioned out of that grotesque toothy closeup of me that had run in the *Twin Cities Reader* the previous November. I actually loved the drag queens. I did *not* love it when they began throwing bright orange traffic pylons at the house and when Campbell began pounding on my door in hysterics. Pete raced out in his bathrobe and scuffled with him for a few minutes. Finally, one of the men outside pulled Tim away in a headlock. It was ugly.

After the incident, the city opted to postpone the vote on the ordinance until after the election. Even so, Loring Park would prove to be my Waterloo, at least as far as support among gay voters. I had always depended on them as a solid part of my constituency. Now many were switching allegiance to Pat Scott, who decreed that the ordinance infringed on people's rights. (Ultimately the ordinance didn't pass. As a result, people in Loring Park still aren't getting any sleep, and they're still dragging their asses through all those trendy little shops with circles under their eyes, cranky as hell.)

But I wasn't in the mood to fight. Right from the beginning, I knew my heart and soul were not in this campaign. I wished that I had stayed out of the race instead of coming back to face almost certain defeat, as well as losing a friend, Tom Hoch, in the process. We were already suffering from a late start, and so the campaign literature didn't get out on time. I took a head-in-the-sand approach to problem-solving. And so on Saturdays when I should have been knocking on doors and counteracting all the negative publicity and mudslinging, I was hitting the flea markets and estate sales with friends. After all, there were treasures to be had, with my name on them.

Strong Woman . . . Tough Job

During the September primary I still held the lead in the race with 47% of the vote, versus Pat's 40%. But by November, election month, she was obviously ahead, and dressing me down on real issues, rather than on my personal life. She talked about the number of votes I had missed on big city council issues and my failure to nip high-rise development in the bud. I made a half-assed attempt to attack her ineffectual record on the school board. I released more campaign literature urging people to vote. "BARBARA CARLSON. A STRONG WOMAN FOR A TOUGH JOB," proclaimed a letter to my constituents.

I watched the election coverage surrounded by friends and family. Pete was there, so was Anne. At 8:41 P.M. I called Pat Scott to concede defeat; she had won 4,222 to 3,888 (While Brian Coyle beat the homeless man by a margin of four to one). I was disappointed, but I was okay. I could accept the inevitable.

The day after the election, the *Star Tribune* ran a photo of me drying Anne's tears. I look at the photo now, and it seems sweet and strange to me. I rather like it—the image of me as a mother ministering to her baby's sadness. And yet Anne stands there stiffly, staring right past me. She isn't used to me touching her.

The paper also ran a vicious editorial cartoon kicking me when I was down. It prompted this letter, which ran a few days later:

"Steve Sack's cartoon the day after the election ridiculing Barbara Carlson was cruel and unnecessary. Barbara may well be colorful and overly flamboyant, but she has also been a dedicated, intelligent, and honest public servant. These virtues are not found in abundance in today's political system.

The Minneapolis City Council will miss her voice of independence.

"I would also add, on a personal note, that Barbara is one of the most caring people I have ever known. She has an unusual capacity to reach and to love people. I have never known anyone who has more true friends."

It was signed Arne H. Carlson, state auditor.

28

Farewell to Flamboyance

Once again, after I left my seat in January of 1990, Minneapolis indulged in another fit of Barbara Carlson nostalgia.
There were editorial reruns of the now infamous cow, my
nightgown and needlepoint and pacifier and pearls. The *Sky-
way News* commemorated my passing with a photo essay.
Barbara munching a cookie. Barbara singing at a symphony
fund-raiser. Barbara with her faithful dog, Humphrey of
Kenwood. Barbara on a big street sweeper. Barbara driving
a tractor. "FAREWELL TO FLAMBOYANCE" was the
headline.

During the next couple of months, I got some rest and
caught up with friends. A few job offers came in, but I
decided to take some time off and bid farewell to my political
life. In March came another ending. My mother died. She
was seventy-five years old.

Jane Duffy—that wonderful, suffering woman who had
kicked her habits of booze and pills so late in life despite
terrific odds. My mother, who had learned to tell me she
loved me, who had nurtured my children when their parents
could find neither time nor peace of mind to fulfill that
obligation. I remember the night we told Tucker who his
father was, how glad he was to learn that she was still his
grandmother and how much he loved her.

I try to remember Jane in the later years as a tiny thing,
dressed so smartly, shopping, sculpting, and making delicious

meals. She made marvelous open-faced sandwiches with avocados. She smoked long cigarettes and laughed, and she told me how proud she was of me. She drove people to the polls on election days. She stayed up nights playing cards with Tucker and gave Anne a new doll every Christmas.

Two years before her death, my mother began to fade. I know now she was probably suffering from Alzheimers. She started forgetting things, and her driving became erratic. None of her children wanted the total responsibility of caring for her and watching her decline. She was back on pills, irritable, and depressed. We took her out of the Calhoun Beach Club and placed her in an apartment with assisted living. It was a wonderful place called the Kenwood near my house, but she hated it. She hated having her independence taken away. She became reclusive. Her only friends were the cleaning ladies and a female companion who was older than she was and crippled.

Finally, against my better judgment, we put her in a nursing home in Golden Valley. Here was a woman who had dressed in the finest clothes and decorated her home with unfailing taste, now living in a cubbyhole. She had a roommate, and only a little curtain separated their living areas. I knew she didn't have long when she began wearing the same dirty blue sheath every day. Other days she wore nothing at all. Often she stayed in her room and sculpted in the nude. You could see the decline in her clay sculptures. The noses were misshapen and grotesque. The eyes were often missing.

She had even lost touch with her grandchildren, who had meant so much to her. I think that through their relationship, she had been given a treasured second chance at motherhood. When we took away Jane's car, she got it in her head that we had given it to Anne. Jane was just furious. For a while, she would scream and spit at Anne when she saw her—more evidence of Alzheimers, though she wasn't diagnosed with the disease. At the time, we didn't know to look for it. Jane knew that she was going to die. Even before she went to the nursing home, I took Anne to visit her. Jane looked at her and said out of the blue, "I am so sorry. I love you."

Jane slipped into a coma and died a few days later on March 16, 1990. I think that if she could have filled out her own death certificate, Jane would have written beside "Cause of Death": "I'm *pissed*. I'm pissed that I'm in a nursing home, and if I can't get my kids to take me out, I am checking out on my own." Strange, I can't recall what the coroner listed as the official cause.

Putting my mother in a nursing home, I feel, was the most cruel thing I've ever done. I really do believe that if we hadn't done that, she might still be alive. But we abandoned her. I feel the same burning guilt that I feel for giving up my children after the divorce. Jane had given so much to my children and me after she got sober, and I returned the favor my putting her in exile. Now she was gone, and there was no chance to make amends for the way I hurt her. She died feeling alone and uncared for.

I called the kids. Anne was still living in Minneapolis and back at the university taking classes. She had made plans to leave for Cancun with friends on the same day as the funeral, and I told her that she should go on vacation as she had planned, that Nana would understand.

Tucker took the news very badly. He hadn't seen his grandmother in a year and a half, and in his shock at hearing she had died, he began to question the turns his life had taken during that time.

After graduating from Brown Institute, a technical college near Minneapolis, he worked in radio for a while but quickly discovered that he could make more money spinning records and emceeing mud wrestling at strip clubs. He had become involved in an unhappy relationship with one of the strippers and was working in Durham, North Carolina, when I called to tell him Jane had died. He stayed there for a club's grand opening over the weekend, and by the time he got to the airport to fly home for the funeral, he was sleep-deprived, nauseated, and stinking drunk.

He piled three hundred $1 bills on the counter to pay for his ticket (he was always paid in $1 bills that came from the strippers' tips at the club) and passed out in the rest room on the plane. He was better by the time he got home, but so worn down. I felt so sorry for him. There was only one person on earth whom he could have shared his pain with, and he had come home for her funeral.

Jane had asked to be cremated, though I insisted that we precede the cremation with an open-casket funeral. Through all my training for dealing with grief, I knew how important rituals were. Too often we don't want to touch or even see our loved ones after they die. You should be able to touch the body, take a last look, accept that the soul is no longer there, and say good-bye properly.

I asked the funeral director if I could dress my mother for the service. He said fine and called the next day to tell me she was ready.

I had purchased for her a while cashmere dress and beautiful gold scarf. When I got to the mortuary, she was lying on a table, with her hair and makeup already done. Her hair didn't quite look right, so I styled it a bit differently and changed her makeup a little bit. The mortician stood by to help.

"I'm ready to dress her now," I said to him.

He took off her shroud.

"First, we put on a bra," he said.

"She never wore a bra when she was alive," I told him. I looked at her, her breasts were small and firm and perfect.

Even now. She had never had surgery on them, but they looked like a young woman's. "She doesn't need a bra," I said.

The man helped me get her into her dress. Then he started to pick her up and place her in the casket. I told him I would do it. I cradled her in my arms. She was so light and small. I placed her in the casket. He adjusted the headrest to put her at just the right angle, and I tied the scarf around her neck.

I asked him to leave me alone for a few minutes with her. I wanted to say a few last words.

"Mother, I want you to know how sorry I am for the difficult times that we had when I was young. I want you to know how proud I am of you and your sobriety, and how much you meant to Anne and Tucker. I really don't think that they would have survived the divorce without you. I think you gave them the constant love and support that they so desperately needed. Arne and I were so wrapped up in our own lives and our own problems, we were not there for those babies. You were. How can I tell you how important you were to us?

"I know you're with Daddy Doc and with Harry, and I'm so glad the suffering is over. I wish I could take back all the years we didn't have together, but I'm so grateful for the other times. I was lucky to have you for a while. You look so peaceful. Rest now. After all the pain, rest. I will always love you."

29

Smoke

My brothers and I decided that since our mother had
brought us into this world, we would carry her out. The
three of us and our spouses carried her casket down the aisle
at the funeral. It was a sight. Three men and three big-
hipped women lugged this big unwieldy box through the
chapel, jockeying our way around the edges of the pews.

I wore a wool dress of turquoise blue.

Overall, it was a beautiful and very personal service. The
grandchildren who attended each read something meaningful. Old friends shared memories. All of Jane's cleaning ladies
from over the years attended. I think Jane must have been
difficult to work for, very demanding, but they all loved her.
At the end, we carried the casket back down the aisle. We
said a final quiet farewell, each of us, and I removed her
jewelry for the last time.

We sent my mother's body to the crematorium, and that
night I had to pick up her ashes. I had signed up for yet
another personal development seminar, so I had to pick Jane
up a little early. She was still smoking when I placed her
urn in the front seat of my car. I couldn't concentrate at
the seminar, I was so worried. I kept thinking, my God, if
someone steals that urn out of my car—it was a VERY pretty
urn—my brothers will never forgive me.

The next day we drove to Anoka with the urn. We stopped
on the bridge over the Mississippi River to scatter some of

my mother's ashes. I touched my mother. I touched her ashes. I sifted through them with my fingers, feeling the bits of bone. The moment was so difficult and profoundly personal. We sprinkled some of the ashes into the river and felt small specks blow back in our faces, like tiny airborne kisses.

We got back in our separate cars and met at the cemetery. The family surrounded Harry's plot. There was a small hole in which her urn and remaining ashes would be placed above Harry's coffin. She always liked being on top. Jane's youngest grandson, Sean, covered her with dirt. I already missed her so much and again wanted to tell her how terribly sorry I was for not caring for her enough at the end. I think of her daily. I believe Jane is now happy and at peace with Harry. I hope that my father is behaving and not seducing the angels.

Voices

Even before I left the city council, various colleagues and my friend Harriet Horowitz, an eccentric, creative woman who loves cats and going to estate sales, were telling me I should consider a career in the media. People were used to seeing me on TV and hearing me on the radio, and they found my strong opinions appealing, whether they were delighted or angered at what I had to say. Even at my most outrageous and most opinionated, I wasn't threatening. I mean, for chrissakes, how much damage could an overweight, middle-aged woman on Prozac do? We would soon find out.

During my council years I had played host at a weekly meeting called Breakfast with Barbara at a restaurant, where I moderated discussions between local political figures and my constituents. Harriet suggested I put my final Breakfast

with Barbara on videotape. Arne showed up to be inter-
viewed. So did Janie Jasin, a motivational speaker of some
reknown. It was terrific fun. During my tenure on the council, I had become used to the cameras, so having the lens
pointed at me wasn't nerve-wracking at all. If anything, I
came more alive for it. Cameras and microphones are demanding creatures. They need a lively personality—a bad
flub or a pause, and you look plain stupid.

My friend Mesa Kincaid, a former radio personality with
a sexy soothing voice, helped me produce a presentation tape
for the radio and made a lot of calls, trying to get station
managers to see me. She worked with me on everything from
enunciation to timing. Many station managers were wary of
my loose-cannon reputation, but I was finally given a one-
day shot on KSTP-AM, a local radio station that was known
for cutting-edge, Rush Limbaugh-type personalities.

It all happened very quickly. By May of 1990, KSTP opera-
tions manager Alan Searle had signed me to a year-long
contract with KSTP. No, I didn't have any hard-core broad-
casting experience, but I had connections and a personality.
He thought that was enough to get me started as a talk show
host. The show would be called *Barbara Carlson and Friends*,
and it would air from nine to eleven each morning.

I had no idea what to do. The stations I listened to the
most were public radio and oldies stations. In the beginning
I was anything but cutting-edge, and *Barbara Carlson and
Friends* was simply too friendly. KSTP wanted a shock jock,
a female Rush Limbaugh, a hormonal Howard Stern, someone who could rile the generally conservative, twenty-five to
fifty-four-year-old males who would become my audience.

I wanted the interviews to be serious, with serious guests.
It would prove to be a very difficult balance, combining my
view of the show with the station's. The poor young lady
who first got saddled with the job as my producer was often

reduced to tears when my Prozac didn't work, and even sometimes when it did. She eventually left for a much more sane existence at a Christian station. Enter Peter Thiele, who would rejigger the show and turn it into a success. I just hated him.

When I'm asked to describe Peter, the first word that comes to mind is "nerd." He was smart, young, and rabidly conservative. By the time I met him, he was operating the board on a late-night show on KSTP. He was given my show with these orders from management: "Be the asshole and change things around." He was, and he did. Thus began my five-year love-hate relationship with Peter Thiele. I would love him one moment and be ready to kill him the next. He had his own ideas about how things should be done, and my directions to him fell on deaf ears. During what should have been the honeymoon of our working relationship, I would get so upset with him that we began scheduling meetings so that our shouting matches could be moderated by KSTP management. Our working relationship got so bad we hired a therapist from the University of Minnesota to come in and moderate our discussions on the air.

Through the course of several bloody battles, he changed the music on the show, made it more contemporary. He tried to find music that fit my attitude and the show's edginess. He introduced a lot of rock, alternative stuff, and heavy metal, the kind of things I just couldn't stand.

But with Peter's help and bullheaded stubbornness, I became more relaxed within a month or so. I became Barbara Carlson, not a sanitized version of her. I realized that with Peter there as a safety net, I could talk about the things I was passionate about. I began discussing whatever was on my mind: Prozac, oral sex, weight (I had put on 50 pounds since I lost the election and was vowing to take it off and keep it off with yet another goddamn liquid diet). Peter produced little teasers—a booming voice announcing, "She *loves* sodomy. She's Barbara Carlson ..." He eventually decided that the theme from *Sesame Street* should be played at the end of the show. Since I could be pretty racy, he decided that the kiddie-show theme would provide a kicky bit of irony.

I was learning to be myself on the air—the secret to being a good broadcaster. The trick, I discovered, was to use my anger and flaws to advantage. Peter and I made good use of our mutual animosity. As far as I knew, Peter was, at the ripe old age of twenty-six, still a virgin, so I teased him mercilessly about it for all the Twin Cities to hear. He did not find this funny and once threatened to sue me for sexual harassment. After that, I simply began calling him "disease free."

Our core guests remained politicians and community leaders, but by August we were adding a little spice to the mix. For example, we invited in the owner of a marital aids store. He came on with his Kama Sutra massage talc, lubes, oils and the biggest dildo I have ever seen.

"This is, uh, *big*, don't you think?" I asked him, when the discussion turned to vibrators.

"Well, Barbara," he said, "most of our vibrators measure about six to eight inches. I'd have to say that *big* is in the eye of the beholder."

This made me laugh. "Well, trust me, ladies and gentlemen," I said to my audience, "I've seen it, and this thing is *big*."

A listener phoned in to ask me if it was possible to become "vibrator addicted."

"Oh, *please* don't tell me that!" I yelled. "You're talking to someone who has so many addictions, that's the *last* thing I need to hear."

Before long I became known as Minneapolis's Mistress of

the Morning. My audience grew to nearly 400,000 listeners a week. They learned to yell back at me, laugh with me, and cry with me. Early on in the show, I shared with them my experience of losing a baby. Many other women whose babies had died of SIDS phoned in to share their stories. It was cathartic and wonderful.

I always wanted to take the show out of the studio and go on location. It was an expensive proposition, which management resisted. But they did agree to let me do the show from the hot tub in my own backyard one day a week. On Fridays, Peter lugged the entire soundboard into my gazebo. Eventually we got a hot tub company to sign on as a sponsor, and the company paid extra for my impromptu testimonials on the air.

As my audience grew, the station's marketing folks began to persuade other merchants to use my eccentricities to their advantage. I was always pooh-poohing the tactics and positions of the animal rights people, so a local furrier became a sponsor, as did a mattress company, probably because I talked so much about sex.

In 1990, just before I hit the airwaves, Arne Carlson had announced his gubernatorial bid. Think of it, soon he would be the most powerful man in the state, and I would have access to hundreds of thousands of listeners. "Please support Arne Carlson," I told Peter during the campaign, which kicked in just as we were going on the air, "because if he wins we'll have a direct pipeline into the governor's office." It was Arne's worst nightmare. It was my dream come true.

30

The Bald Box

I have never liked having celebrity guests on the show because, while they're billed as celebrities, I hardly ever know who the hell they are. Plus, they're seldom bright, and instead of having an issue to debate or a quirky sex-related sideline to discuss, they simply have a movie of TV show or record to promote. They aren't there to be interesting; they see the media as a vehicle for free advertising. Boring. Nevertheless, we have booked a few. One of the first to share my microphone was an actor named Tom Wopat, who had apparently been on a TV show a few years back. Peter tried to brief me about Tom's career. He said the show was called *The Dukes of Hazzard* and that it was about a couple of hunky rubes who solved crimes or some darn thing. I wasn't impressed.

Tom Wopat had been hired by some corporation to tour the country promoting Rogaine, which is supposed to stimulate hair growth. Celebrities apparently make a lot of money doing this kind of thing (and though I find the practice of endorsing a product in such a way a teensy bit corrupt, I would do it in a heartbeat). Peter said that my audience would like Tom Wopat, so he insisted on having him on the show. He promised me that if it got too boring, Tom would bring on his guitar and sing.

So Tom came on, and I informed Tom that I had never heard of him and that I never watched TV because I found it mind-numbing. He laughed along good-naturedly. Then we began discussing Rogaine. I pulled his hair to make sure he wasn't wearing a toupee. Tom shot Peter a glance, as if to say this wasn't going well. His publicist sat in the studio, just horrified. Finally I decided that if we were going to have to talk about Rogaine, then we would *talk* about Rogaine.

"Can women use it?" I asked.

He said he thought so.

"Well, then I could use some," I told him, "because I've gone through menopause and lost all my pubic hair. My husband says I've got a bald box."

This was not what Tom expected. He just didn't know what to say. So, no more Rogaine discussion. His publicist jumped in and suggested that he go out to the car and get his guitar and sing a song, so he did. Tom hasn't been back.

Politicians have always been my favorite guests. I'm at my best with them, be they friend or foe, and during my first year on the air, I was blessed with a gubernatorial election. All the candidates agreed to appear on the show except incumbent Rudy Perpich, who was razzed mercilessly in absentia.

Even Arne came on. He had remarried again, this time to a bright, young attorney named Susan. Before meeting Arne, Susan had worked for a state Republican senator in St. Paul, so she knew the ins and outs of politics. Arne had made an aborted run at the governor's office back in 1986, and now he was back. Arne's lack of warmth threatened to put off some voters, but he was great at going on the attack. When Paul Wellstone, a DFL candidate, tried to unseat him as state auditor in 1982, Arne surprised him during a debate by pulling out an old tape in which Wellstone could be heard admitting that he had trouble reading charts and graphs. Wellstone was put in the position of denying to reporters that he had ever been treated for a learning disability. I thought the tactic was just brilliant.

I supported Arne wholeheartedly in the race. But the Independent Republican party, still at the mercy of its rabid anti-choice wing that cared so much less about the quality of politicians than their stands on abortion, endorsed anti-abortion nominee Jon Grunseth to run against incumbent DFLer Rudy Perpich (also anti-abortion). Soon, however, reports began to surface that Grunseth, the IR's family-values man, had allegedly gone skinny-dipping with a bunch of teenagers nine years earlier. He denied the charges but I was just beside myself with glee. It was the most fun I've ever had in politics. Daily reports about his misbehavior kept my show humming, while a Republican legislator was trying to organize others to force Grunseth off the ticket. Grunseth refused to go. In October, two weeks before the election, Arne reentered the race as a write-in candidate.

Even though he was a Republican, DFLers liked Arne's fairly liberal bent, his position on civil rights, and his pro-choice stance. Plus, DFLers didn't seem particularly loyal to their incumbent candidate, Perpich. This was 1990, when the general population was beginning to blame fat-cat incumbents and political establishment figures for the sorry state of federal and state governments. Just two years later, we would replace George Bush, a member of America's political royalty, with a slow-talking good old boy from Arkansas.

IR loyalists saw Arne as a solid, reliable, down-to-earth member of the party. Maybe he was more liberal than they would have liked, but at least he wasn't screwing teenagers. Still, some pundits on the political scene figured that Arne's candidacy would simply divide the IR vote and give Perpich a free ride. Plus, Arne risked alienating his party further by announcing his intentions to run at such a late date and thereby throwing a wrench into the IR political machine.

But on election night in November I watched Arne graciously accept the voters' approval. He won. God, I was proud. Proud of him. Proud of me. Would he be up there making an acceptance speech if he had never met me, Barbara Duffy from Anoka? Maybe. Maybe not. But I was certainly a *part* of it, whatever our feelings for each other were now. I had devoted myself to so many of his campaigns when we were married, and I had publicly endorsed him on this one. Friends tell me that I was crying that night he won. But I don't remember that. Nor do I remember what I wore.

Oscar

Susan Carlson became the first lady of Minnesota, while I happily remained Mistress of the Morning. People have asked me over the years whether I am sad that I'm not in the position of first lady. I worked hard to get Arne there, but no, I am not. I will never play second fiddle to any man again. I have held political office, have been successful in my own right. I am not an appendage of some man's success. I would have made a dreadful first lady. I feel proprietary about Arne's success because we shared some very important years. During our time together, I had my children, I formed friendships, and I went through recovery.

Arne would tell you that I should put our relationship behind me, forget about it, and *for God's sake, stop talking about it*. That's easy for a man to say. I think that a man's self-worth more often comes from a career. A woman more often prides herself on her relationships. As rocky as our marriage was, I still worked hard at it. I still find myself defending him when he has a disagreement with Tucker, for theirs has always been a case of tough love. And sometimes I feel such a connection to Arne Carlson that I forget I'm not married to him.

Of course, it doesn't thrill Arne that on my radio show I have never deprived myself of the advantages of knowing the most private personal details of the governor's life. But it is a constant source of delight to the Twin Cities. Even when I complain about him, I always support Arne politically. I think my listeners sense my residual tenderness and respect for Arne. My personal revelations abut him certainly haven't hurt him. Maybe the public needs to know that their governor is also human. The general public does not know Arne Carlson. They see him as cold, only interested in the sports teams of the University of Minnesota. It's up to me to tell Minnesota that he's more interesting than that.

"Who is the real Arne Carlson?" I asked him during an appearance on *Barbara Carlson and Friends* soon after he took office. I had seen him smiling too much for the cameras, and I knew that wasn't the real Arne Carlson. "I don't like you nice," I told him. "I like you nasty and in there and standing up for your beliefs and the issues and the people you care about. I want you to forgo this sweet new persona. When you're nice you make me just want to throw up."

"Well, *you're* very, *very* nice," he jabbed.

We sparred and laughed and got great coverage. The *Star Tribune* ran the interview verbatim in a story about us the next day. I closed the show that day by saying I had voted for him. "Just because we can't live together does not mean we can't be supportive of each other," I said. "I think he can be a fabulous governor. I think he can go down as one of Minnesota's finest."

Arne wasn't so amused when, after he won the election, I discussed his penis on the air. The big news of the day was Gennifer Flowers, the woman who claimed to have had an affair with Bill Clinton. She said that she named his testicles, "the boys," and that Bill called her breasts "the girls."

"You know, Peter," I said at the beginning of the show. "I have had two husbands and gave names to their penises."

I must say this for Peter: He knows an opportunity when he hears it.

"Oh?" he said slyly. "And would you care to share with us what those names are?"

"Well," I said. "Pete's is named Dupont."

"And what might the governor's be called?"

"Oscar."

Now, why it was called Oscar in the first place, I cannot recall. But within minutes of the broadcast, across water coolers in offices all over Minnesota, Oscar was the talk of the town, a celebrity in his own right. Not the kind of tidbit people soon forget.

Another Fix

Over the years I've shared my hot tub with everybody from an overweight conservative think-tanker to strippers of both male and female varieties.

With Peter constantly working the phone, cajoling and persuading and conning people we wanted on the show, we played a pivotal role in the firing of a Minneapolis superintendent of schools. I took the fight directly to my listeners and gave out school board members' home phone numbers so listeners could call and demand his replacement. I successfully crusaded in favor of a homeless shelter downtown and got the city council to stop dragging its feet and allow the

zoning change required to build it. I refereed an on-air debate between the director of an abortion clinic and the local
leader of Operation Rescue.

And before God and the Twin Cities, I swore off liquid
diets. No more. I just couldn't take them. Someone suggested
I look into something called the gastric bypass or stomach
stapling. *Ta-da!* Another fix.

I met with Dr. Henry Buchwald at the University of Minnesota Hospital and Clinic. Dr. Buchwald is handsome, Jewish, and one of the country's leading experts on tummy-
tucks—just my type. I had a choice of the gastric bypass and
vertical banded gastroplasty. Both are used fairly frequently
on patients who weigh in at 100 more pounds than they
should.

Dr. Buchwald explained to me that 80 percent of his patients reported excellent results and another 5 percent reported good results. The bypass means just that—food is
rerouted, bypassing about 90 percent of the stomach and the
first part of the small intestine. If you agree to this procedure,
you can suffer diarrhea and light-headedness. But you do
lose weight, and fast.

The vertical banded gastroplasty is a less drastic procedure,
but it's more trouble for the surgeon. A silastic band is tied
around a stapled off segment of the stomach, leaving only a
small compartment available to hold food. Very small meals
leave you feeling full. Dr. Buchwald warned me over and over
that too much food, eating too fast, or a bite larger than a
fingertip would cause nausea. This occurs because all the
food has to pass through a little tiny ring attached to the
band. If it gets backed up in the stomach, you have to
throw up.

I chose the gastroplasty. Vomiting aside, it sounded more
reasonable than the bypass.

During my ensuing physicals, we discovered a hernia between my chest and abdomen, as well as stones in my gall bladder. I was a mess, but healthy enough for surgery, and we decided to take care of the stones and the hernia and gastroplasty in one fell swoop.

I scheduled my stomach surgery for February 24, 1992. I was under the knife for three hours, and while he was in there, Dr. Buchwald found a benign muscle tumor in my stomach. So he got rid of that while he was at it. But the operation went smoothly and left only a little scar.

Dr. Buchwald was right about the vomiting. One extra bite of something delicious, and the waves of nausea washed over me. I decided, why should I give up this food? Why should I give up French fries and steaks and candy bars? I thought, why not chew the food and not swallow it? Just spit it out! And my colleagues thought the pacifier was weird.

My radio audience thought my adventures in gastroplasty were just hilarious. But they didn't have to live through it. The management at KSTP still remembers the days when I snacked all through talent meetings, then turned and spit the orange, mushy remains of Chee-tos into a cup. It ruined many meetings. I carried my cups everywhere. Friends stopped going to restaurants with me. I thought it was quite clever and effective, because I began to drop pounds. But then I came to the conclusion that I would have to choose between having friends or spitting out chewed food. I chose the friends.

There were other ways to outsmart the gastroplasty, but they proved to be more fattening. Dr. Buchwald had warned me about how patients managed to cheat the operation, to keep me from falling into these bad, self-destructive patterns. He told me that the surgery wouldn't do any good if the patient drank calories in nondiet soda or sat for a long time and ate very slowly or munched constantly small amounts of fattening snacks.

I chose munching.

Today I suck down buttery candies in the car, nibble on potato chips during the show, eat handfuls of cheese-flavored popcorn in the afternoons at home, and enjoy soft, digestible, fattening desserts. So I gained back the weight and have kept it to this day. Only *now* I can't get through a meal without excusing myself to throw up at least once.

I have also tried vitamins, and for several weeks consumed seventy-five vitamins a day instead of sugar and candy. I felt fabulous, but got bored, so I quit. Some say I should concede defeat and simply accept my weight problem. Though sometimes when I catch myself in the mirror or when I get tired of wearing slimming black seven days a week, I consider yet another stomach operation. It's called the intestinal bypass. With that one, you bypass 90 percent of the small intestine. This causes malabsorption, so you have to take vitamin supplements. That is, when you're not pooping. But I've always loved a challenge. There must be a way to cheat that one, too.

31

Black and White

My first and so far only suspension from the airwaves occurred in the summer of 1992. It started when I decided once again to engage in my favorite charitable pasttime—playing yenta. I am proudly responsible for many successful matings and marriages in Minnesota. So I decided to stage my own version of *The Dating Game* on my show. I invited single listeners to join me on location while we broadcast the festivities live. It was turning out to be great fun and, as a result, I was in a festive mood. At one point, a black female anchor named Carolyn Brookter from KSTP's TV station was on the line, ready to do a short news break.

I introduced her and, in my exuberance, queried, "I know I shouldn't ask you this, but have you ever slept with a white man?" The reporter was not amused. Carolyn Brookter was a well-known, serious news entity and had been in the Twin Cities for years. She was furious. She was simply doing her job for KSTP news. She was not supposed to be a part of the riotous action on location, and she was appalled that I would ask such an insensitive question. She wanted me fired.

I can understand her rage, but I still don't think it was the worst thing I've ever said. I think that all levels of relations between the races are fascinating and worthy of discussion. Maybe not in a humorous way over the airwaves, but interesting nonetheless. Really. Show me a group of African-

American female friends who haven't asked each other the same question.

Even the most well-meaning white people remain shamefully unenlightened about the gross level of routine discrimination suffered by the black community. We have no idea how it feels to be a black man, boarding an elevator and watching all the white ladies clutch their purses a little tighter, or hearing the thumping of an automatic door lock when he walks by someone sitting in a parked car. I've suffered sneers and jokes from men because I'm fat, I've listened to enough of my friends discuss their fear of losing their jobs or housing simply because they're gay, so maybe I can begin to understand how much racism hurts. My question to Carolyn was insensitive and hardly an opening for lively debate. I feel bad about it, but it did start a healthy dialogue at the time.

But anyway, Carolyn did not find my question amusing, nor did KSTP. The African-American community did not find this amusing, either. And so I was suspended for two weeks. It doesn't feel good to be called a racist. When your employer is, in essence, calling you one, and when you've hurt someone, regardless of your intentions, creeping guilt comes in and distorts the sounds of your heart and conscience. I sat home for those two weeks and worried. I didn't go out, and by the time I returned to the studio, I was a wreck. I forgot to take my Prozac that morning, so that only made matters worse.

I looked at my microphone and imagined all the thousands of listeners out there waiting to hear if I would redeem myself or fall on my ass. My tummy hurt like hell. I downed a Diet Coke for a jolt of energy and took a healthy supply of vending-machine potato chips into the studio with me. The lights clicked on.

"Ohhhhhh, it's been a while," I breathed into the mike. "Did you miss me?" I wasn't sure if they had.

I apologized for offending Carolyn and anyone else who had been hurt by my remark. It's always a tough balancing act, the public apology. You want to convey how sincerely sorry you are for whatever you're sincerely sorry about. But never, *never* try to convince your audience that you're sorry for something you're really not. No one will buy it. After my apology, the controversy dissipated, but only for a while.

Hostile

During the ensuing weeks on the radio, I had all kinds of discussions with my call-in listeners about prejudice. We talked about the way we look, whether it be fat, thin, black, white, blond, or brunette, and the way people perceive each other. I was confronting my own prejudices and demons. I had many biases—I like people who are educated in private schools, I would never speak to a woman who wore white shoes after Labor Day, I hate polyester in all forms, and I have negative feelings about people who ride motorcycles and defile their bodies with tattoos.

And so I, the Kenwood matron, with her designer clothes and pearls and furs, decided to fly in the face of propriety by having a tattoo stenciled on my ass. I would embrace and display the very thing that I judged others negatively for having. How would it feel, I wondered, to have a tattoo and pearls at the same time? It would be a testament to the fact there's more to all of us than meets the eye. And it was a good publicity stunt.

I chose a design of two red lips bound by a zipper, with my station's call letters and the word "Not!" carved alongside it. I asked a local tattoo artist to give it to me on the air. I didn't expect that getting a tattoo would *hurt,* and so while the needle etched my bottom, I groaned into the microphone.

The zippered mouth was meant to be ironic, of course. No one knows just *how* deep the irony in this symbol is better than my children do.

It has never been easy for them to grow up with two public parents. Neither Anne nor Tucker ever took advantage of having the governor for a father. They never asked him to find them jobs or get them into schools. But they have suffered the disadvantages. The local papers have played up Tucker's hippie-ish appearance and wondered on their pages whether he would embarrass the governor at inauguration time. That must be humiliating.

When Anne was involved in a minor traffic accident (she dented someone's fender on Crosstown Highway 62 while she was creeping along in heavy traffic) the *Star Tribune* informed everyone that she was being investigated for a hit and run. The governor's office had to respond, trying to explain that she hadn't realized any damage had been done to the other car.

Anne and Tucker seem to ignore the spotlight pretty well, even when it is glaring on them. It never shone more brightly on Anne than during her wedding. In 1992 Anne met Andrew Davis, a handsome, bright, articulate man in his twenties who worked in Washington, D.C., for Democratic congressman James Oberstar. They had a long-distance romance, but in spite of that, it seemed to get serious right away. She introduced me to Andrew. He sat down and matched me word for word and story for story, making it clear that he wasn't going to take any bunk from the mouthpiece of Minnesota. They became engaged, and I gave them my blessing on one condition. I asked them to promise never to put me in a nursing home. Anne said she planned to put me away as soon as possible, but Andrew assured me he wouldn't let her do it, so I was crazy about him.

Of course, the population of Minneapolis knew that Barbara and Arne would have to join forces for their daughter's wedding and sensed that drama was afoot. They got all they expected and more.

Andrew's parents were from Ely, Minnesota, where they owned a company called Tom and Woods' Moose Lake Wilderness Canoe Trips. They graciously offered to help with the expenses of this large wedding. Arne and I were both grateful. Arne went on to send me a letter, detailing what was expected of me and what I would pay for. It was a formal letter, typed on his official stationary.

I was pissed. Here was this arrogant s.o.b. telling the mother of the bride how to act, what to say, and what to pay for. Of course, I saw it as his attempt to control me. Well, I was furious. So I read his goddamn missive over the air. In retrospect, I probably shouldn't have, but I enjoyed every second of it. There was no response from Arne, but the next day a *Star Tribune* gossip columnist named Cheryl Johnson, who goes by the name of C.J. in print, recounted the incident. She then informed her readers that I would probably be excluded from some of the wedding festivities because Arne was still so angry that I had divulged the name of his penis.

I ran into C.J. at the theater one evening.

"Please try not to write any more about the kids," I pleaded. "They're trying very hard to maintain their privacy, and it's an emotional time for all of us."

She gave me her word that she would back down, and I felt relieved.

Imagine my surprise to read *this* a few mornings later: "Governor Arne Carlson, a politician who likes a tight budget, has a daughter with expensive tastes in wedding gifts." Then C.J. recounted Anne's bridal registry in print, from the $699 Mitsubishi TV to the $150 fondue pot.

"We don't recall former first daughter Mary Sue Perpich Bifulk's bridal registry rambling on for seven pages," C.J. added. I was just furious. I took the microphone at KSTP and wondered aloud how C.J. would feel if I said nasty things about her? How would she feel, for example, if I were to call her a "hostile black bitch?"

The second I said it, I knew that I had done something awful. I felt terrible, and during a break I told the station manager that I said something terribly inappropriate.

I returned to the air and said that the color of C.J.'s skin had nothing to do with this. I was careful to note that she remained, however, a bitch. We got a few irate phone calls about it, but no more than usual. The KSTP senior management was fit to be tied; some wanted me fired once again. But the station ultimately decided that sending C.J. an apology would suffice. I would not be suspended again.

Through a great deal of fault of my own, I and my little girl's wedding were now fair game for C.J.'s poison pen. C.J., in fact, said that she'd never promised not to write about the kids. Whatever. Until the wedding took place in April of 1993, C.J. took shots at every move we made. When a gubernatorial communiqué about the wedding was issued, C.J. made much of the fact that I was listed as Barbara Carlson-Anderson. Quoth C.J.: "The thinking in the executive branch is that Babbler enjoys zinging Arne on her talk show because she can't quite get over the fact that she didn't hang in there long enough to suck up attention as the First Lady of Minnesota." Touché.

Gracious, Kind, and Nice

Obviously Anne and Andrew had been nervous from the start about the tension between Arne and me while planning the wedding. But despite all the drama caused by me, Anne and I were growing closer. I was her mother, and she wanted me to be a part of the event. I desperately wanted to be there for her, since I had let her down so many times in the past. We shopped estate sales to furnish the little house that she and Andrew had bought, and I watched her juggle the guest list, trying to include Susan and her family and Pete and me. Both Susan's daughter, Jessica, and Pete's and my granddaughter, Cici Anderson, were in the wedding.

Anne and I shopped for her wedding dress together, and we found a gorgeous off-the-shoulder gown with a cathedral-length veil trimmed with pearls and lace. She helped me choose my outfit—a custom-made blue piqué dress and coat. During our time together planning her wedding, I realized how genuine and generous Anne is. She found the time amid all the prewedding chaos to construct elaborate gift baskets for the thirty-eight out-of-town guests who showed up.

At the time, Anne was also struggling with a severe case of endometriosis. This is a common disease among women of child-bearing age, in which tissue similar to endometrium, which is shed during menstruation, forms outside the uterus. It causes internal bleeding, can be very dangerous, and can quite possibly affect a woman's ability to produce children. There are no absolute cures. I was there for Anne during that time, and I saw her drop her guard against me—a guard against her fear of being abandoned by me once again. Just as I had been given my mother back late in life, Anne had rediscovered her mother. And I had rediscovered my beautiful daughter.

A couple of days before the wedding ceremony, a reporter from the *St. Paul Pioneer Press* called to see if the Twin Cities could expect Arne and me to shoot off any fireworks at each other inside the sanctuary of the Hennepin Avenue Methodist Church in Minneapolis.

"I'm going to be very gracious, kind, and nice," I promised. "This is my daughter's wedding day, and I think both the governor and I are trying very hard to make this a wonderful day."

After I thought the interview was over, I promised the reporter that I wouldn't try to kill Arne—"the cheap bastard."

Apparently the quote was too good to resist, and it showed up in print on the day of the wedding. As punishment, Andrew and Tucker decided that I would be banished from the place of honor—the main pew, right on the aisle where the mother of the bride is customarily seated. No one informed me of this until Tucker took my arm and led me toward the front of the church.

"When you get to the front, turn left," he whispered.

"Into the second pew?" I asked.

"No, Mom, all the way around to the left . . ."

Suddenly I realized what was happening, but there was nothing I could do. Tucker led me to the front, made a sharp left, and took me around to the side. My nose was in the air, I was sailing like the proud Queen Mary. I would not cause a scene, but I was livid. So I sat there and stewed. I looked around at the guests. Lots of Arne's political cronies, people who didn't know Anne, people who were there because they wanted to be close to the governor, were mingling with Anne's real friends and loved ones. Of course, this was to be expected in a wedding of this size, but it was one more thing for me to be angry about. I couldn't help but remember Kristin's funeral, when local politicos I didn't know showed up ostensibly to mourn the passing of my child.

The wedding march began. Anne made her regal way down the aisle. She was beautiful.

I saw her smile at me as she turned from the altar at the end of the ceremony. Her smile said to me thank you, all was forgiven.

There was a magnificent wedding reception at the governor's residence. Arne even allowed me to enter through the front door. Although I was tearing up by the time I made my toast, I was able to wish my daughter and her husband luck and serve them one last reminder:

"Remember, Andrew dear, you have promised to *never* put me in a nursing home."

32

Shut Up

As soon as Anne and Andrew returned from their honey-moon, Anne discovered that she was pregnant. Don't think that all the old biddies weren't counting the months before the baby showed up. But on January 12, 1994—a little over nine months after the marriage—my beautiful granddaughter Alexandra came kicking and screaming into the world.

Anne had an extremely difficult pregnancy, months on IVs, and months on bed rest. Arne was terrific, offering her a room in the governor's mansion where the staff could look after her while Andrew was working. Arne even gave me full visiting rights—though I had to enter through the back stairs—on the condition that I didn't use any information I gathered at the mansion on the radio. I agreed and stuck to my promise. I had other things to worry about, like Anne's health. Anne hemorrhaged several times throughout the pregnancy. There were so many times when we wondered if the baby would make it.

One night Anne swore she heard a rat in the wall of her room at the mansion, which damn near sent her into labor too soon. Finally, after many collective prayers, Anne went into labor a month early. Her pains began on a Sunday and lasted for a couple of days. I remember Arne's driver calling from a Gopher basketball game on the night of the birth asking if the baby was ready yet. Well, dear little Allie held off until the game was over. On Wednesday night, when

Allie was good and ready, Arne, Susan, Jessica, Andrew, Tucker, his current girlfriend, and I joined Anne in the delivery room. Pete had begged off, saying he'd stay home with Humphrey and save his strength to help us when we got home. Andrew brought his little video camera, and Tucker videotaped the entire birth.

I wore a Lanz nightgown and pearls.

Andrew and I each pushed on Anne's feet, as she bore down and Allie made her way down the birth canal. I started to sing the University of Minnesota fight song, to keep Anne's mind off the pain.

"Minnesota, hats off to thee, firm and strong . . ."

"Shut up, Mother," Anne growled.

And then we could see the baby's head, and the doctor told Andrew to touch it softly with his finger. It was just astounding. The head popped out.

"My God! It's not breathing!" I cried.

"Shut up, Barbara," the doctor snapped, "and let me get the rest of this baby out."

Well, the rest of Allie popped out, and to my great relief, she was just as healthy as she could be. So slimy and beautiful and perfect. Here was a brand-new life, it was just amazing. They let Anne hold her and showed Andrew how to cut the umbilical cord. Then it was my turn.

I took her in my arms. I loved her immediately. I held her close and whispered, "Allie, I want you to know that I am your grandmother and that I am going to be the most important person in your life." That's what I told her, knowing I could never be the *most* important one in her life. Still, I planned to be right up there.

My little dog Humphrey did not share in the joy. The first time the kids visited with Allie at my house, he went into a slump. He dragged his hindquarters about, hid under the bed, and whined. I didn't know *what* was happening. I thought he was really sick, and Pete was out of town, so I was terrified that he'd come home and I'd have to tell him that the dog had died. So I rushed Humphrey to the dog hospital. I couldn't find my glasses, so I didn't find the place until about one A.M. While we were waiting, poor Humphrey pooped right in the middle of the floor. I just knew this was the end.

"Oh, Humphrey," I pleaded, holding the dog in my arms, "please don't die. *Please* don't die. Your daddy will kill me."

The doctor took x-rays and couldn't find anything wrong. I paid the bill and took the poor little wheezing, whining creature back home. Over the next few days Humphrey's condition did not improve. I carried him up and down the stairs. I carried him outside so he could relieve himself and prayed that he would hold on until Pete returned.

I took him back to the vet for more tests, and again they discovered nothing wrong with him.

"What changes have gone on in the family?" the vet asked me.

"We have a new baby granddaughter," I answered.

The vet looked at me for a moment, smiled reassuringly, and said, "Humphrey is fine, but he is very, very angry. Let me tell you what's next on your agenda. He is going to poop on your bed."

"Humphrey, you do that, and it will be your last action as part of the Carlson-Anderson family," I said, glaring at the little beast. So Humphrey and I had a little powwow when we got home. The next time Allie came over, I held her and Humphrey both, one in each arm. He growled for a while and slowly realized, after hundreds of dollars in vet bills, that Allie was not going to totally replace him. At last he made peace with her.

Humphrey's hurt feelings aside, I think that more than anything, that baby has helped bring my family together.

Allie is a treasure that Anne shares with me. She is also a very personal link to my ex-husband.

Allie. How can I begin to describe the happiness that this child has brought into our lives? Her laughs, her hollers, and her gurgles are music to my ears. I love her more than I ever thought possible. There is not a day when I do not wake up thinking about her and hoping to see her. I buy her clothes and toys and outdoor equipment with great abandon. Nothing is too good for this baby. I think it takes me back to my own childhood when I felt like the center of the universe, the one tiny person for whom the planet spun on its axis.

Allie has allowed me to be a mother once again, to do it right this time, and a second chance to be a mother to my children. The last time I loved this deeply, the child died. I had a conversation with Anne about this, because we all know that to love this deeply is to risk pain and loss. I now know that if anything happened to Allie or my two surviving children, that I would survive. I can take the risk of loving absolutely and unconditionally—a lesson that I wished I could have learned sooner, for the sake of my children.

I am still trying to make amends with my children for my shortcomings as a mother. I believe that I will continue to do so for the rest of my life. I know they love me and that they've forgiven me, but for my own peace of mind, I must try to remind them constantly that I won't leave them again.

Anne and Tucker both live here in the Twin Cities now, close to me, sometimes closer than they'd prefer. My relationship with Anne turned around when she got sick before the wedding, and she realized then that I was committed to caring for her and being a mother. Now that she's a wife and mother herself, our relationship has reached a deeper level. We spend a lot of time together now as friends.

Tucker got out of the titty bar business, which thrills me.

He's now the house manager of the Orpheum and State theaters, where road companies of Broadway shows move in and out. He's happy, too smart for his own good sometimes, and finding his way through his twenties. He has a long list of women. He was engaged at one time and once dated an exotic dancer, whom he took to Arne's first inauguration, which I thought was just delightful. She had just had her breasts augmented and happily showed them to all my friends upon request. I have liked all the women in Tucker's life and I hope there's one out there from whom he can accept happiness and devotion. Like his mother, he likes to push the envelope. Life won't always be easy for him, but he'll have fun living it.

What do I like best about Tucker? His sense of humor. Only a parent can tell you how wonderful it is to have an adult child who can make you laugh. Not very long ago, I slumped into a depression, and he called me. "Mom," he said, "would it make you feel better if I let you cut my hair on the air?" He knew I just hated his long hair, but he never listened to my complaints. What he was really saying when he called was, "Mom, I'm here for you." So I took him up on his offer, and one day on my show I took a pair of scissors and snipped off all the hair brushing his shoulders. Then I wrote him a check for the barber who could clean up my butchery and style his hair properly. It was a funny gesture by Tucker, but also sweet and generous and thoughtful. It meant a lot to me, and I soared right out of my slump.

Fortunes

I'm almost at the end, and my story wouldn't be complete without telling you the rest of Tommy Weiser's story. After he moved to Palm Springs, his fortune ran out. Just before interest rates began escalating during the Carter administration, he had purchased a bunch of commercial properties in Minneapolis and four hundred residential units in Palm Springs. He was heavily leveraged. Various schemes to regain his financial footing failed. He has gone from palaces to hovels and back a couple of times. If I kept an address book, I'm sure I'd have twenty-five numbers for him.

Yet Tommy has never broken, never stopped playing host to humanity, and even in more austere circumstances, his home has remained open to anyone in need of laughter and company. During and after my marriage to Arne, I would visit Tommy in Palm Springs, lie by the pool with him and his friends, and laugh, realizing that I hadn't laughed in months before I got there. It was during a visit there in 1982 that I heard about AIDS for the first time.

It wasn't called AIDS then, of course. It wasn't called anything. "I'm scared," a friend of Tommy's told me one afternoon by the pool. "My friends are getting sick. Nobody knows what it is, nobody knows the cause, nobody knows the cure. It's just death. Death is stalking us."

During the thirteen years since, Tommy's life has been decimated by the disease. In 1983, he took in his first AIDS victim. The man was an airline pilot and had lived his entire life in the closet. When he got sick, he was evicted from his home and disowned by his family. Tommy cared for him and saw him out with dignity. After his friend died, Tommy dedicated the rest of his life to caring for AIDS victims.

He has a lover, a former Marine named Carl Burgmeier. (His brother, Tom Burgmeier, was an all-star pitcher for the Boston Twins and is now the pitching coach for the Kansas City Royals.) They've been together for a quarter century. Tom and Carl care for up to six AIDS patients at a time in their home. They take in people who have nowhere else to go, or need a family environment to help them get better, or die in peace, whatever the case may be.

Two years ago Tommy called and told me that he was HIV positive because he had had unprotected sex. I still don't understand my initial reaction. I was angry. I couldn't speak to him for a year. I suppose it was easier to be angry than to care and worry. And then it dawned on me that I had lost a year of intimacy with this wonderful man—a year, when time seemed most precious. I called him.

"I love you, Tommy," I said. "I can't stay mad at you."

Any sane friend would have hung up on me, but not Tommy. We spoke as if no time had gone by. The gulf closed with generous, easy forgiveness. When I gave him money last year to pay for some dental work, he sent my new granddaughter a gorgeous antique quilt covered in colorful butterflies. It had been a gift from his eighty-two-year-old aunt, who spent nearly three years meticulously stitching it by hand, despite crippling arthritis.

Besides the sentimental value, Tommy could have sold the quilt when he needed money. But now it sits on my daughter's bed, a soft, quiet symbol of my friend's generosity and style. How can my daughter adequately appreciate the gift, having known Tommy only from distance? How will my granddaughter love it enough, never having known him at all? But I know Tommy Weiser, and that quilt is magnificent.

33

The Dead

I have now been given more time on this earth than my father was given. I plan to keep going for at least four more decades and grow old like Isabel Miller did. Isabel was the queen of Mitchell, South Dakota, and a good friend of my grandparents. She was a woman of great class and fabulous intelligence. She drank like a fish and drove like a madwoman. She wore her hair in a bun, and when she got old, her eyes drooped so badly she couldn't see. To remedy the situation she held them open with tape. Whenever you popped in on old Isabel, she'd answer the door with big bug eyes and tape on her forehead. She died at age ninety-five one night when she was cooking dinner. The only thing different I want is to be in bed with a man when I go—preferably at my lake house.

It was 1991 when Pete and I found our paradise. It was a little rundown shack right on Potato Lake near Spooner, Wisconsin. Pontoon boats glide on the lake in the summer and tiny ice-fishing shacks dot its surface in the winter. We bought it for $15,000, and Pete began rebuilding. He doubled the size of the main house, converted a small barn into guest quarters, and added a sauna for himself. The kids love coming up, going out in our pontoon when the weather is pretty, and sledding when it snows. It's wonderful. Pete spends most of the week out there, and I join him on weekends. We have etched out an ideal relationship for ourselves. It took me fifty years to be able to do that. It took Pete seventy. So I figure we've earned it.

Occasionally I'll steal a week and spend it up at the lake. I make soup, bake bread, watch the birds, and read sitting by the fire. In that house, I am as happy as I have ever been. There I can look at my soul and talk to God. Life is not about tranquillity, and if you are ever lucky enough to find it, know that it is a gift. The lake house is my gift, built lovingly by my husband.

In my quiet moments I think about Kristin, my mother, and my father. I think of them as angels now. They watch over me. I can feel them as surely as if I were looking at them. I feel Harry sometimes when I'm alone, driving in the car, and he embraces me.

I talk to the dead. I celebrated Allie's first St. Patrick's Day with her. I dressed her in an adorable little outfit, hand-painted with the words "Kiss me, I'm Irish" on the front. I held her and told her all about how we celebrated St. Patrick's Day back in Anoka. I told her about her great-great-grandfather, who would put on his green suit and green tie and green underwear and green socks and hand out green carnations.

I was singing "When Irish Eyes Are Smiling" to Allie and noticed she was weeping quietly. Suddenly I realized all my Irish relatives were in the room with us. I couldn't see them, but I could feel them. I could tell you exactly where they were standing. My father was there. So was Uncle Patrick and Aunt Mary, all of the Duffys. I began to cry, too. Anne came home from shopping, walked in the door, and saw us sitting on the sofa with tears rolling down our cheeks. She sat down in a chair next to us without saying a word.

"What happened?" she said quietly.

I just said, "They're here."

Going Home

One afternoon, not long ago, I visited the old Duffy residence, which is now owned by a physician and his family. I sat in my new black Chrysler out by the curb for a while and looked at the old place. The red bricks had been painted gray, and the garage had been moved forward, cutting into the front yard where we once played touch football on cold fall Saturdays. After a minute or two, I got out and knocked on the door.

A very nice woman of around forty answered and said she already knew that I had grown up there. "It's so funny that you're here," she said. "I'd been meaning to call and invite you out."

She and her two teenage daughters showed me around, told me about the remodeling they had done and what they planned to do. I showed them where the liquor cabinet once stood, and walked through the screened-in porch where Bruce used to hide when he played hooky from school. The pool was still there, and the deck where we danced, and the river beyond that.

"It's all still here," I told them. "Nothing's changed."

We went upstairs to my old bedroom, littered with one of the daughter's clothes and books that she was packing for college. The balcony, which had provided my escape on so many nights as a teenager, was removed several years ago. I stood in the guest room where Arne and I slept the night our baby died. The new owners left me there for a few minutes, and I sat on the bed quietly. What a relief to know those days were over. There was green carpet in the master bedroom—the same shade of green, coincidentally, that Jane had once painted her walls. I could still see her lying in bed watching TV, sipping from the glass of scotch on her nightstand.

I could see her standing at the top of the stairs with a shotgun in her tiny arms.

"That's where Jane stood the night she was going to shoot me," I said to the nice lady and her girls, and they laughed nervously.

As I walked out to my car, I took one last look at the place. It had been taken care of, I thought, and it was full of love and peace.

I will end the story of my life with Lou. He called me in 1992 from New York. I hadn't spoken to him in about fifteen years. He told me that he was sober. He said he wanted to see me again. He didn't ask me to resume our affair, but my old feelings for him were still there. I went a little crazy. I knew that I was still capable of giving up everything to be with him—my career, Pete, my kids. So I was afraid of seeing him again.

One afternoon I drove out to the Anoka cemetery and sat by Harry's grave and asked for advice. I could hear my father's voice.

"Do not do this," the voice said. "You've worked hard to get your life in order. You're sober. You're successful. You're happy. Your children are doing well. You have a husband who loves you. Why would you even consider it?"

I sat bundled up in my fur coat and argued with a ghost. "This is *not* what I came out here to hear, Harry."

"You know this is a mistake," he said. "You know this is going to fail. But I want you to know that I'll always be here for you."

"Of course you'll be here," I told him. "You're dead, and this is your final resting place. Where *else* would you be?"

I got back in the car and drove away sobbing. Harry was right again.

Two months after I visited Harry's grave, I hadn't heard from Lou. I called his office, and his secretary told me that he had suffered a heart attack and died. Maybe Harry had a little more control on the other side than he had had here. There really are no words to describe the feelings I had upon hearing that Lou was dead. My grief for Lou was so complicated. Maybe I wanted him so badly because I couldn't have him. Or maybe he actually was that thing called a soul mate. The possibility of sharing part of this life with him was now dead and buried. But I was given a gift at this time, too. Relief.

A year or so after Lou died, a nationally known psychic from Sioux Falls, South Dakota, named Donna O'Day was booked on my radio show. On the air, she asked me if I cared to speak to any of my dearly departed. I immediately started to shake, and tears welled up in my eyes. I wanted to speak to Lou, whom I had not seen during the last seventeen years of his life. The old hunger, pain, and yearning returned. I asked Donna to ask Lou the question that I had so often asked him myself.

"Did he ever really love me?" I wanted to know.

I closed my eyes. My breathing changed, and I suddenly sensed a spirit entering the room. (Remember this was all taking place live, on the air.) Donna concentrated for a moment.

"He says, 'Of course I loved you, you silly fool,' " Donna said. " 'Do you think I would've put up with the phone calls, the hysteria, and the visits without caring about you? I loved you. I told you I would never stop loving you. But I had responsibilities, a wife, and three beautiful daughters.' " This did me in; Donna knew nothing about Lou, had no idea that he had three kids.

"He's beginning to fade," said Donna. "But he has one

last thing to say. 'Keep your shoes together.' " Donna looked surprised. "I'm not sure what that could mean. Do you have a messy closet?"

I was immediately transported back to that night so many years ago, to that carriage in Central Park. I wept and whispered, "I know what he's saying."

"He's gone," said Donna.

"I know," I said quietly. "And my heart is breaking."

Lou was a metaphor for many things in this broad's life. When I was married to Arne, I saw Lou as a way out, and I continued to see him that way, as an escape from unhappiness and guilt. He was the Emerald City, bigger than just a man I loved. When he died, I was left standing in the midst of my life, with no way out. But I didn't feel trapped there. At last I realized that it really wasn't a bad place to be.

I still talk to Lou. He visits me when I'm driving and holds me the way Harry does. He doesn't visit me at home, because I don't think Pete would appreciate it. After he died, I was in New York for a meeting. I had gone out to dinner and was in a cab headed back to my hotel. It was a clear winter night, and the lights along Park Avenue were crisp and bright. I passed by Lou's old office building and the bars we used to visit together. And suddenly he was there with me, sharing the memories. The driver must have thought I was nuts because I began talking to him aloud and sobbing. I spoke to Lou about how much I cared for him, told him how much I missed him, and thanked him for leaving this world before I had the chance to throw everything away for him.

And then he was gone. I sat back and cried, feeling overwhelmed with loss, as well as gratitude. So much of my life has been spent—is spent—seeking love, hoping to be loved.

But by way of making peace with Lou, I had learned life's secret: Love isn't a passive thing. There is greater joy in loving than in being loved. I sat still in that cab and watched the lights go by, feeling so smart and sober. Then I reached into my purse.

Goddammit, *what* did I do with my glasses?